튜즐 당구 시스템

튜즐 당구 시스템(Tüzül Billiards Systems)
by Murat Tüzül

Korean Copyright ⓒ 2020 Global Contents, Publishing Co., Ltd.
Publishing by arrangement with Optimus Billiard Agency, Seoul, Korea
All rights Reserved.

이 책의 한국어 판권은 옵티머스빌리어드 에이전시와 독점계약한 글로벌콘텐츠에 있습니다.
저작권법에 의해 한국 내에서 보호를 받는 저작물이므로
어떠한 형태로든 무단 전재와 무단 복제를 금합니다.

튜즐 당구 시스템

무랏 튜즐 지음 | 박천수·박지수 옮김

TÜZÜL BILLIARD SYSTEMS

MURAT TÜZÜL

글로벌콘텐츠

목차

감사의 말 / 06
서문 / 08

part 01 튜즐 시스템(회전)

테이블값의 계산 / 12
득점을 위한 올바른 선의 결정 / 19

1. 튜즐 시스템 – 단쿠션 출발 / 22
2. 튜즐 시스템 – 장쿠션 출발 / 43
3. 튜즐 시스템 – ¼ 테이블 응용 / 63
4. 튜즐 더블레일 시스템 / 73
5. 튜즐 더블레일 시스템 – ¼ 테이블 응용 / 82
6. "튜즐 – 몰" 시스템 / 88

part 02 튜즐 시스템(무회전)

1. 튜즐 무회전 시스템 / 98
2. 튜즐 무회전 시스템 – ¼ 테이블 응용 / 110
3. 튜즐 부가점 시스템 / 118

용어 / 132
부록 / 133

감사의 말

현대 당구의 발전에 작은 기여를 할 것으로 기대되는 튜즐 당구 시스템은 저의 생각을 당구 동호인들과 공유하고자 하는 목적으로 출간하였습니다.

튜즐 당구 시스템을 사용함으로써 제게 많은 용기를 북돋워 주신 세계 당구 챔피언 토브욘 브롬달과 세미 세이기너에게 감사드립니다.

책을 쓴다는 것이 이처럼 어려운 일인지 처음에는 알지 못했습니다. 이제 제가 알고 있는 모든 당구 동호인들이 제게 여러 방면으로 도움을 주어 왔다는 것을 깨닫고 있습니다.

제게 이 여정의 모든 과정에서 도움과 지원을 주신 한스 쿨레겜, 올라프 레이플린, 에르달 아카르, 일한 귀벤, 알리 시난 무틀루, 외머 카푸르, 에르뎀 사힌, 알버트 페사, 네제 키다치, 외저 키다치, 마르타 세라밋자나, 알도 메디나, 나치 귀찬 교수, 파루크 윅셀, 에스라 타르한, 수에 켈릭, 귈센 데게너에게 특별한 감사의 말씀을 드립니다.

ACKNOWLEDGMENTS...

Tüzül Billiards Systems Book, which I hope will make a small contribution to the development of the modern billiards, is prepared with the aim of sharing my thoughts with billiard lovers.

I am grateful to World Billiards Champion Torbjorn Blomdahl and to Semih Saygıner for encouraging me by adopting Tüzül Billiards Systems.

In the beginning, I would have never thought that it would be so difficult to write a book.

I now realize that all billiard lovers I know have supplied me with a valuable feedback in one way or the other.

I also want to give my special thanks to Hans Coolegem, Olaf Reifflin, Erdal Acar, Ömer Kavur, Erdem Şahin, Albert Pesah, Neşe Kıldacı, Marta Serramitjana, Ali Sinan Mutlu, Aldo Medina, İlhan Güven, Salim Şen, Prof. Dr. Naci Güçhan, Esra Tarhan, Gülşen Degener, Özer Kıldacı for helping and supporting me at every stage of this adventure.

서문

당구 동호인 여러분,

튜즐 당구 시스템은 2개의 파트, 튜즐 시스템(회전) 및 튜즐 시스템(무회전)으로 이루어져 있습니다. 이 시스템에 대해 자세히 들어가기에 앞서, 저는 이 책에서 자주 접하게 될, 그리고 우리가 "테이블값"이라고 부르는 개념에 대해 간략하게 언급하고자 합니다. 테이블값은 튜즐 시스템(회전)의 계산에 사용되는 중요한 요소이며, 이 시스템의 토대를 이루고 있습니다. 테이블값의 개념과 그 계산과 사용에 대해서는 다음 장에 자세히 설명되어 있습니다. 이 개념에 대해 완전하게 이해하지 못하면 튜즐 시스템(회전)을 효과적으로 활용할 수 없다는 점을 강조합니다.

쓰리쿠션 당구의 훈련에서 사용되는 다른 시스템들은 테이블과 라사지의 품질, 스트로크 기법 및 큐팁 접촉지점 등과 같은 다양한 요소들에 대해 어떤 표준을 요구합니다. 이러한 표준들은 튜즐 시스템(회전)에서는 불필요합니다. 테이블과 당구공 및 플레이어의 스트로크 기법 등을 고려해서 얻게 되는 테이블값은 이러한 종류의 표준들에 대해 고려할 필요가 없게 만들어줍니다. 간단히 말해서, 테이블값을 토대로 하는 튜즐 시스템(회전)은 모든 종류의 테이블에 적용될 수 있습니다. 튜즐 시스템은 이러한 점에서 다른 시스템들과 차별화되는 기본적인 특징을 가지고 있습니다. 그러나 튜즐 시스템을 효과적으로 사용하기 위해서는 다른 시스템들과 마찬가지로 일정 수준의 연습과 능력이 요구됩니다.

튜즐 시스템(무회전)은 계산하기는 쉽지만, 무회전 볼의 샷을 만들어내는 능력을 요구하기 때문에 활용하기가 더 어려울 것으로 생각됩니다. 위에 언급한 모든 플레이어들도 인정하듯이, 무회전 볼 기술은 쉬워 보이지만 실제로는 어렵습니다. 튜즐 시스템(무회전)을 효과적으로 활용하기 위해서는 정확한 무회전 볼의 샷을 구사할 수 있는 능력을 갖추어야 합니다. 시스템을 공부하는 데에 있어서 이러한 점을 염두에 둘 것을 권합니다.

이 책에서는 가능한 한 간결하게 설명하고, 설명의 분량을 최소화하기 위해 노력하였습니다. 이 시스템의 활용 범위를 고려할 때, 되도록 많은 그림 자료들을 사용하는 것이 이 시스템의 공부에 더 도움이 될 것으로 생각됩니다.

튜즐 당구 시스템이 독자 여러분의 당구 실력 항상에 도움 되기를 바랍니다.

PREFACE

Dear billiard lovers, Tüzül Billiards Systems are analysed in two main chapters: Tüzül Systems (english) and Tüzül Systems (dead ball). Before going further into the details of these systems, I briefly want to mention a concept that we will frequently meet in this book and that we will call "Table Value". Table Value is a key factor that is used in the calculations of Tüzül Systems (english) and that constitutes the basis for these systems. The following chapter explains in detail what the concept of Table Value is, how it is calculated and used. What I want to emphasize here is that an incomplete perception of this concept may hinder the effective use of Tüzül Systems (english).

The other systems used in Three-Cushion Billiards disciplines require some standards in the variable factors such as the quality of the table and the cloth, the stroke technique and the cue-tip contact point. These types of standards are not required in Tüzül Systems (english). The Table Value that we will get by taking the table, the balls and the stroke technique of the player into account saves us from considering these kinds of standards. Briefly, Tüzül Systems (english) based on the Table Value can be applied in all kinds of tables. This is the basic characteristic that distinguishes Tüzül Systems (english) from the other systems. But we have to accept that the effective use of Tüzül Systems also requires a certain level of experience and ability as in all other systems.

Although their mathematical side is easier, Tüzül Systems (dead ball) are systems that I consider more difficult to apply because they require the ability to make dead ball shots. As all above-the-line players would accept, dead balls technique seems easy but is in reality difficult. In order to use Tüzül Systems (dead ball) effectively, one has to acquire the ability to make standard dead ball shots. I would suggest considering this point in your system studies.

I have tried to keep explanations as brief as possible and to minimize the amount of text in the book. Considering the usage areas of the systems, I think that the use of more graphical examples will also facilitate your studies. I hope Tüzül Billiards Systems will have positive effects on your playing capacity.

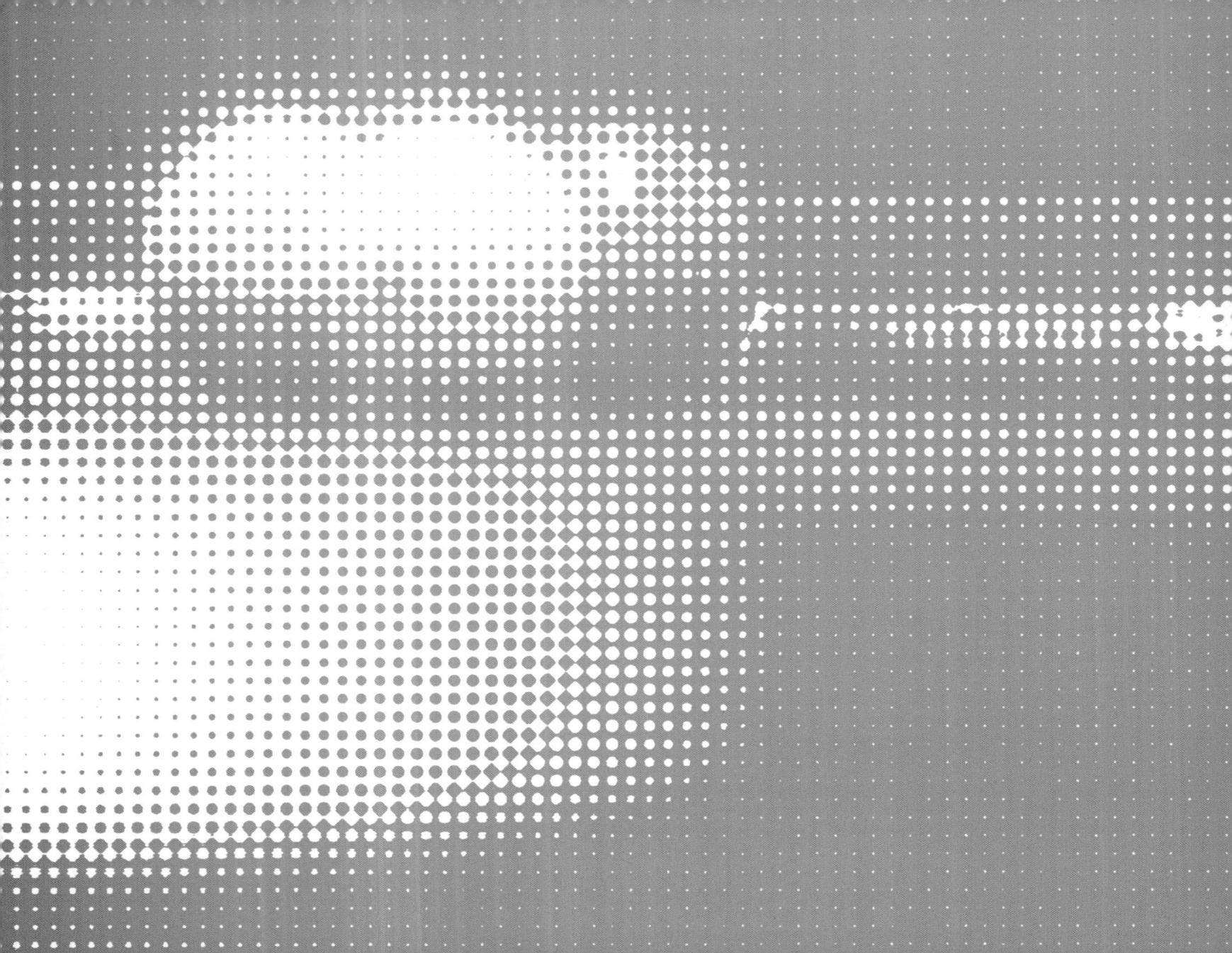

part 01

튜즐 시스템
회전

::: 테이블값의 계산

튜즐 당구 시스템 북의 튜즐 시스템(회전) 파트에서 시스템의 계산에 사용되는 테이블값의 개념은 쿠션의 특성, 회전량 및 플레이어의 스트로크 기법에 따라 얻어지는 값이다.

테이블값을 계산하는 데에 있어서 특정 회전과 속도를 사용하여야만 하는 것은 아니다. 중요한 것은, 플레이어가 선호하는 회전량과 속도에 따라 테이블값이 어떻게 될 것인가 하는 점이다. 특히 강조하고 싶은 점은, 테이블값에 대한 올바른 수치는 없다는 것이다. 기본적으로, 테이블값은 플레이어가 사용하는 스트로크 기법, 속도 및 회전량, 그리고 특정 시점에서의 테이블 상태에 따라 산정된다. 예컨대 동일한 테이블일지라도 두 플레이어의 테이블값은 다를 수 있다. 이는 두 플레이어의 플레이 특성이 다르다는 것을 의미한다. 이 시스템을 적용하는 데에 있어서, 동일한 공 배치를 해결하고자 하는 두 플레이어가 서로 다른 각을 이용하여 동일한 도착점에 이르게 할 수 있다. 즉, 두 플레이어는 서로 다른 테이블값을 사용하여 서로 다른 첫 번째 레일 목표점을 정하여 동일한 도착점에 도달할 수 있다. 이는 튜즐 시스템(회전)이 다른 시스템들과 차별화되는 중요한 특징이다.

테이블값의 계산에 사용되는 스트로크 기법에 있어서 추천하는 방식은 큐팁과 당구공 사이에 긴 접촉시간을 가져오는 비교적 부드러우면서도 속도감 있는 샷으로서, 이는 당구 용어에서는 팔로우스루 스트로크(follow - through stroke)라고 불리운다. 중요한 것은 모든 샷에서 동일한 테이블값을 얻는 것이다. 다시 말해서, 플레이어는 항상 동일한 샷을 구사해야 한다. 예컨대 만약 플레이어가 동일한 기법을 사용하였는데 어떤 샷에서는 15라는 테이블값을 얻고 다른 샷에서는 13이라는 테이블값을 얻었다면, 이는 무엇인가 잘못되었다는 것을 의미한다. 이 경우, 플레이어는 항상 동일한 값을 얻을 수 있도록 일정한 샷을 구사하는 연습에 집중해야 한다.

그림들(GRA1, GRA2, GRA3)은 상이한 세 가지의 큐팁 접점을 사용할 때 상이한 값이 얻어지는 세 가지 계산 예를 보여주고 있다. 중요하게 고려해야 할 사항은, 플레이어에 따라 그리고 테이블에 따라 이 값들은 달라진다는 것이다. 플레이어는 선호하는 큐팁 접점에 따라 원하는 만큼의 많은 테이블값을 얻을 수 있다. 플레이어는 이 시스템을 적용할 때 자신에게 가장 유리한 테이블값을 사용할 수 있다. 튜즐 시스템(회전)을 적용하는 데에 경험과 기술이 쌓이면 계산 없이도 테이블값을 알아낼 수 있게 될 것이다.

라사지가 새로 교체되고 미끄러운 테이블에서는 오래된 라사지에 비해 테이블값이 작게 계산될 것이다. 예컨대 극단 회전을 통해 얻어지는 값이 새 라사지의 테이블에서는 14~15 또는 그보다 낮을 수 있고(GRA1), 반면에 꺾이는 특성의 다른 테이블에서는 동일한 플레이어가 17~18 또는 그보다 높은 값을 얻을 수도 있다. 이러한 점은 이 시스템의 효과적인 적용에 문제가 되지 않는다. 연습 시 이러한 점을 염두에 두기를 권한다.

테이블값은 공식에 부합되기만 한다면 어떤 출발각에 대해서도 결정될 수 있다. 적용하는 각도와 무관하게, 플레이어는 공식을 적용하기만 하면 동일한 최종값에 이를 수 있다. 그림들(GRA1, GRA2, GRA3)은 단지 예시적인 것일 뿐이다.

::: CALCULATION OF TABLE VALUE

The Table Value concept used in the calculations of the systems in the Tüzül
Billiards Systems Book -System Tüzül (english) chapters is a value obtained according to the characteristic of the cushions, the degree of spin used and the stroke technique of the player.

It is not obligatory to use a certain spin and speed while calculating the Table Value. The important thing is what the Table Value will be according to the degree of spin and the speed preferred by the player. The point I especially want to emphasize is that there is no correct numerical value for Table Value. The basic thing is that the Table Value is calculated on the stroke technique, the speed and the degree of spin used by the player and the table conditions at a specific time. For example, the Table Values of two players at the same table could be different. This means that the shooting characteristics of these two players are different. In the system applications, players aiming to solve the position would get the same reach point via different angles. That is to say that, two players with different Table Values can reach the same reach point with different first rail aiming points. This is the major characteristic distinguishing Tüzül Systems (english) from other systems.

My proposition for the stroke technique used in the calculation of the Table Value is a relatively soft but speedy shot that will provide a longer contact between the cue tip and the ball which is called in billiards terminology a follow-through stroke. The main thing is to get the same Table Value at every shot. In other words, the player has to make the same shot every time. For instance, if the player gets 15 as Table Value in one shot and 13 in another by using the same technique, this shows that there is something wrong. In that case, the player has to concentrate on making the same shot to obtain the same value in his practices.

The graphs (GRA 1, GRA 2, GRA 3) show three calculation examples with three different cue-tip contact points where different values are obtained. The main point to be considered is that these values may vary according to the player and the table. The player may have as many Table Values as he wants according to the cue-tip contact points preferred. He can use the most advantageous Table Value for the positions in his system applications. Players who have a certain experience and skill in applying the Systems Tüzül (english) will become capable of estimating the Table Value without any calculation.

With a new and slippery cloth, smaller Table Values will be calculated compared to an old cloth. For example, the values obtained with extreme english may be 14-15 or even lower in a new cloth (GRA 1), whereas the same player may get 17-18 or even higher in another perpendicularly reacting table. This does not cause any problem in the effective application of the systems. I suggest that you consider this point during your practices.

The determination of the Table Value may be done with any starting angle, on

condition of being in line with the formulation. Regardless of the angle you apply, you will reach the same end-value when you apply the points to the formula. The graphs (GRA 1, GRA 2, GRA 3) are only given as examples.

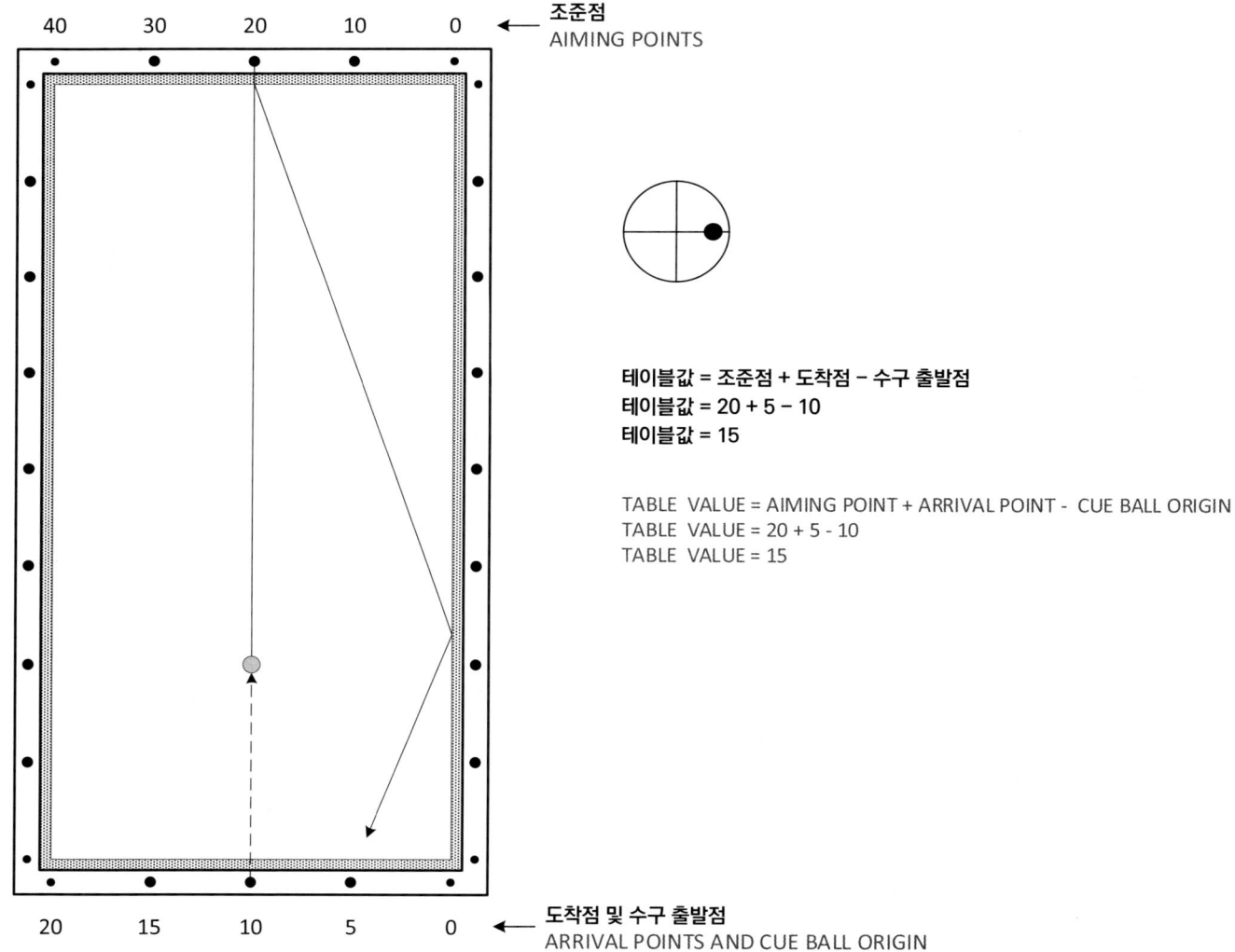

- GRA 1 -

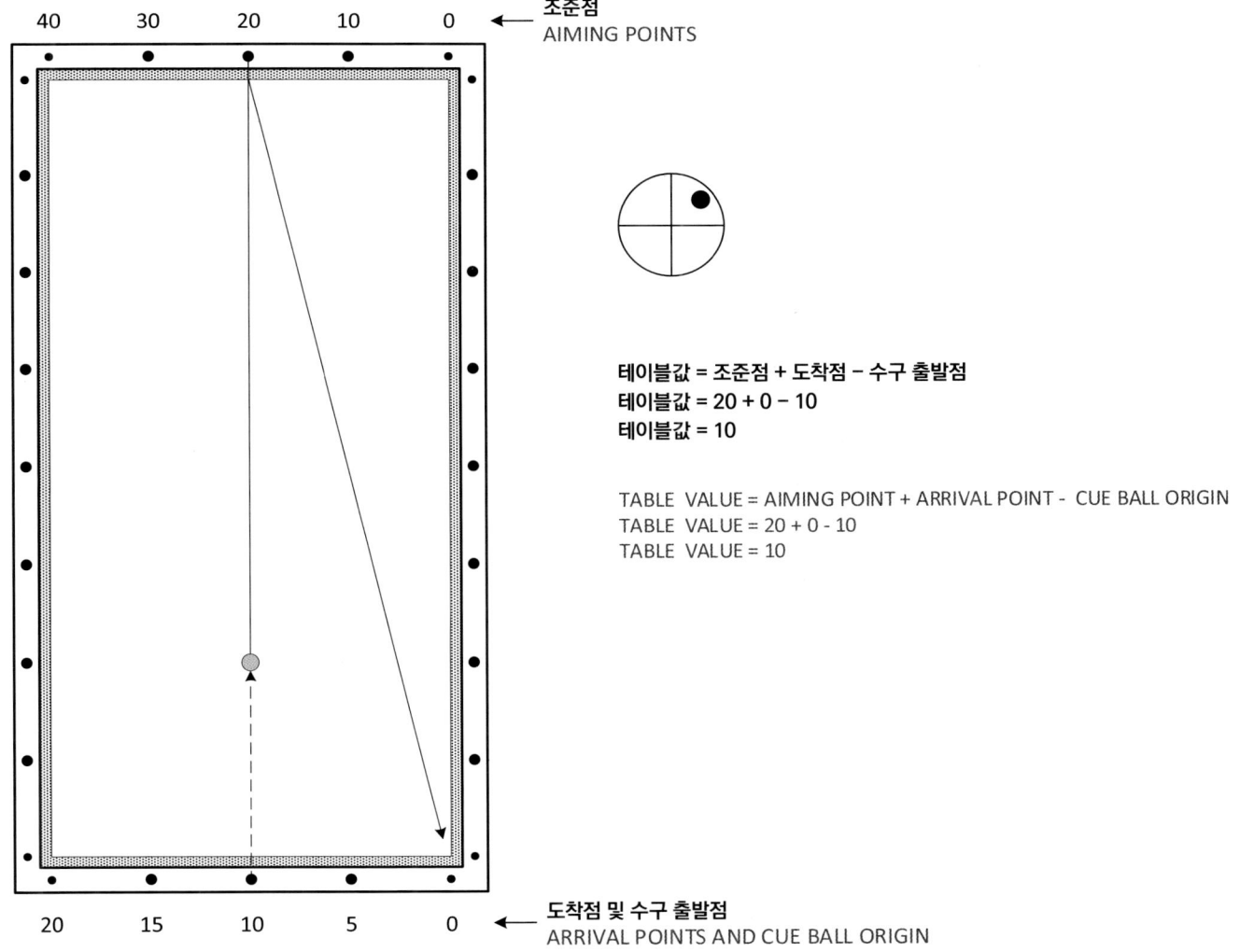

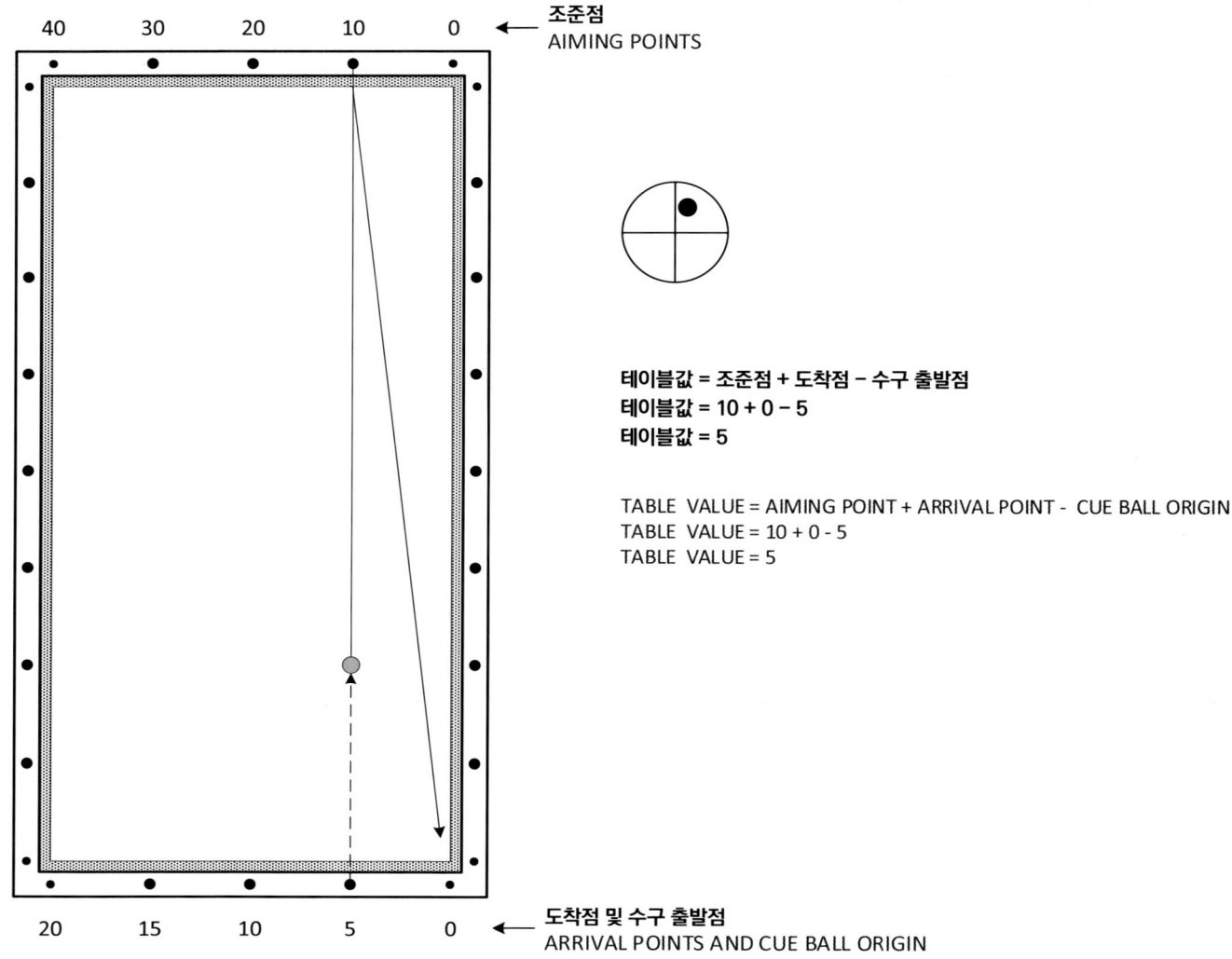

⋮⋮⋮ 득점을 위한 올바른 선의 결정

이 시스템 적용의 첫 번째 단계는 도착 쿠션의 지점을 결정하고 그에 따라 공식에서 미지수의 개수를 줄이는 것이다.

뱅크샷(쿠션을 먼저 맞추는 샷)의 경우에는, 수구의 중앙을 지나는 가상선을 그리되 한쪽 끝이 조준 쿠션을 그리고 다른 쪽 끝이 출발 쿠션을 향하도록 함으로써 등식에 부합되는 방향을 찾는 시도를 한다.

수구가 먼저 적구를 맞추고 목표 쿠션으로 진행하는 경우에는, 가상선은 적구로부터 약 3cm(당구공의 지름)가량 떨어진 지점을 지나도록 그려짐으로써 등식에 부합되는 방향이 구해진다.

조준 쿠션으로부터 출발 쿠션까지의 가상선에 의해 결정되는 수치가 등식에 부합되는 값인지 여부는 시행착오 방식을 통해 점검할 수 있다.

가상선에 의해 결정된 조준 쿠션의 지점과 출발 쿠션의 지점을 테스트한 결과 등식에 부합되지 않는다면, 가상선을 시계 방향 또는 반시계 방향으로 이동시킴으로써 등식에 맞는 값을 찾을 수 있다.

등식에 부합되는 값을 결정한다는 것은 그에 앞서 결정되어 있는 도착점에 이르도록 하는 조준점을 결정한다는 것을 함께 의미한다.

이러한 방식에 대한 경험이 증가할수록 시행착오가 줄어들고, 등식에 부합되어 득점이 가능한 올바른 선을 찾아내는 것이 쉬워지는 것을 느끼게 될 것이다.

그림의 예들은 등식에 부합되어 득점 가능하게 되는 올바른 선이 결정되는 과정을 세 개의 가상선에 대한 시도를 통해 보여준다.

::: THE DETERMINATION OF THE RIGHT LINE TO MAKE POINT

The first step in all system applications is to determine the arrival cushion point and to decrease the number of unknowns in the formula accordingly.

In bank shots (which first touch the cushion), a hypothetical line is drawn passing through the centre of the cue ball and one end of which shows the aiming cushion, while the other end shows the departing cushion, in an attempt to find the direction of the shot which will balance the equation.

In the applications where the cue ball first hits the second ball and then goes to the aiming cushion, a hypothetical line is drawn which passes the second ball at a distance of about 3 cm (the radius of the ball) and the direction which will enable the equation to be balanced is sought.

The trial & error method enables us to check whether the numerical values determined by the hypothetical line from the aiming cushion to the departing cushion, are the same values as in the balance equation.

If the aiming and departing cushion points determined by the line we are testing do not lead to a balanced equation, we can rotate our line clockwise or counter-clockwise in order to find the values which will fit the equation.

The determination of the values which will balance the equation also means the determination of the aiming point which will enable us to reach the previously determined arrival points.

As your experience on this subject increases, you will see that the number of trial & error will decrease accordingly and finding the right line to make the point that will balance the equation will become easy.

The graphical example shows how the right line to make the point that balances the equation is determined after three trials of the hypothetical line.

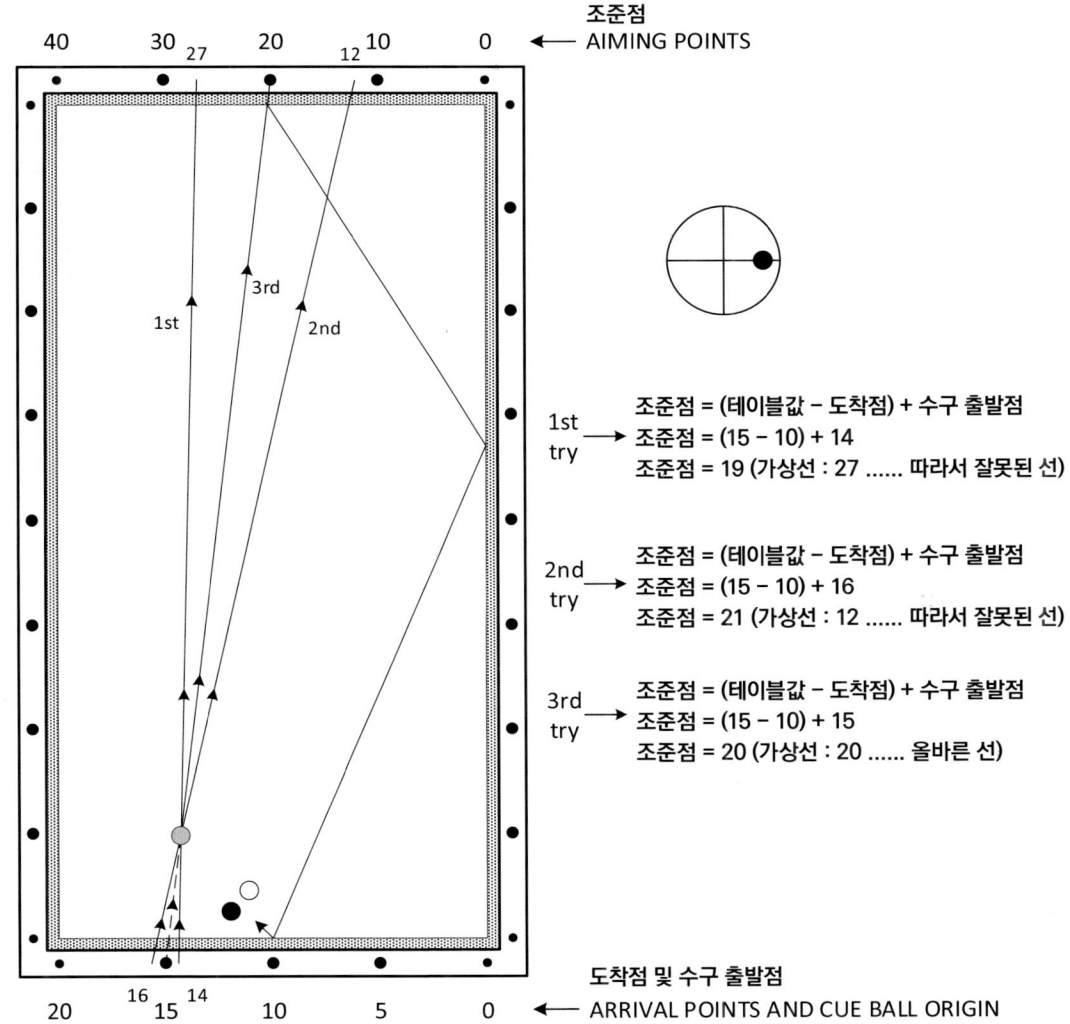

1. 튜즐 시스템 - 단쿠션 출발

이 시스템은 수구가 커브를 수반하는 단쿠션-장쿠션-단쿠션 경로에 따른 수학적 해결 방법이다. 최근에 애용되는 어떠한 커브에 대해서도 적용 가능하므로 그 활용 범위가 매우 넓다. 앞에 언급한 바와 같이, 동일한 스트로크 기법을 사용하더라도 상이한 테이블에서 상이한 테이블값을 얻을 수 있다. 게임 중에는 테이블 값을 얻기 위해 이전에 구사한 것과 동일한 샷을 구사하는 것이 필수적이다. 수구가 커브를 수반하며 첫 번째 쿠션에 도달하게 되면 각도에서는 어느 정도의 편차가 발생한다. 이 시스템은 이러한 커브 스트로크 기법을 선호할 경우 이 편차를 감안하는 경우에만 효과적으로 적용될 수 있다.

1. SYSTEM TÜZÜL -STARTING FROM SHORT CUSHION

This is a system which mathematically solves the short cushion-long cushion-short cushion line of the cue ball that carries a curve. Its usage area is very wide due to its applicability with any recently preferred curve. As mentioned before, although having used the same stroke technique it is possible to obtain different Table Values on different tables. It is essential to make the same shot as the one which we made to establish the Table Value during the game. The fact that the cue ball reaches the first cushion via a curved movement causes a certain loss of angle. To apply this system effectively is only possible if this loss is considered when such curved stroke techniques are preferred.

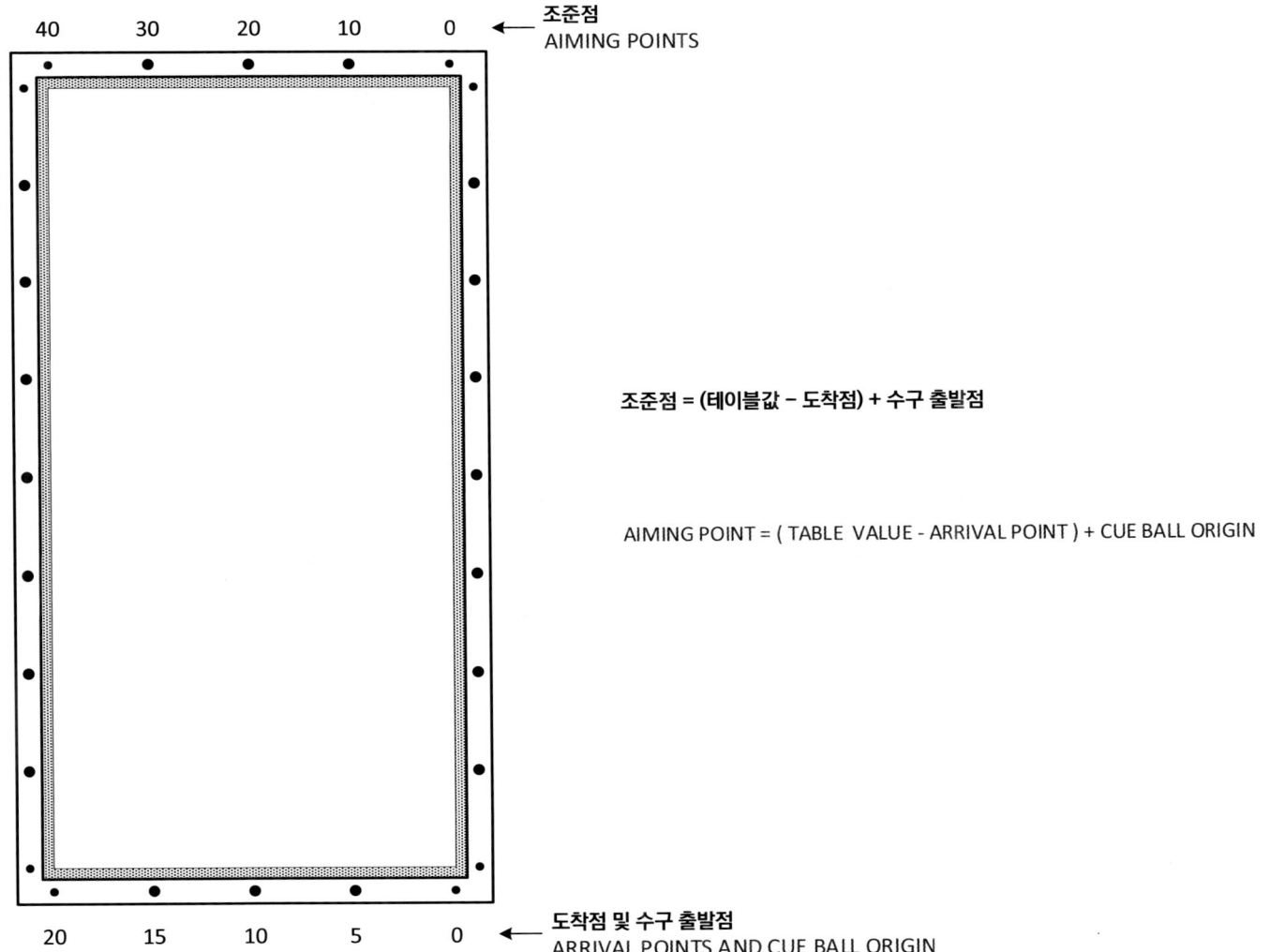

조준점 = (테이블값 − 도착점) + 수구 출발점

AIMING POINT = (TABLE VALUE - ARRIVAL POINT) + CUE BALL ORIGIN

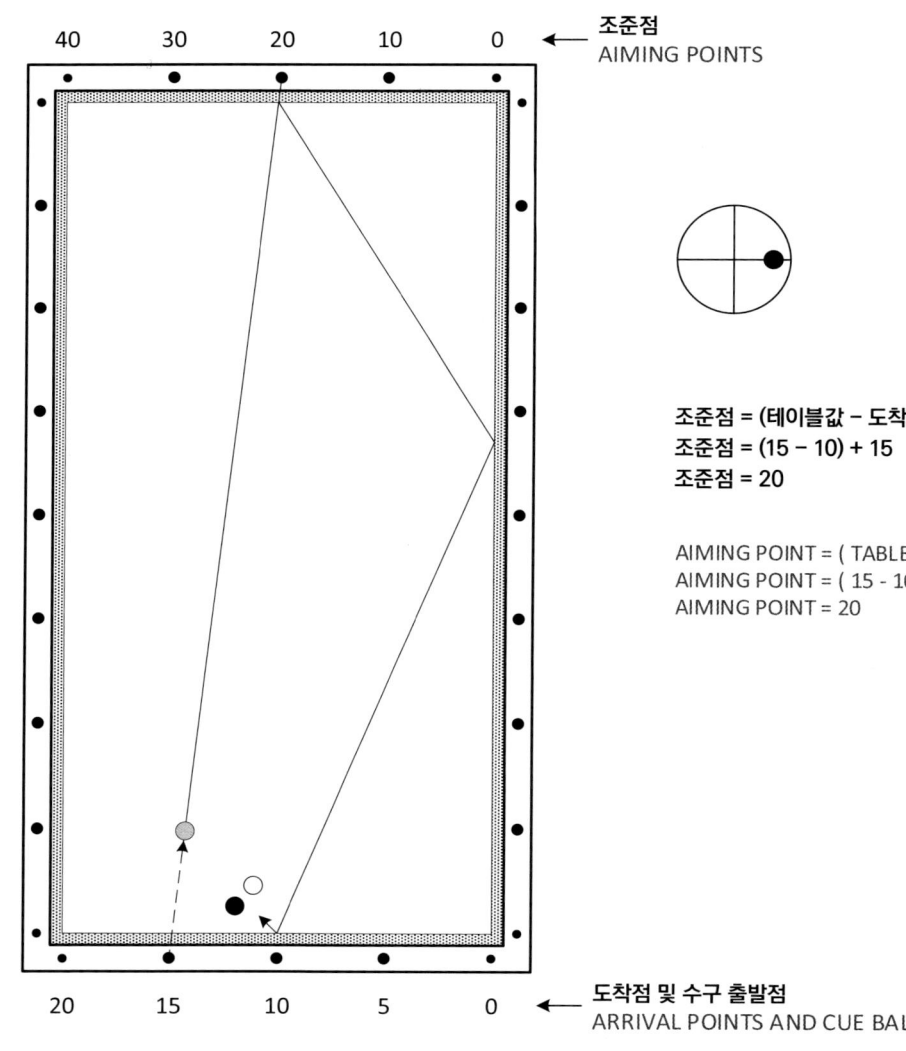

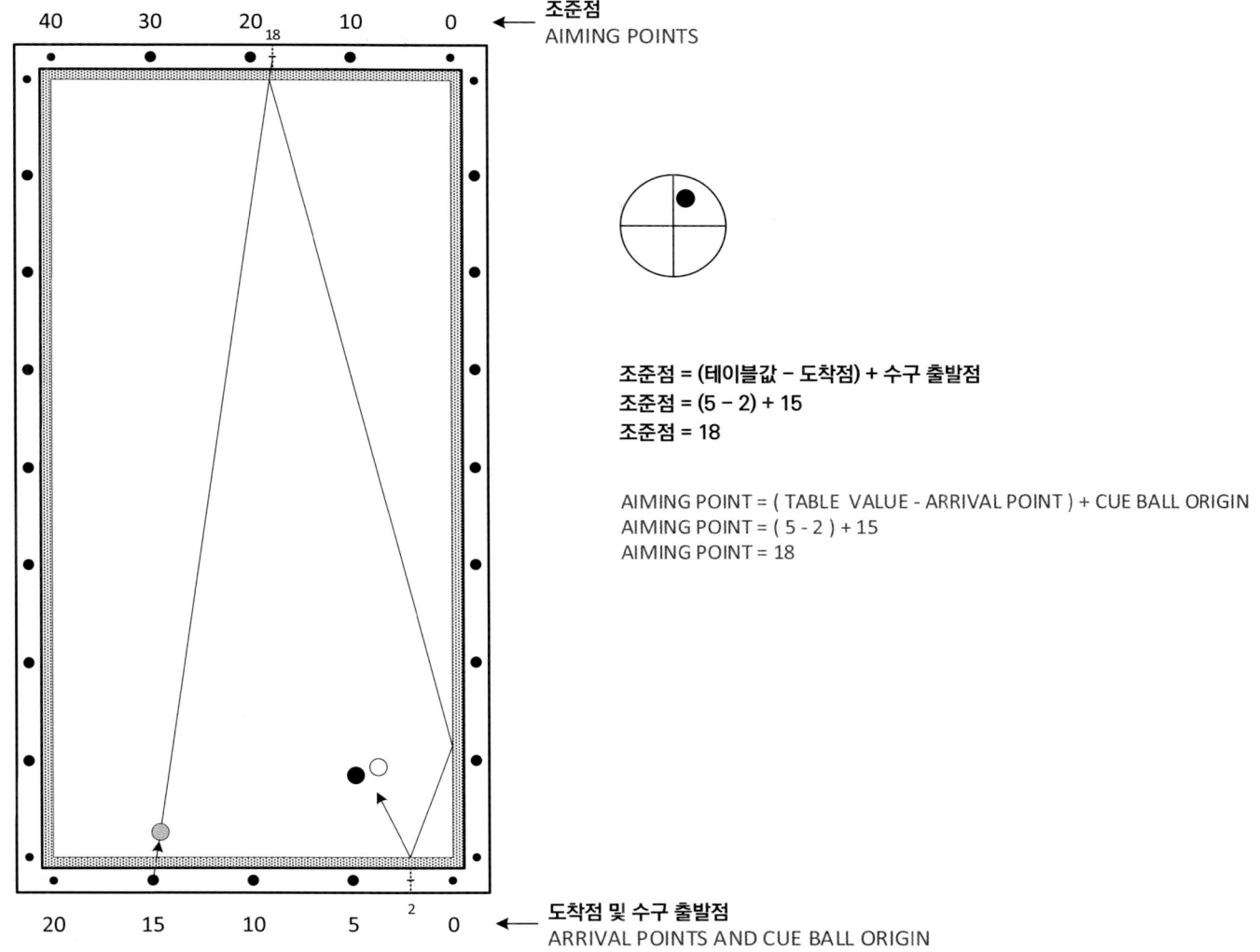

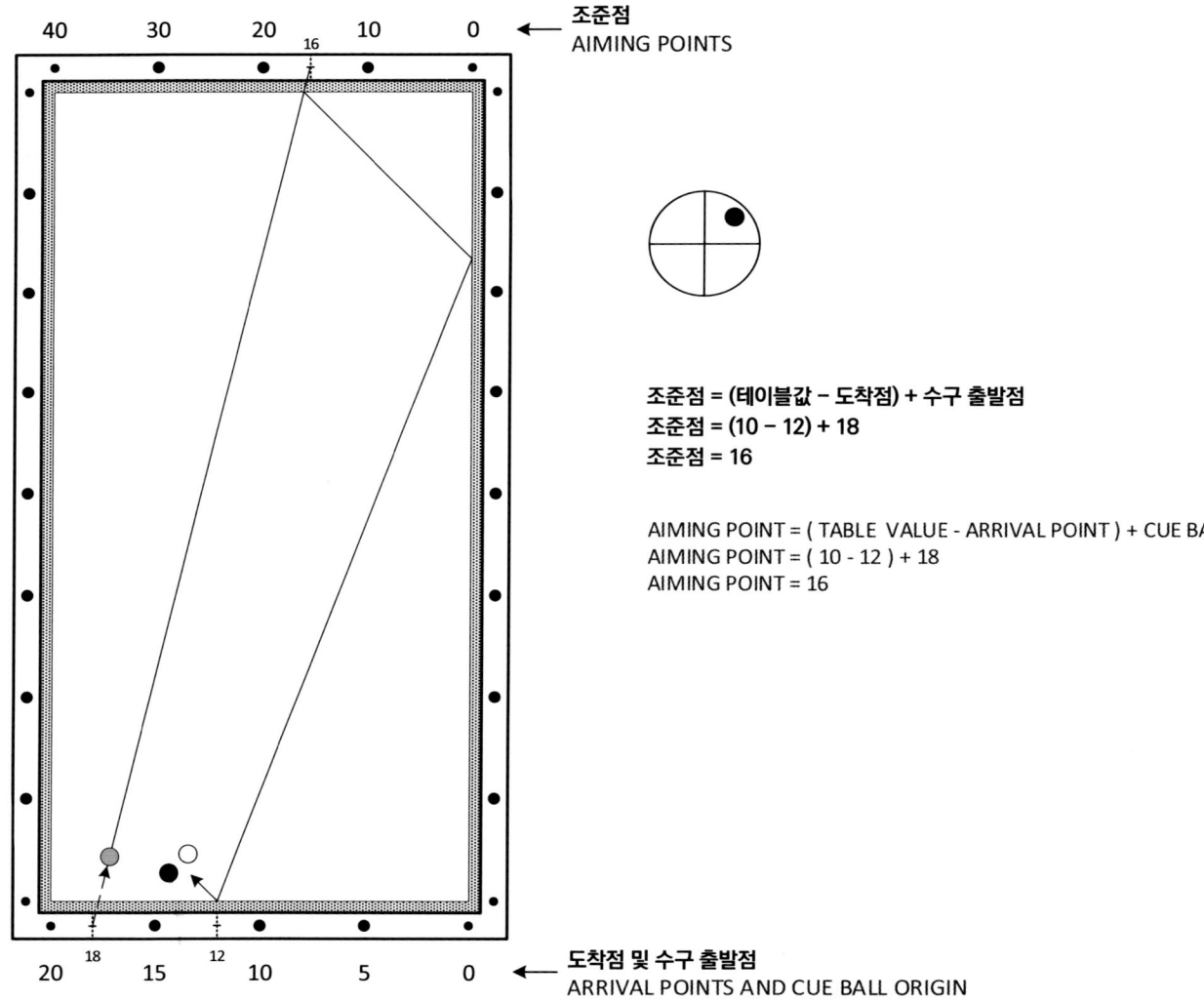

조준점 = (테이블값 − 도착점) + 수구 출발점
조준점 = (10 − 12) + 18
조준점 = 16

AIMING POINT = (TABLE VALUE - ARRIVAL POINT) + CUE BALL ORIGIN
AIMING POINT = (10 - 12) + 18
AIMING POINT = 16

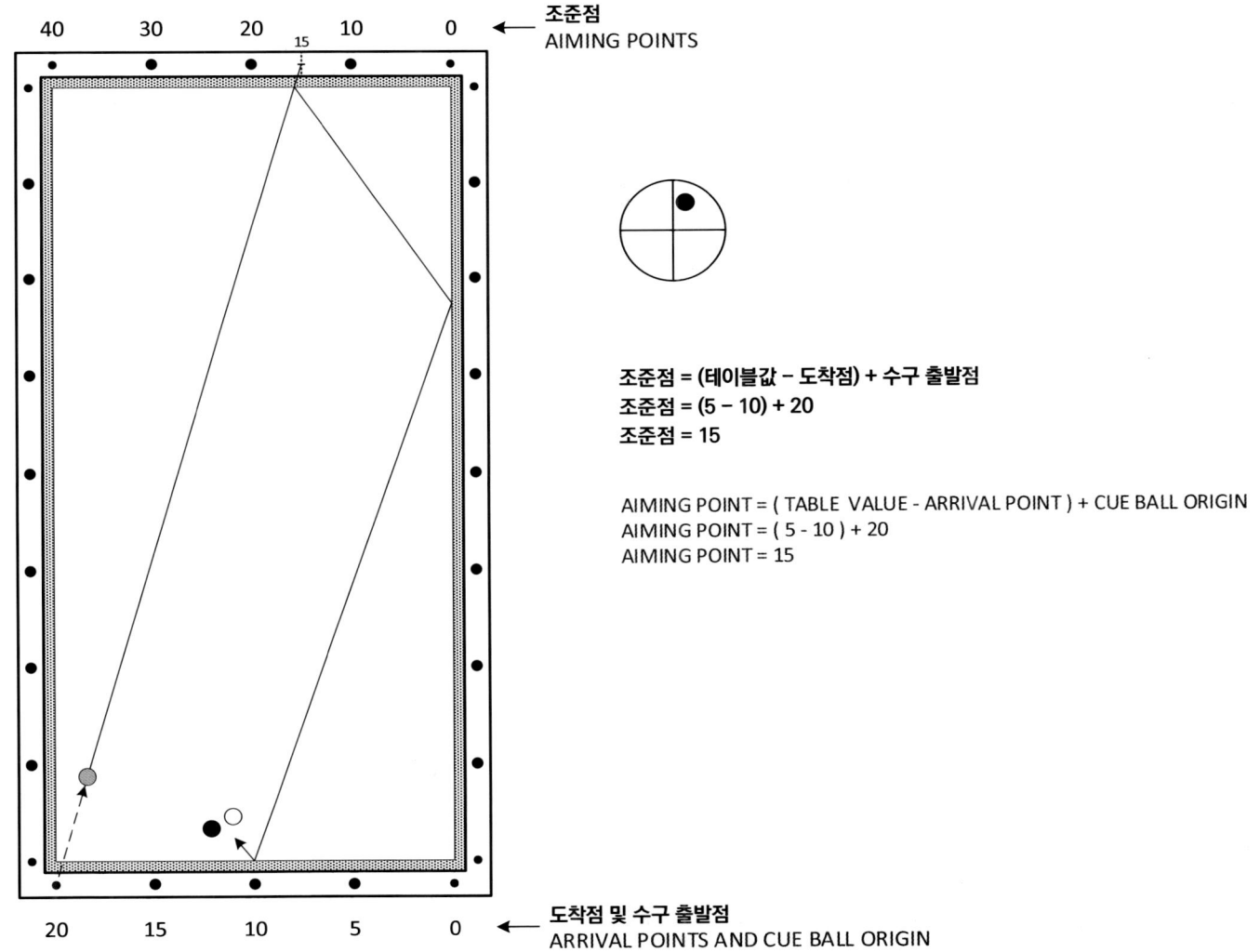

조준점 = (테이블값 - 도착점) + 수구 출발점
조준점 = (5 - 10) + 20
조준점 = 15

AIMING POINT = (TABLE VALUE - ARRIVAL POINT) + CUE BALL ORIGIN
AIMING POINT = (5 - 10) + 20
AIMING POINT = 15

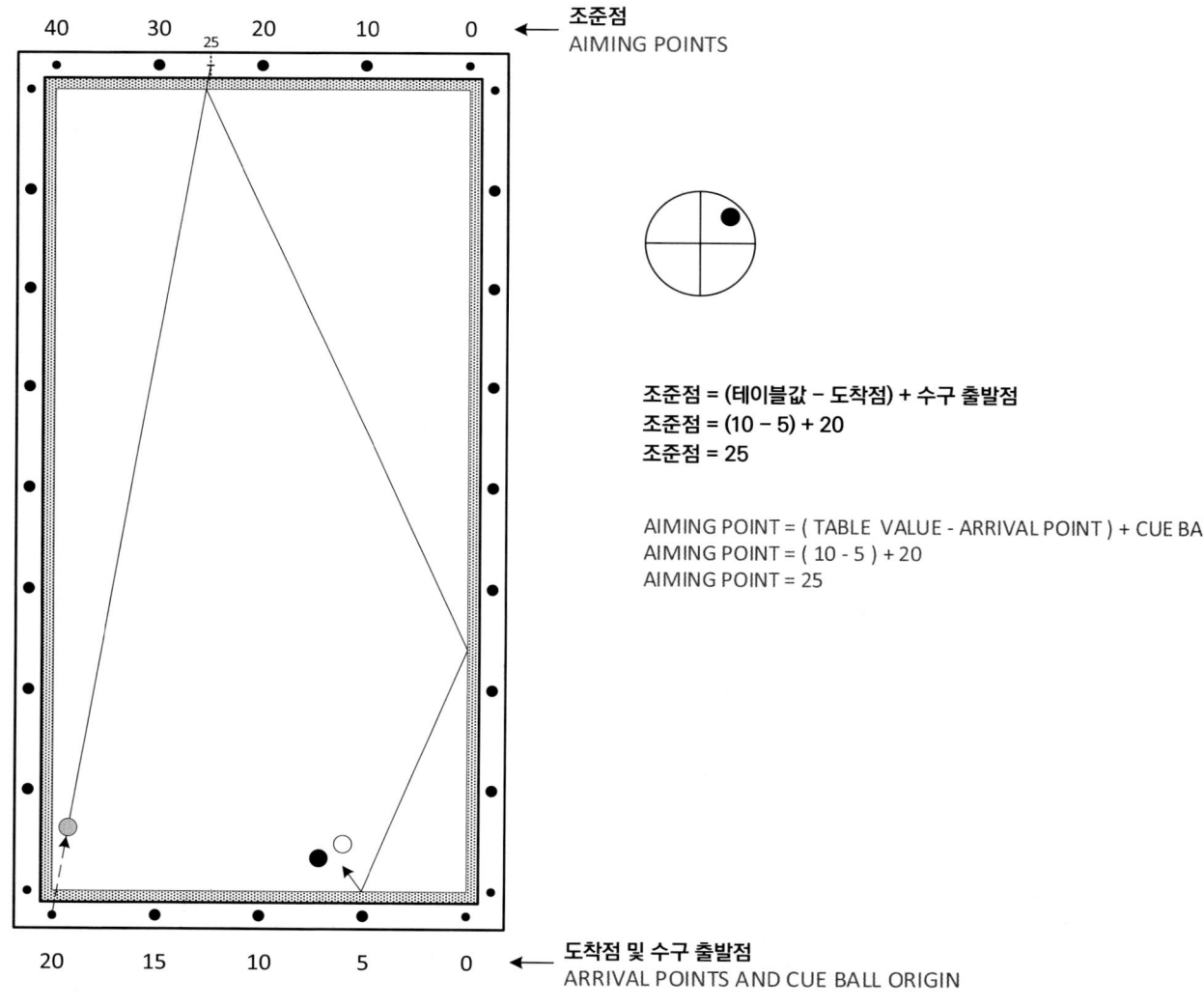

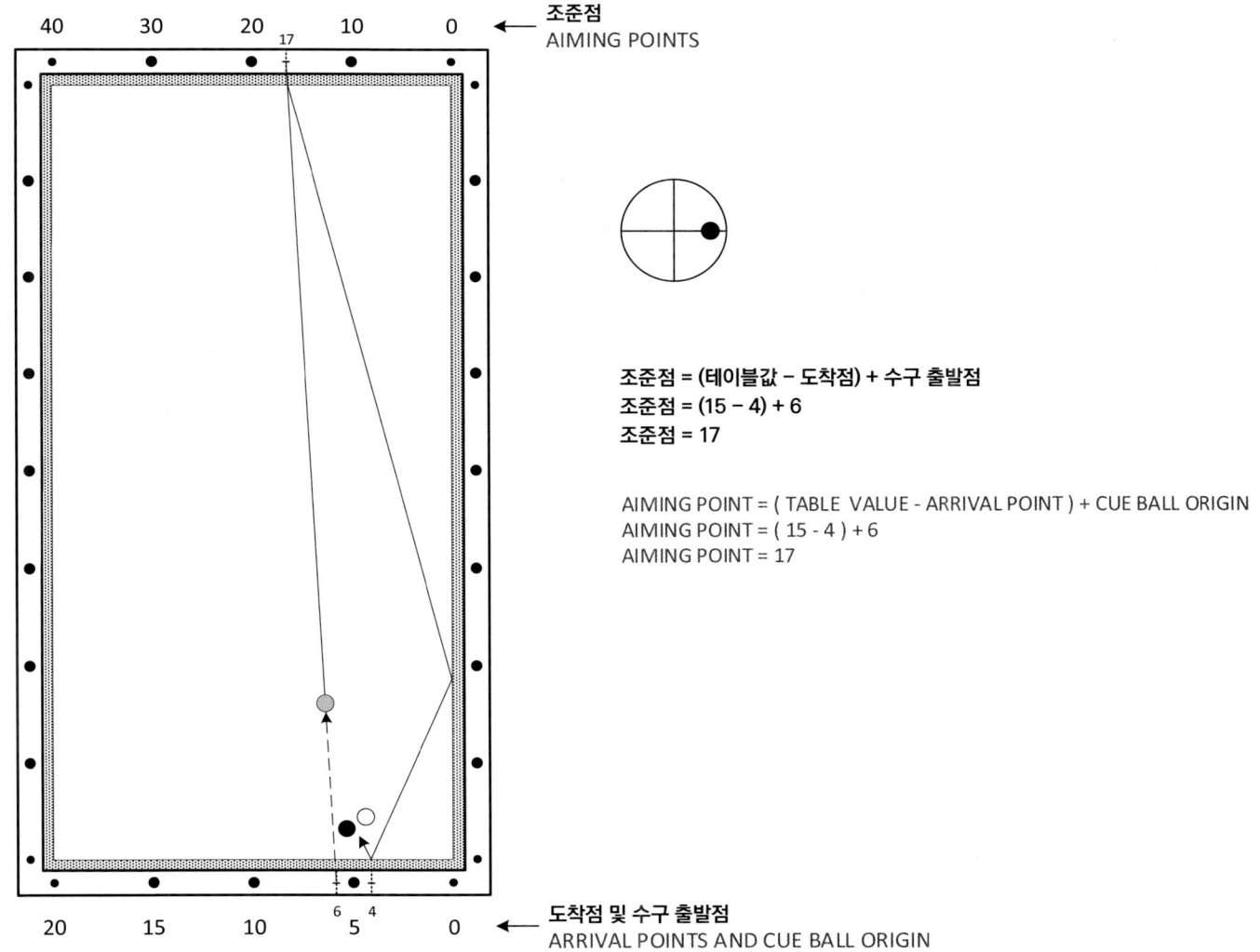

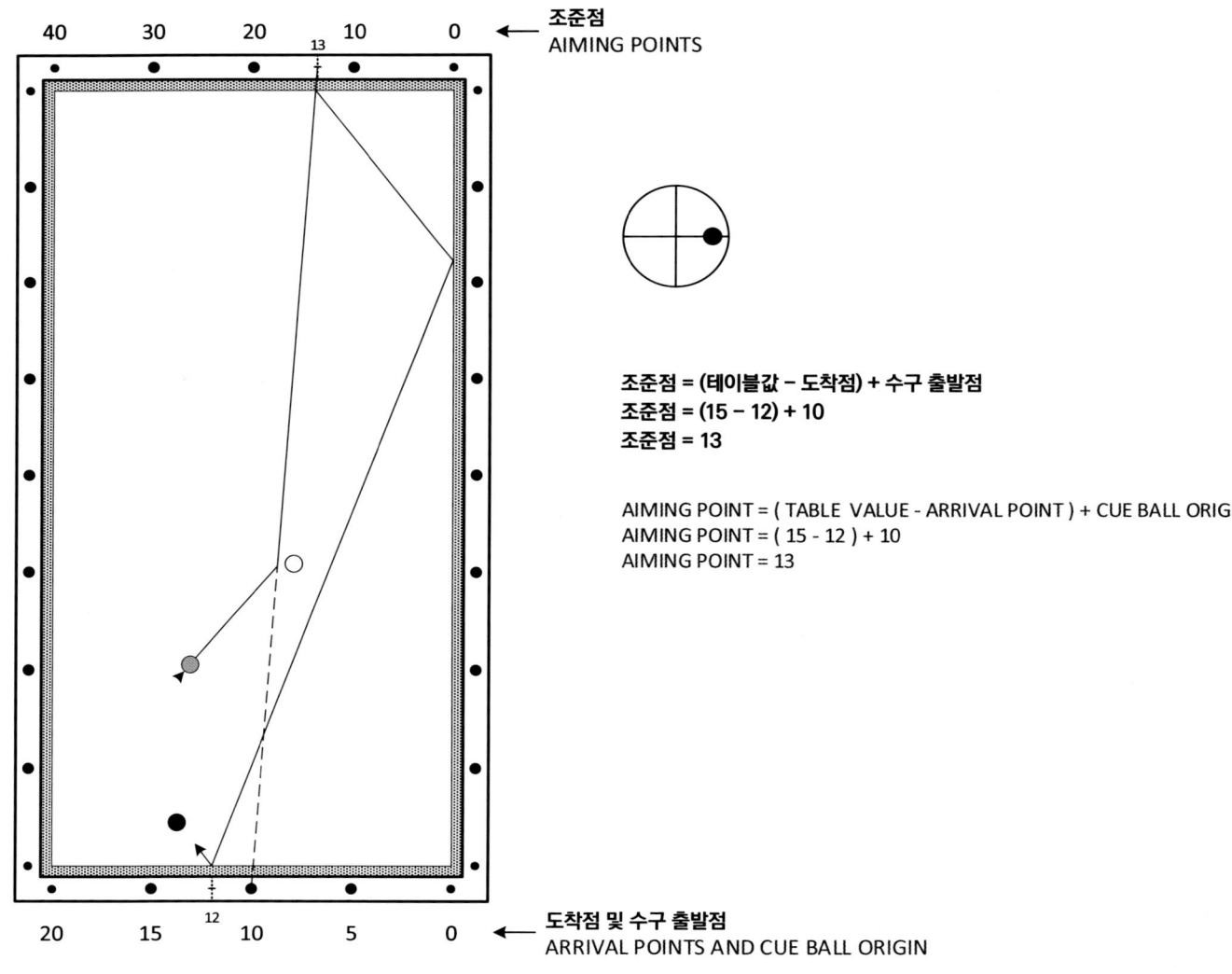

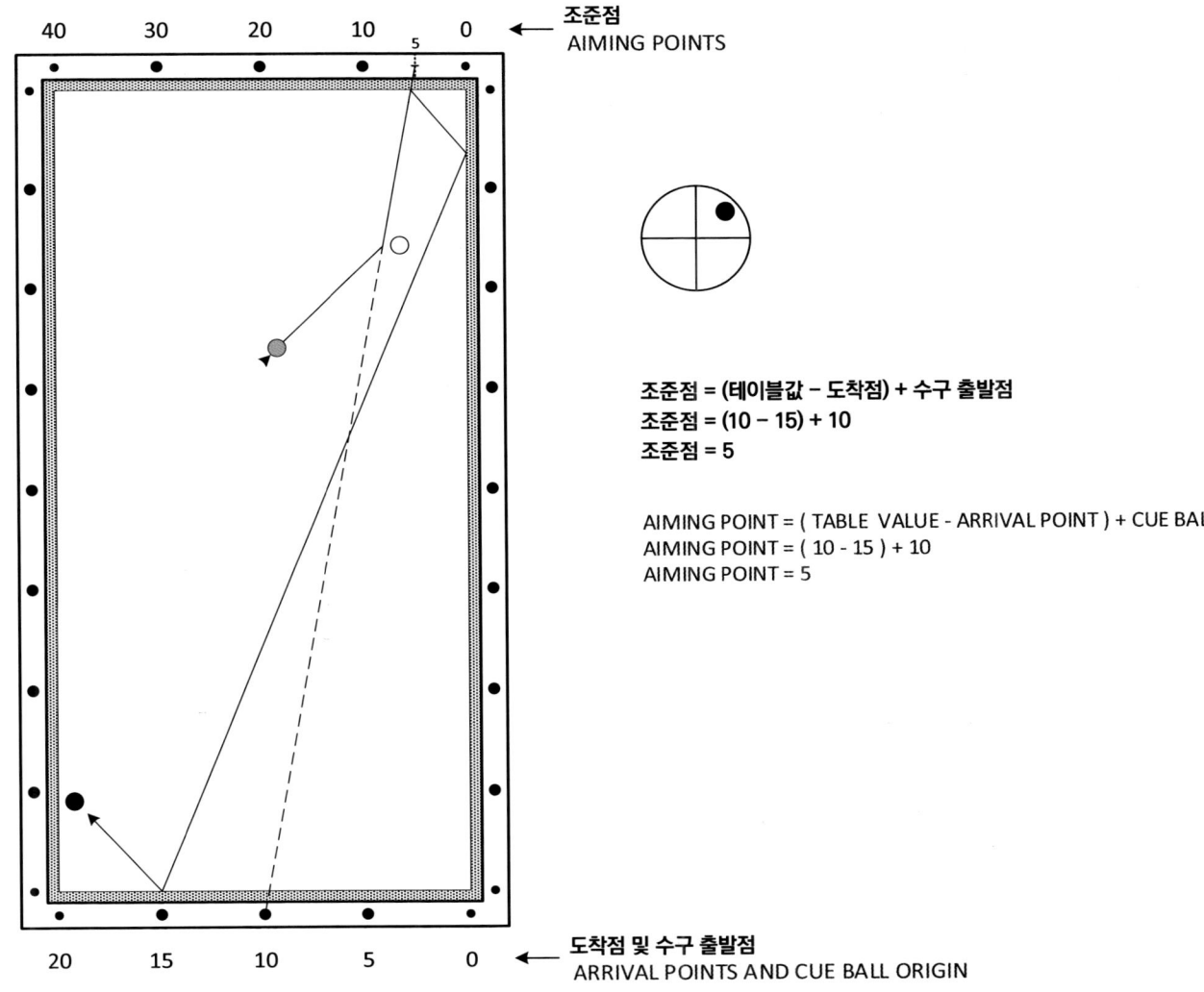

조준점 = (테이블값 − 도착점) + 수구 출발점
조준점 = (10 − 15) + 10
조준점 = 5

AIMING POINT = (TABLE VALUE − ARRIVAL POINT) + CUE BALL ORIGIN
AIMING POINT = (10 − 15) + 10
AIMING POINT = 5

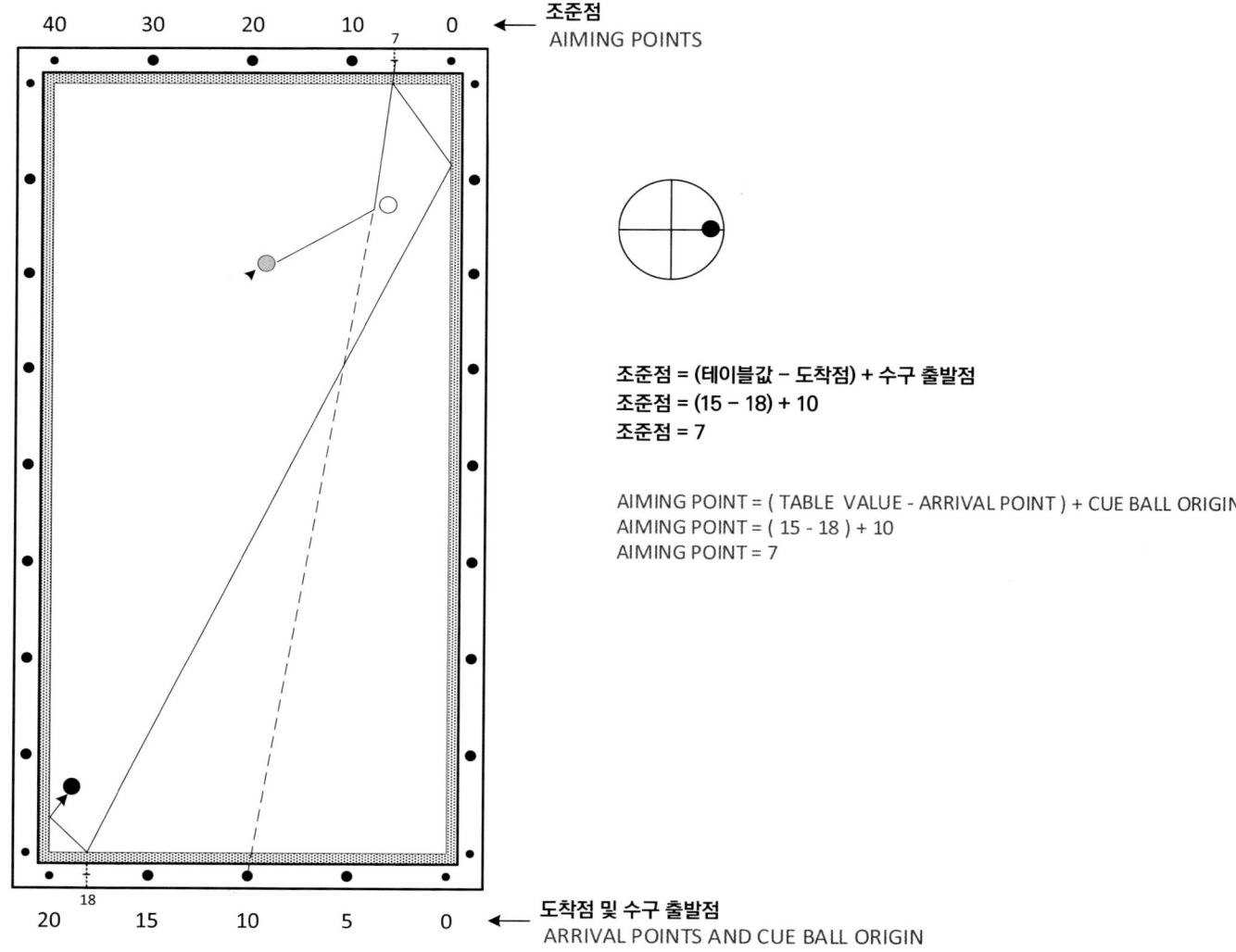

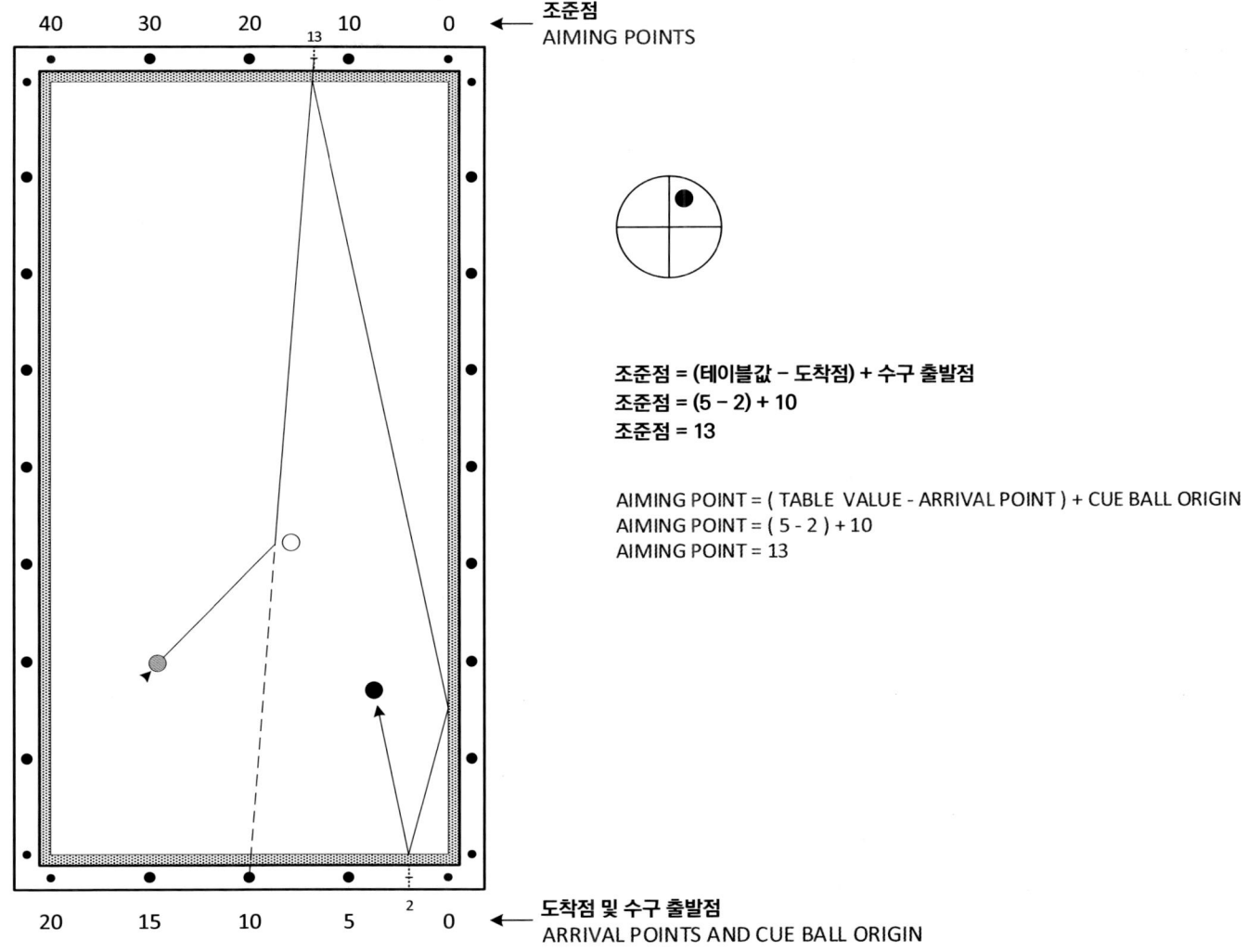

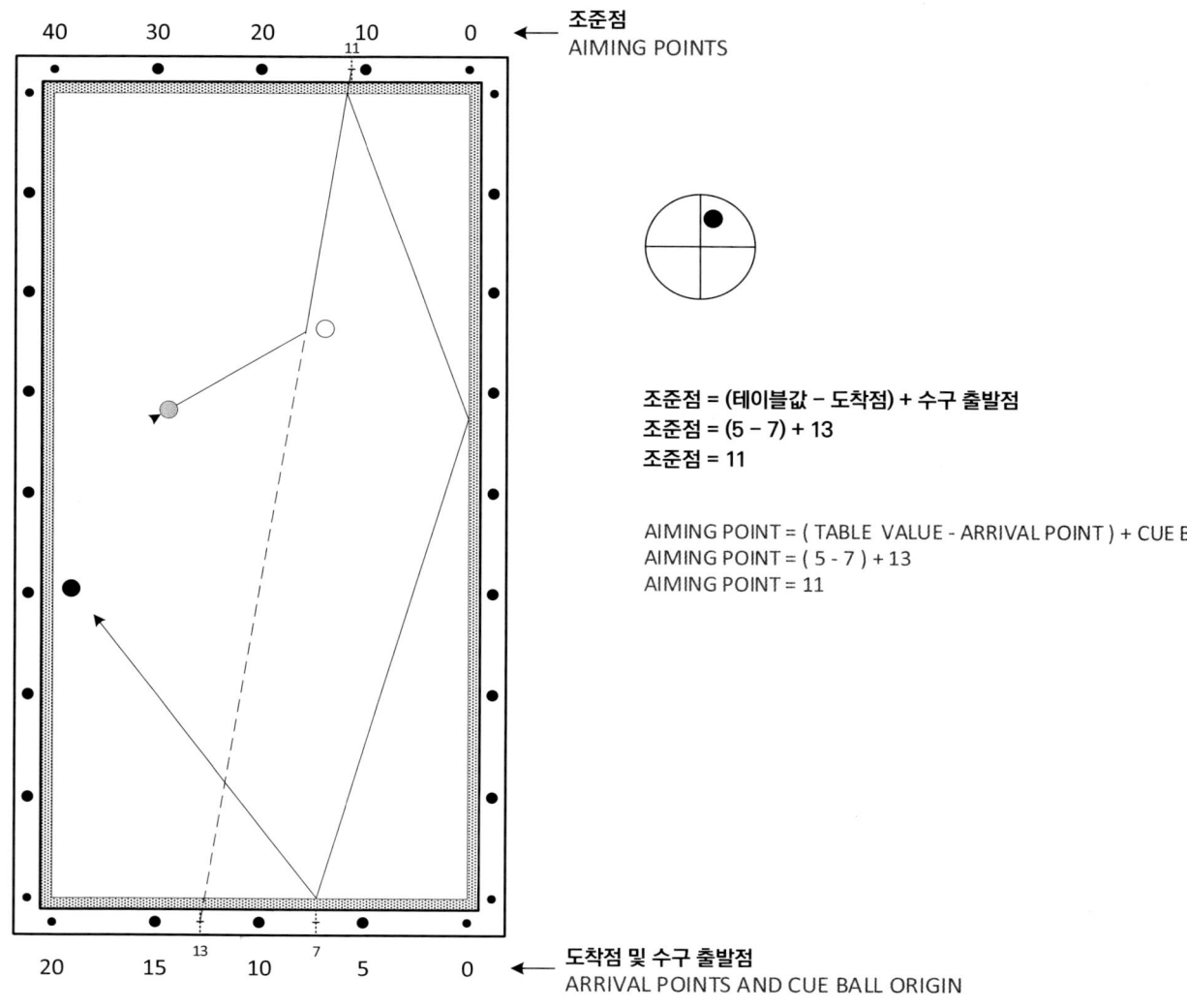

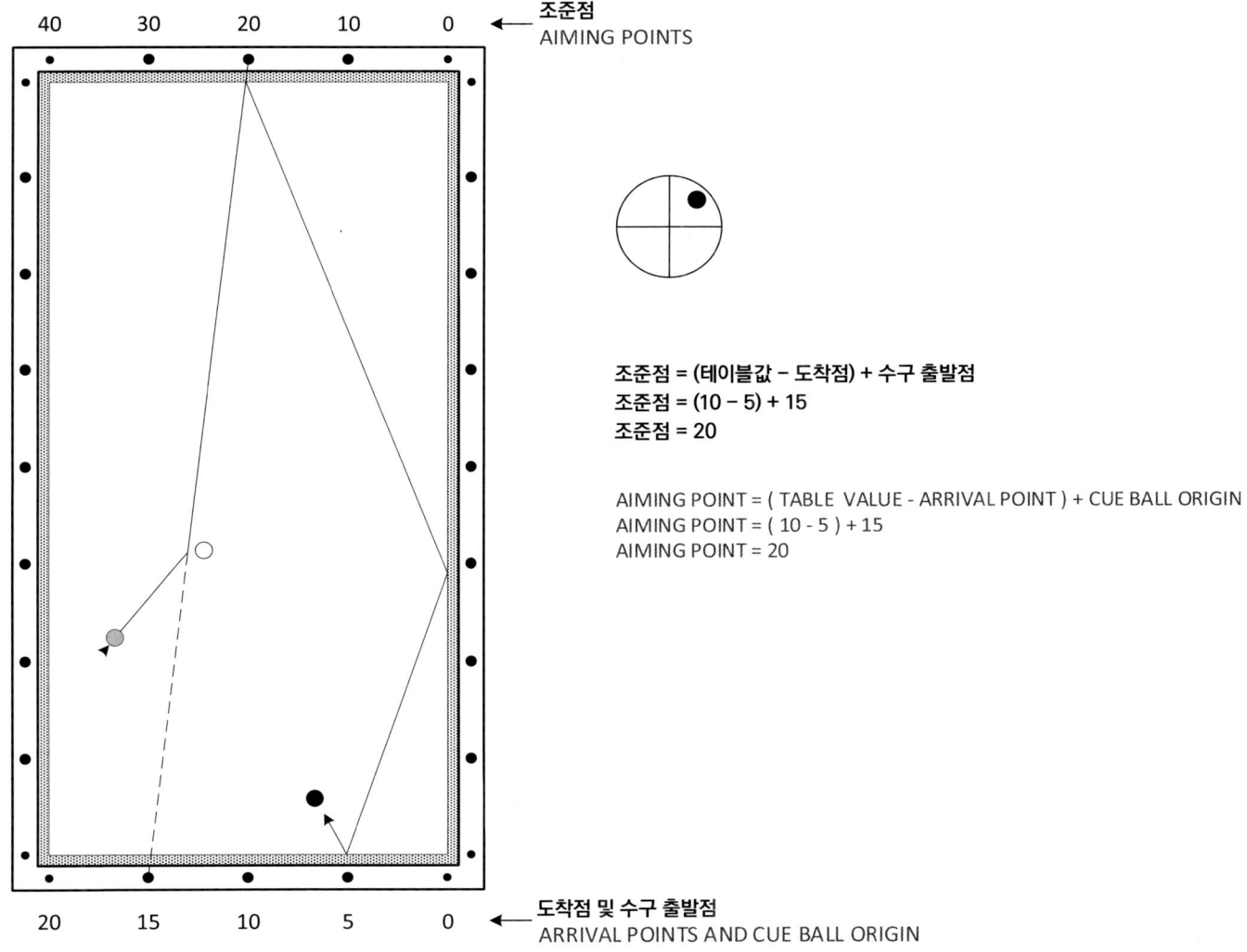

part 01 튜즐 시스템(회전) / 35

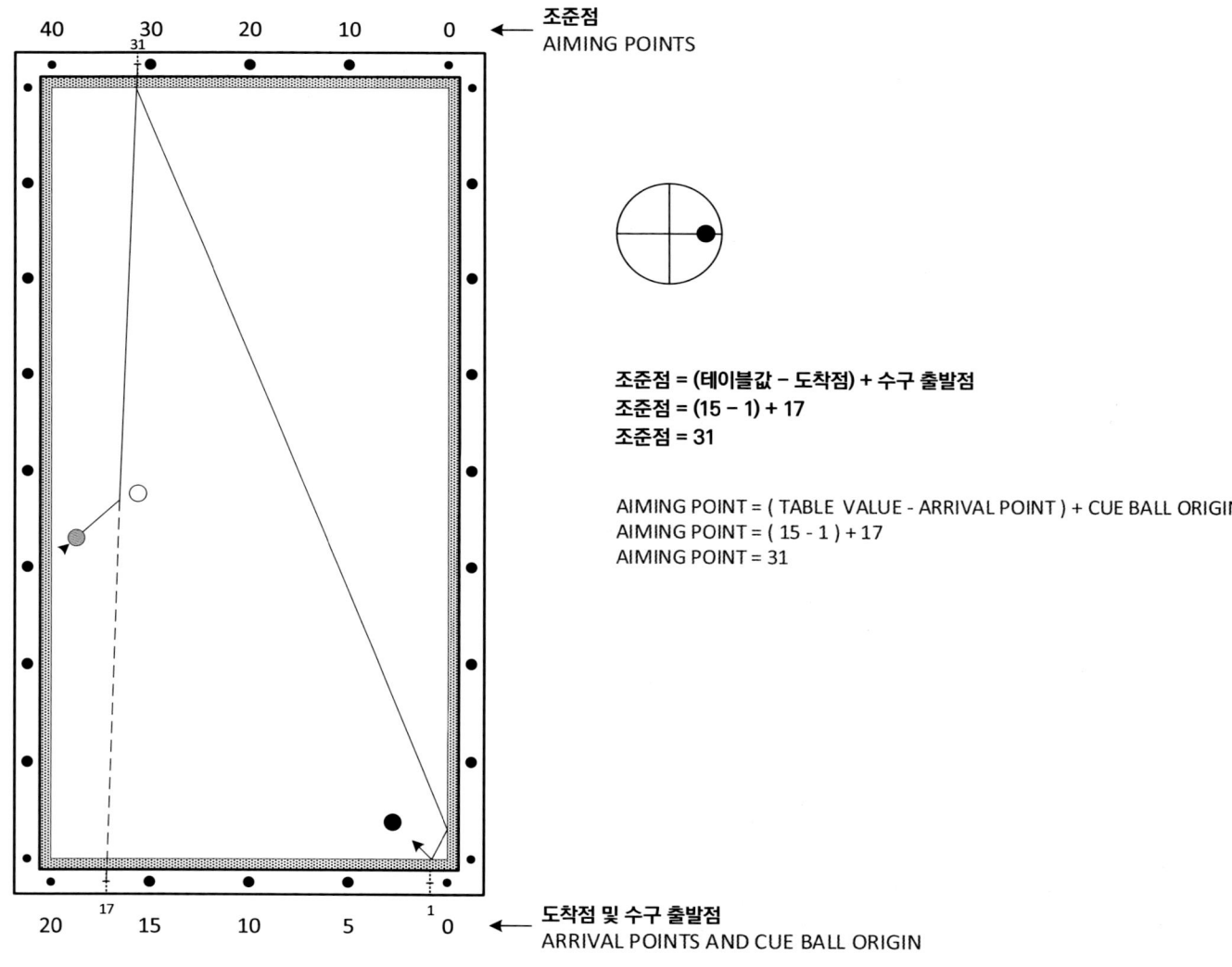

조준점
AIMING POINTS

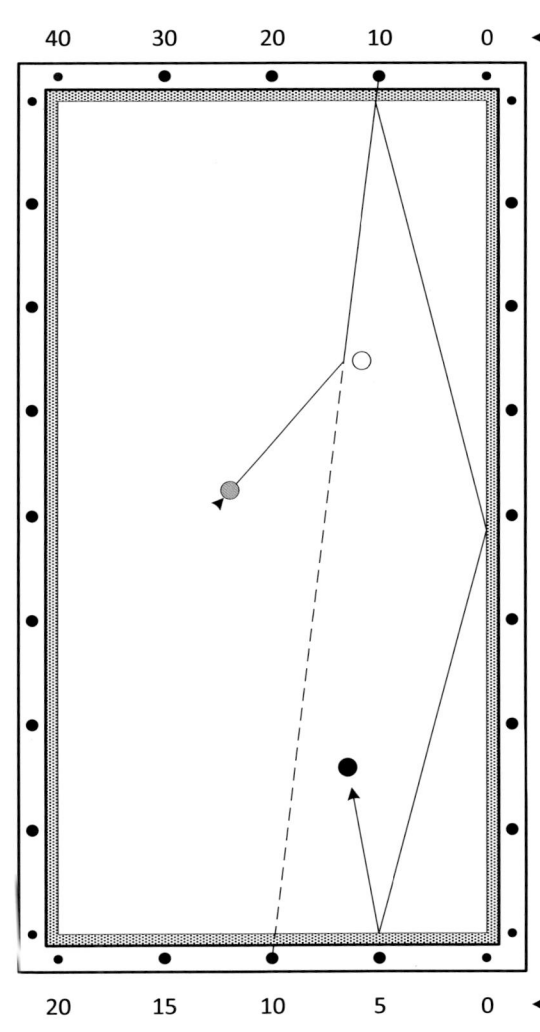
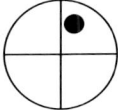

조준점 = (테이블값 − 도착점) + 수구 출발점
조준점 = (5 − 5) + 10
조준점 = 10

AIMING POINT = (TABLE VALUE − ARRIVAL POINT) + CUE BALL ORIGIN
AIMING POINT = (5 − 5) + 10
AIMING POINT = 10

도착점 및 수구 출발점
ARRIVAL POINTS AND CUE BALL ORIGIN

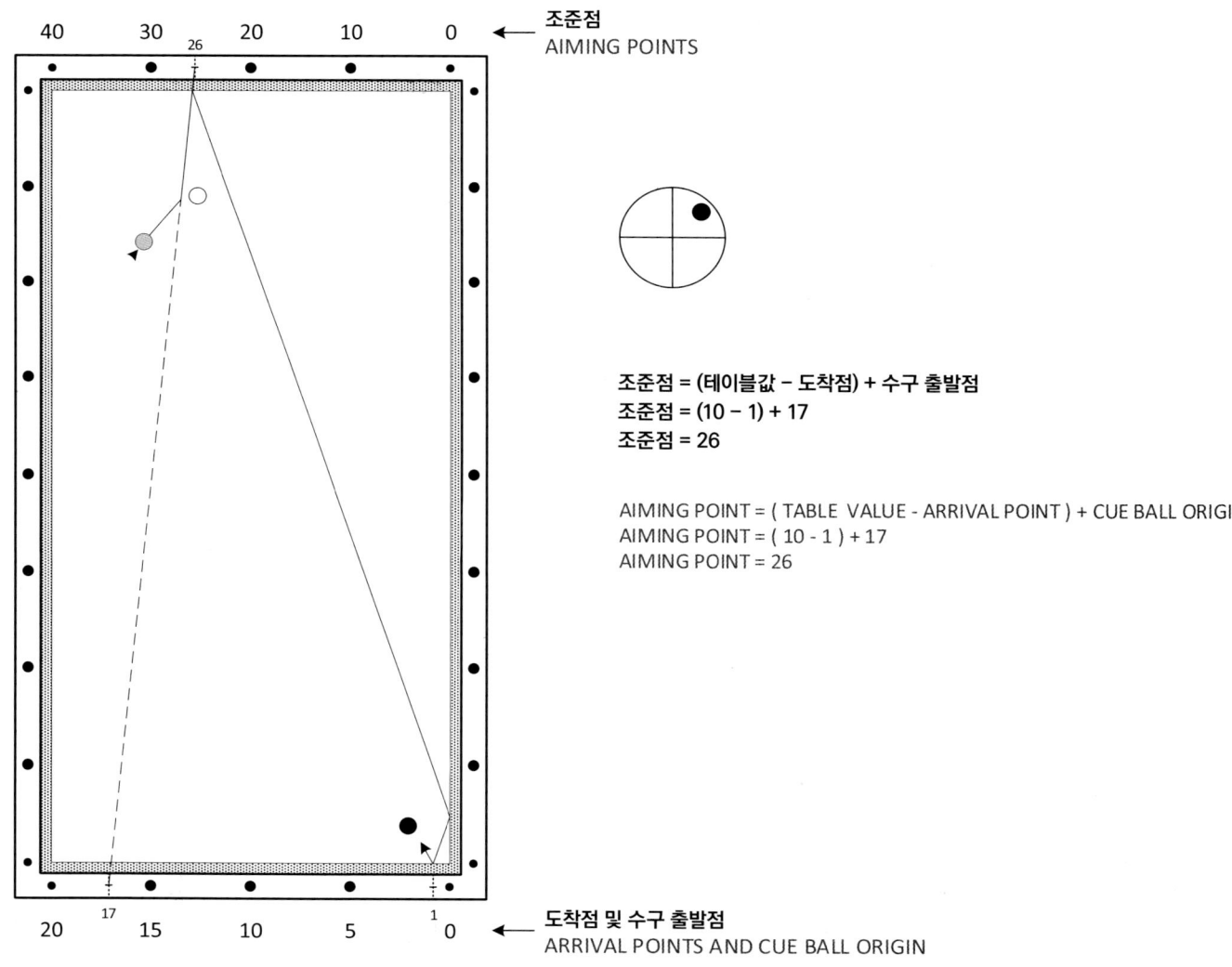

조준점 = (테이블값 − 도착점) + 수구 출발점
조준점 = (10 − 1) + 17
조준점 = 26

AIMING POINT = (TABLE VALUE - ARRIVAL POINT) + CUE BALL ORIGIN
AIMING POINT = (10 - 1) + 17
AIMING POINT = 26

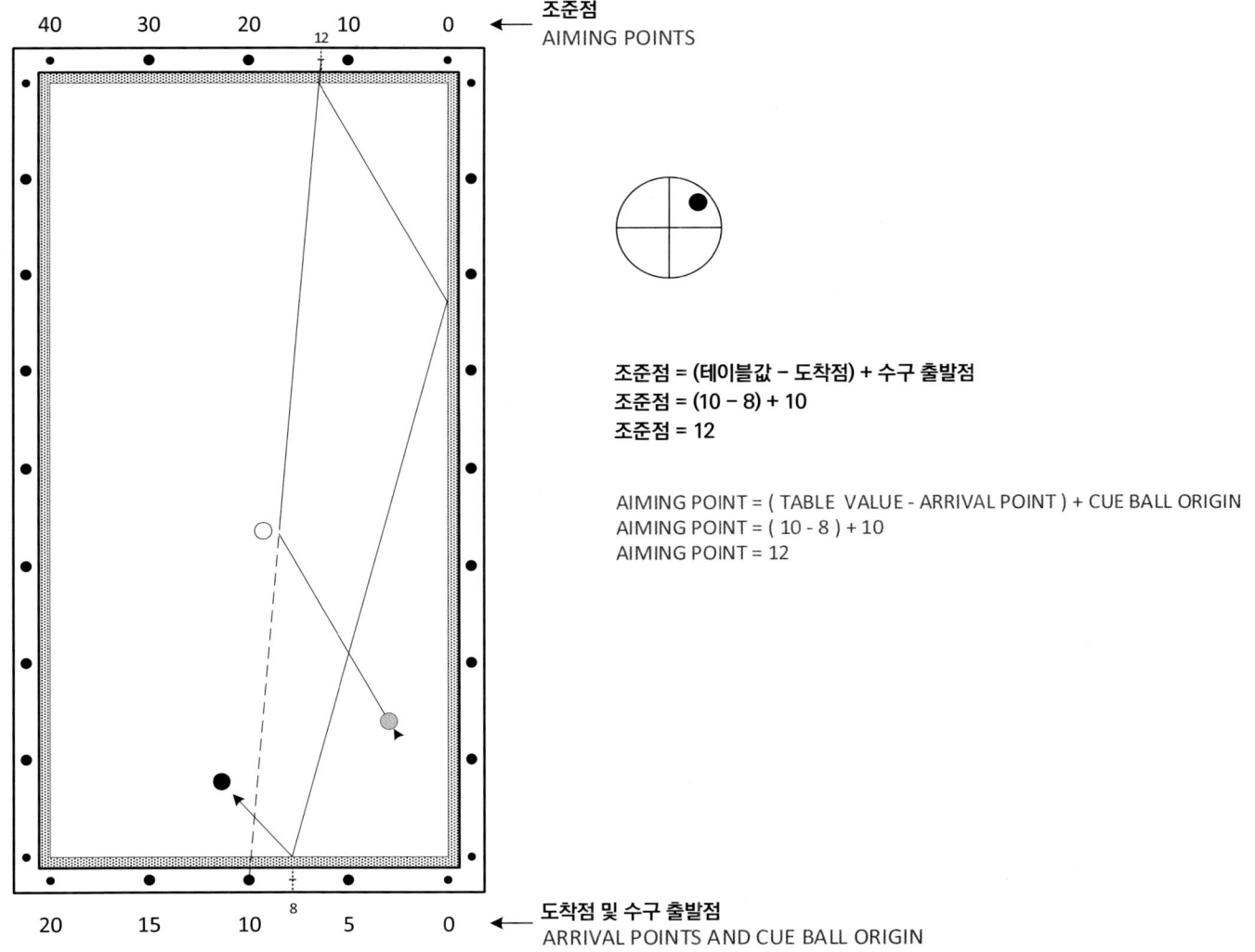

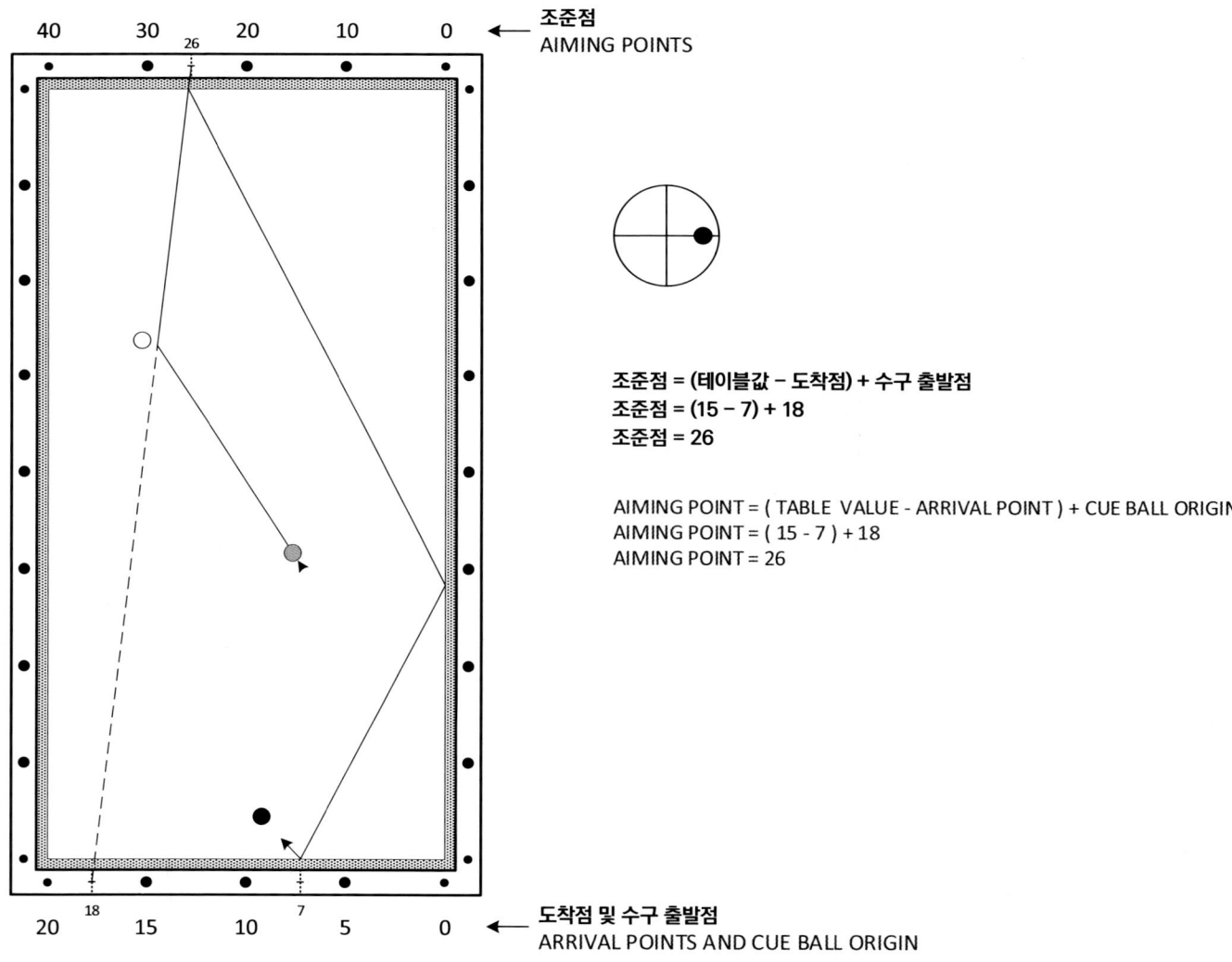

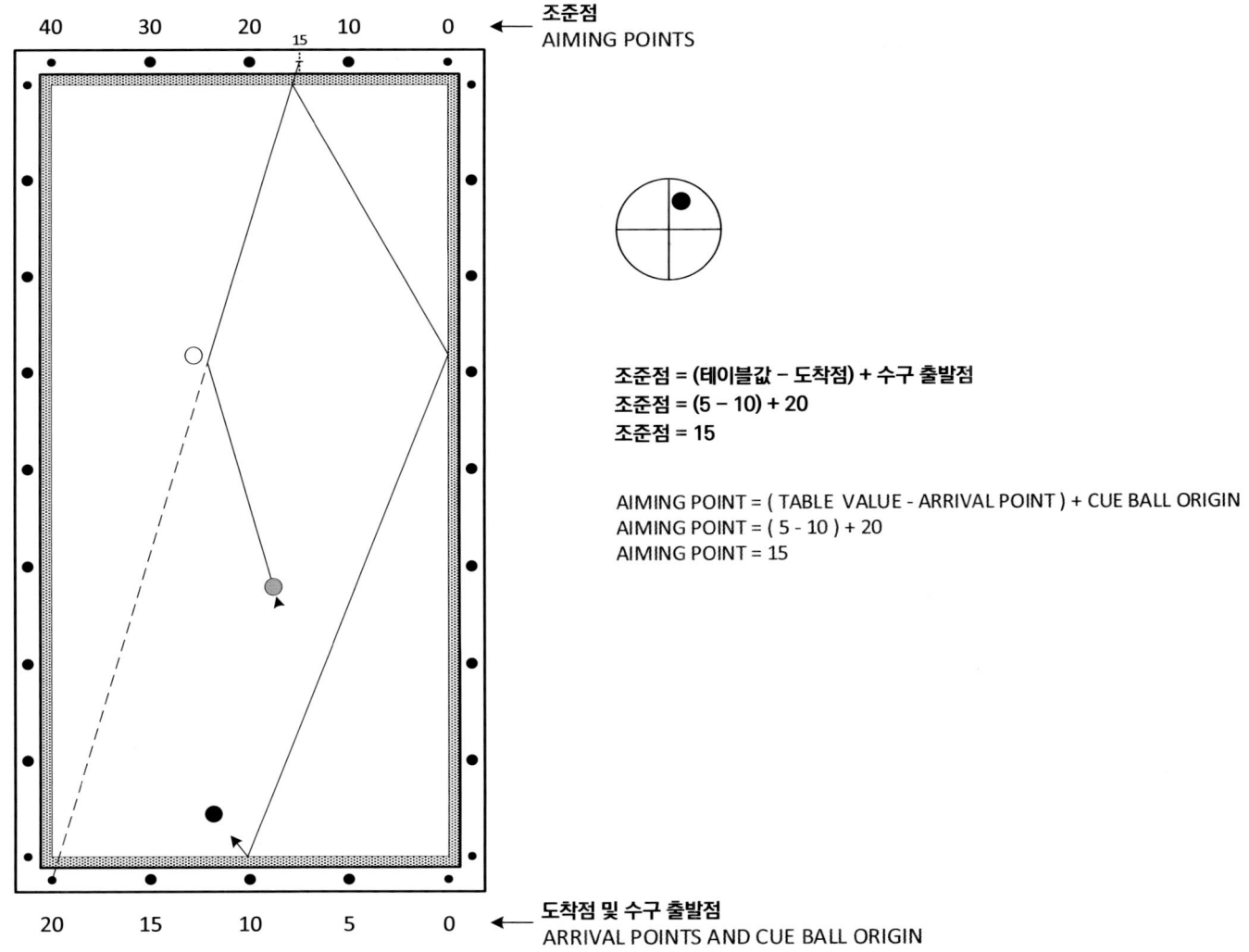

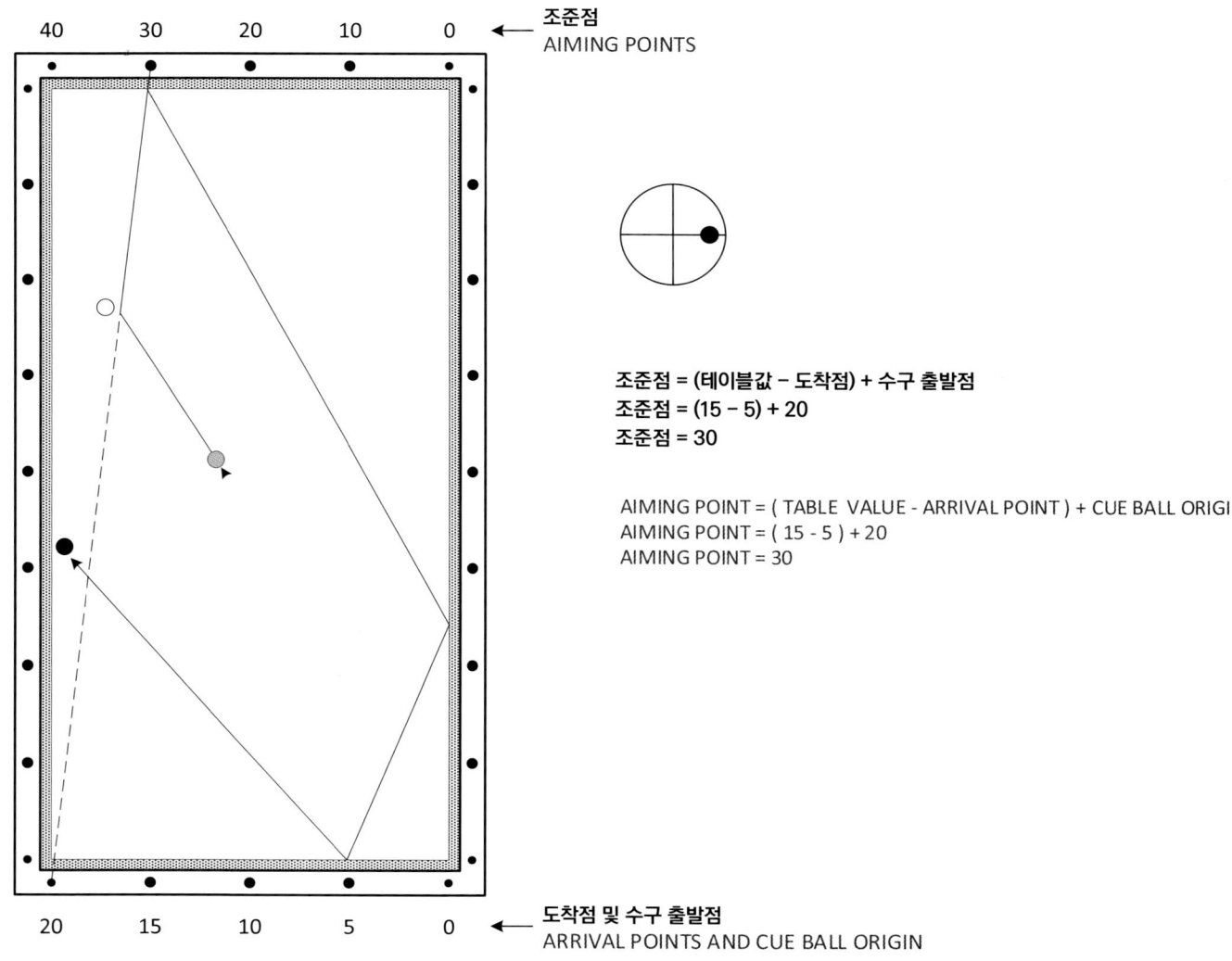

2. 튜즐 시스템 - 장쿠션 출발

튜즐 시스템 - 장쿠션 출발은 그 명칭에서도 알 수 있는 바와 같이 회전을 준 단쿠션-장쿠션-단쿠션 경로에 대한 해결을 위해 사용되며, 큐의 뒤쪽이 장쿠션을 향하고 있는 경우에 수구의 출발점을 계산하는 방법이다. 튜즐 시스템 - 단쿠션 출발에서 수치화한 그림들에 부가하여, 수구의 출발점이 장쿠션에 배치되어 있다. 사용되는 스트로크 기법은 모든 튜즐 시스템(회전)에서 테이블값을 확인해야 한다.

2. SYSTEM TÜZÜL -STARTING FROM LONG CUSHION

System Tüzül –Starting From Long Cushion is used -as understood from its name- to solve with a curve, the short cushion-long cushion-short cushion line, while calculating the cue ball's origin point, in case the back of the cue is towards the long cushion. In addition to the figures on the numbering graph of System Tüzül -Starting From Short Cushion, cue ball origin points are aligned on the long cushion. The stroke technique that should be used has to verify the Table Value as in all Tüzül Systems (english).

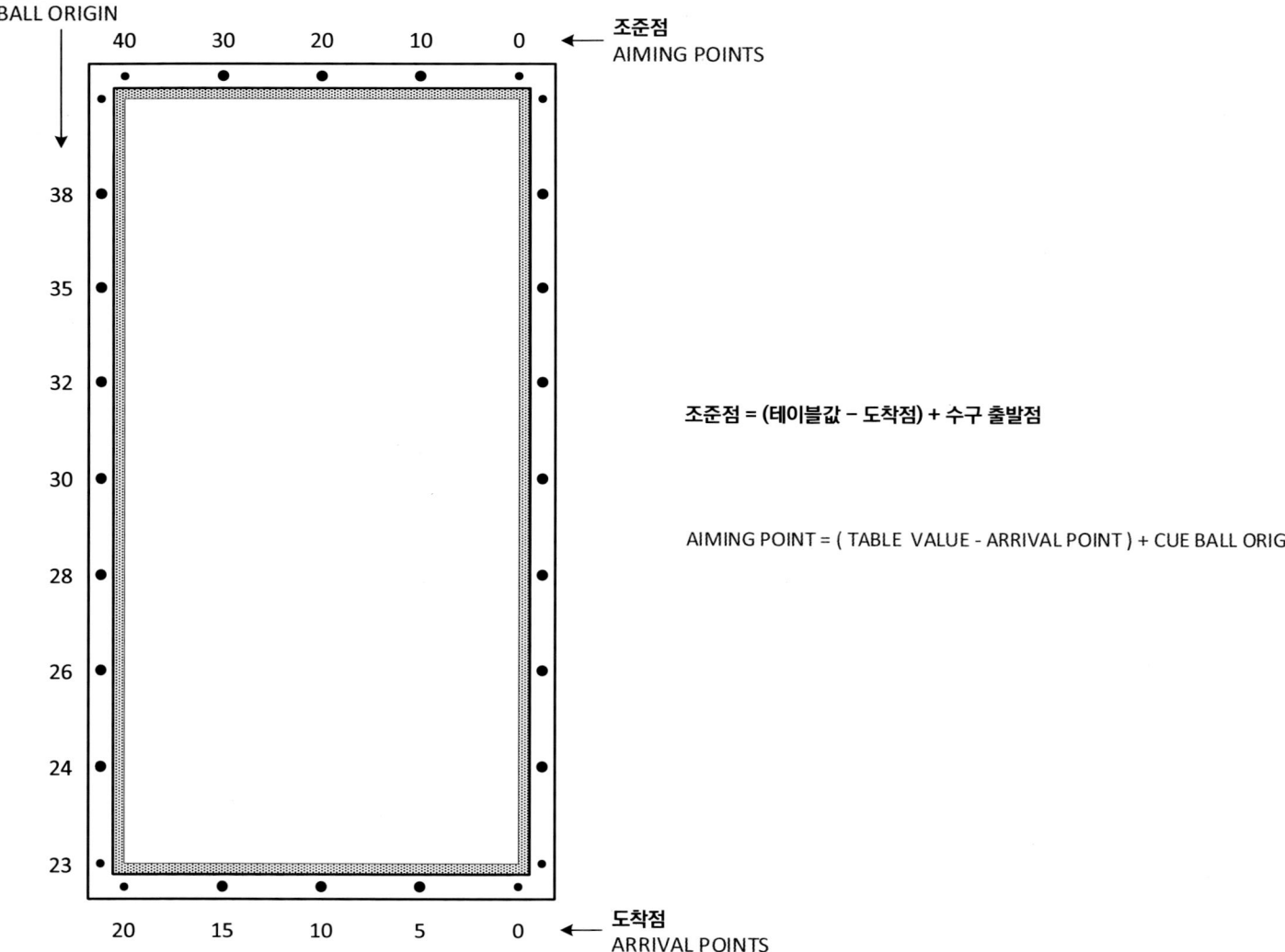

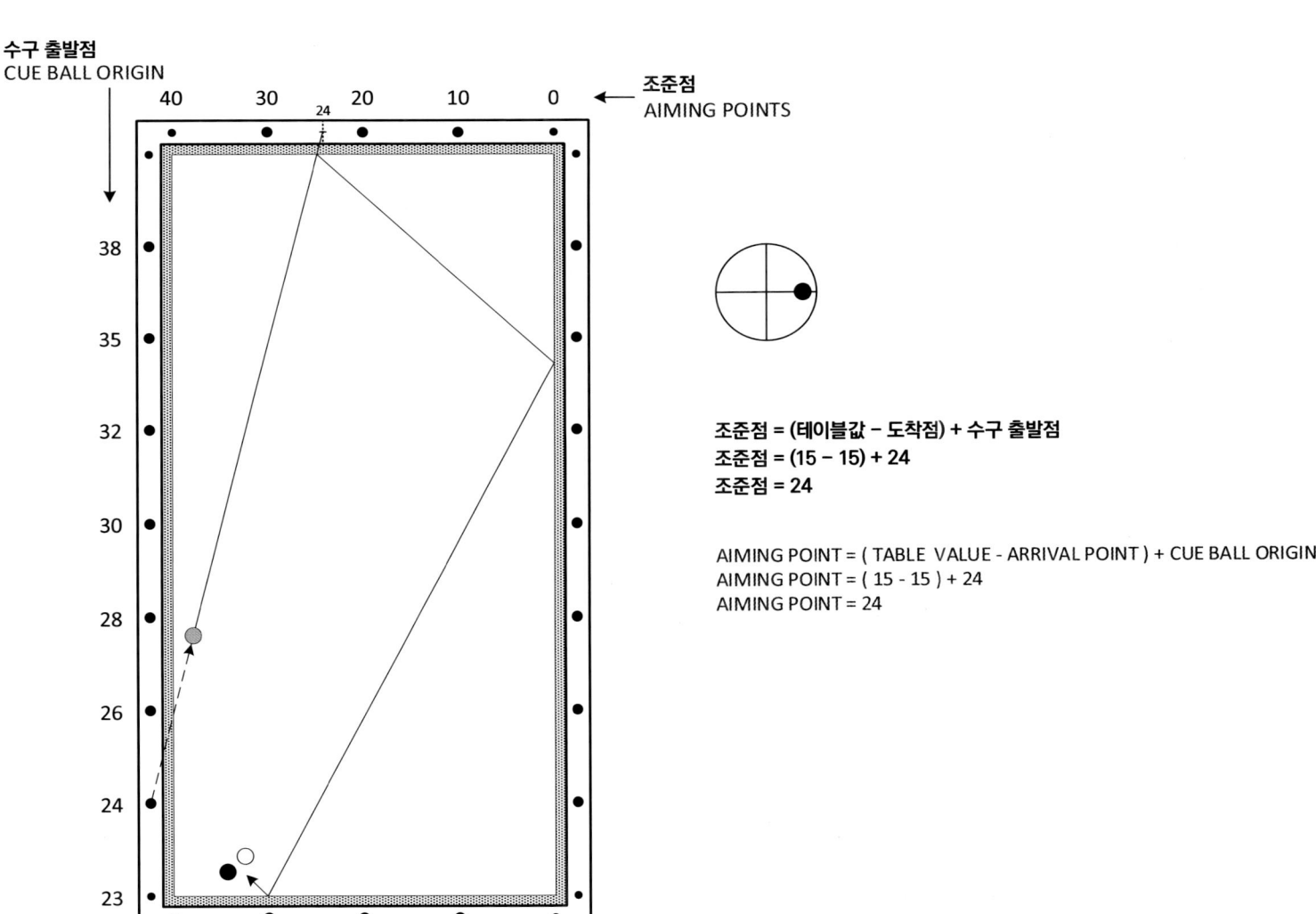

조준점 = (테이블값 - 도착점) + 수구 출발점
조준점 = (15 - 15) + 24
조준점 = 24

AIMING POINT = (TABLE VALUE - ARRIVAL POINT) + CUE BALL ORIGIN
AIMING POINT = (15 - 15) + 24
AIMING POINT = 24

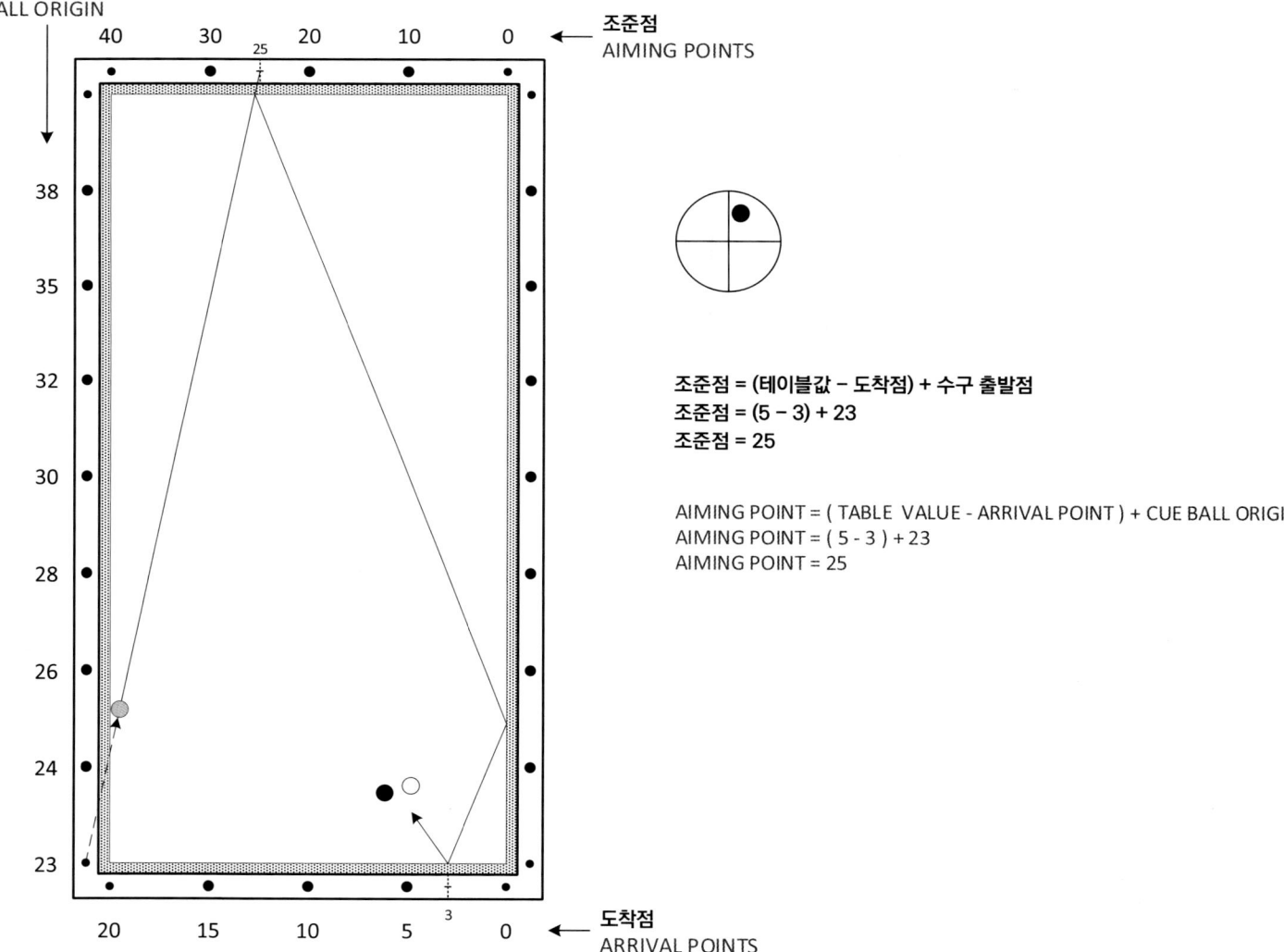

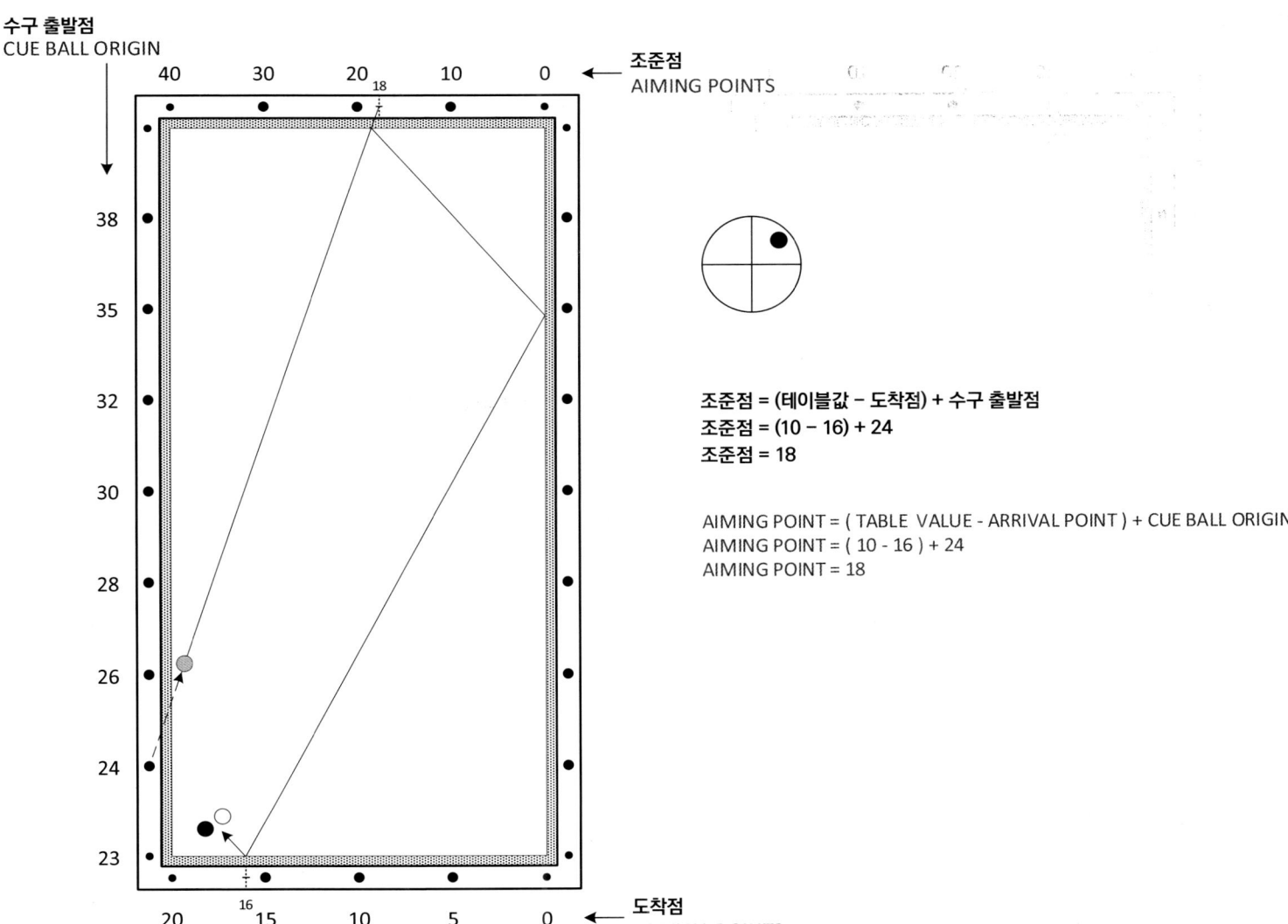

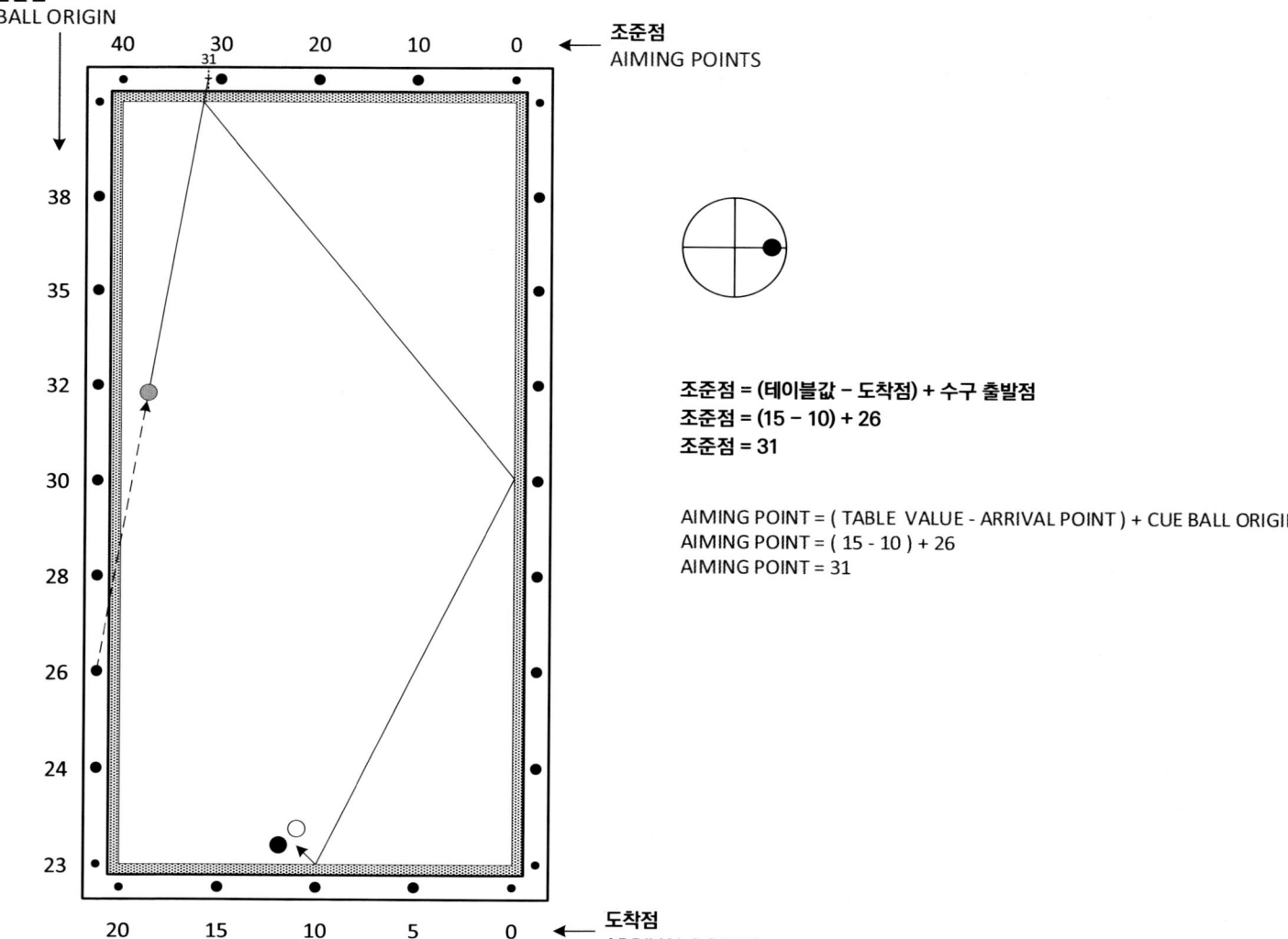

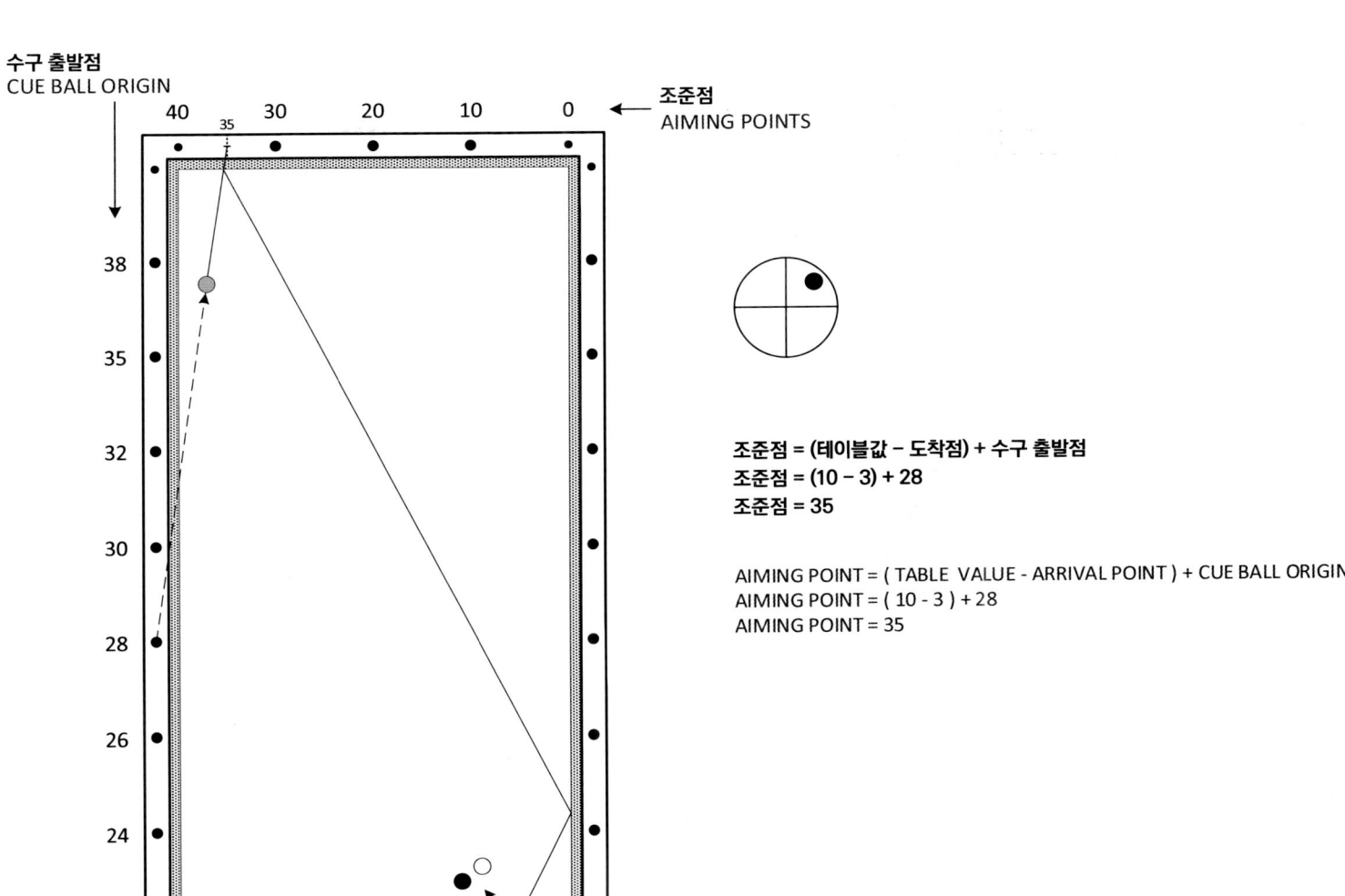

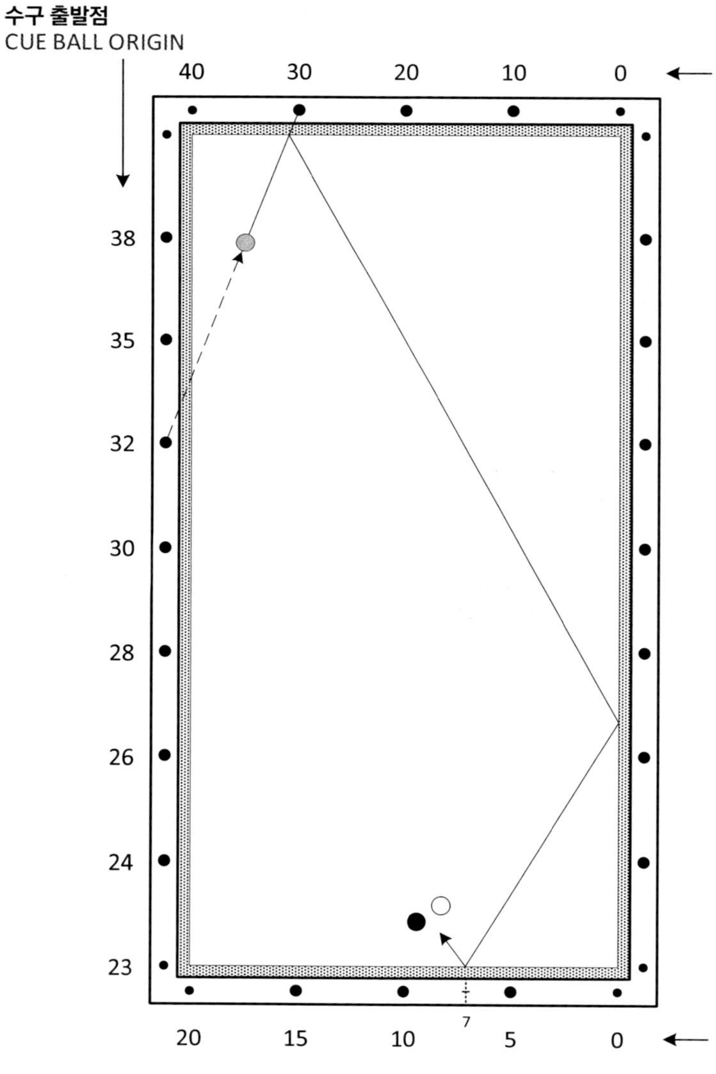

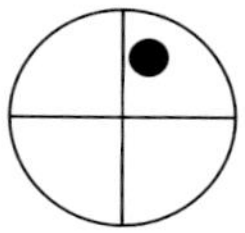

조준점 = (테이블값 − 도착점) + 수구 출발점
조준점 = (5 − 7) + 32
조준점 = 30

AIMING POINT = (TABLE VALUE − ARRIVAL POINT) + CUE BALL ORIGIN
AIMING POINT = (5 − 7) + 32
AIMING POINT = 30

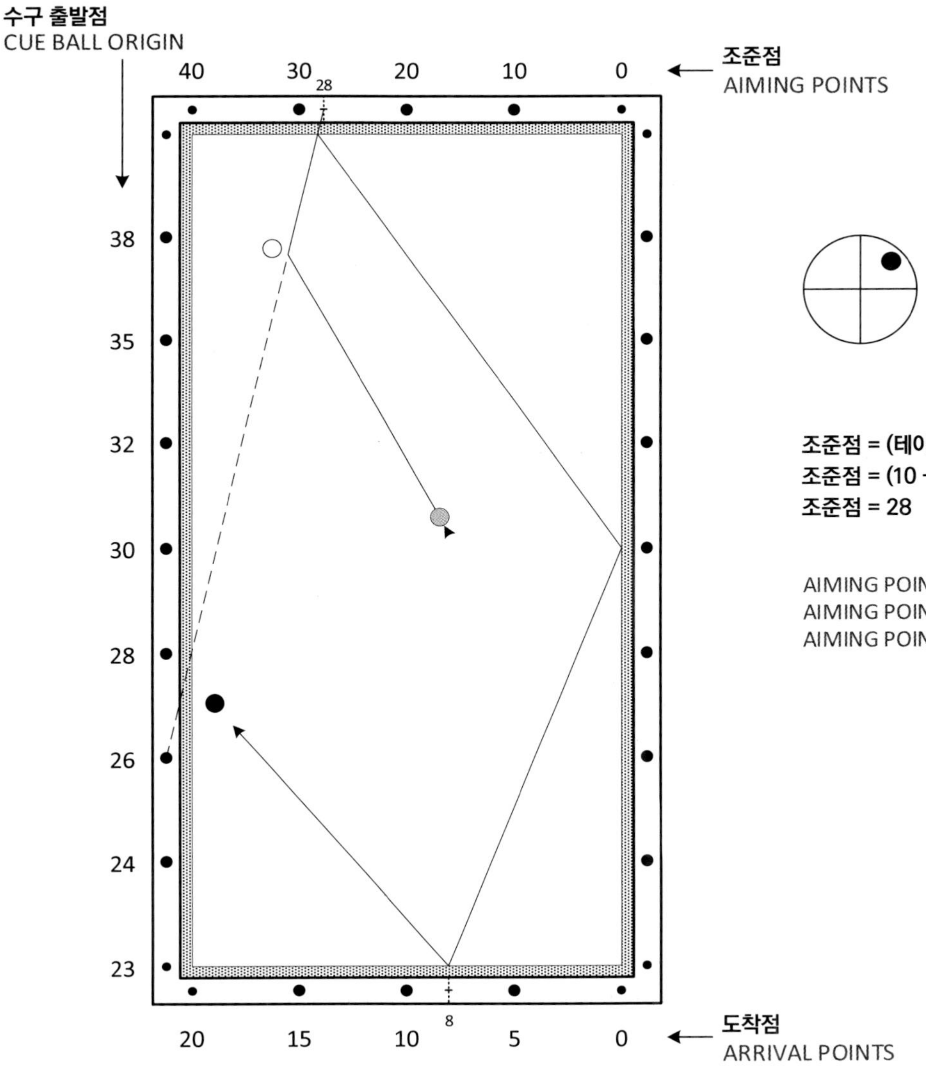

수구 출발점
CUE BALL ORIGIN

조준점
AIMING POINTS

도착점
ARRIVAL POINTS

조준점 = (테이블값 − 도착점) + 수구 출발점
조준점 = (10 − 8) + 26
조준점 = 28

AIMING POINT = (TABLE VALUE - ARRIVAL POINT) + CUE BALL ORIGIN
AIMING POINT = (10 - 8) + 26
AIMING POINT = 28

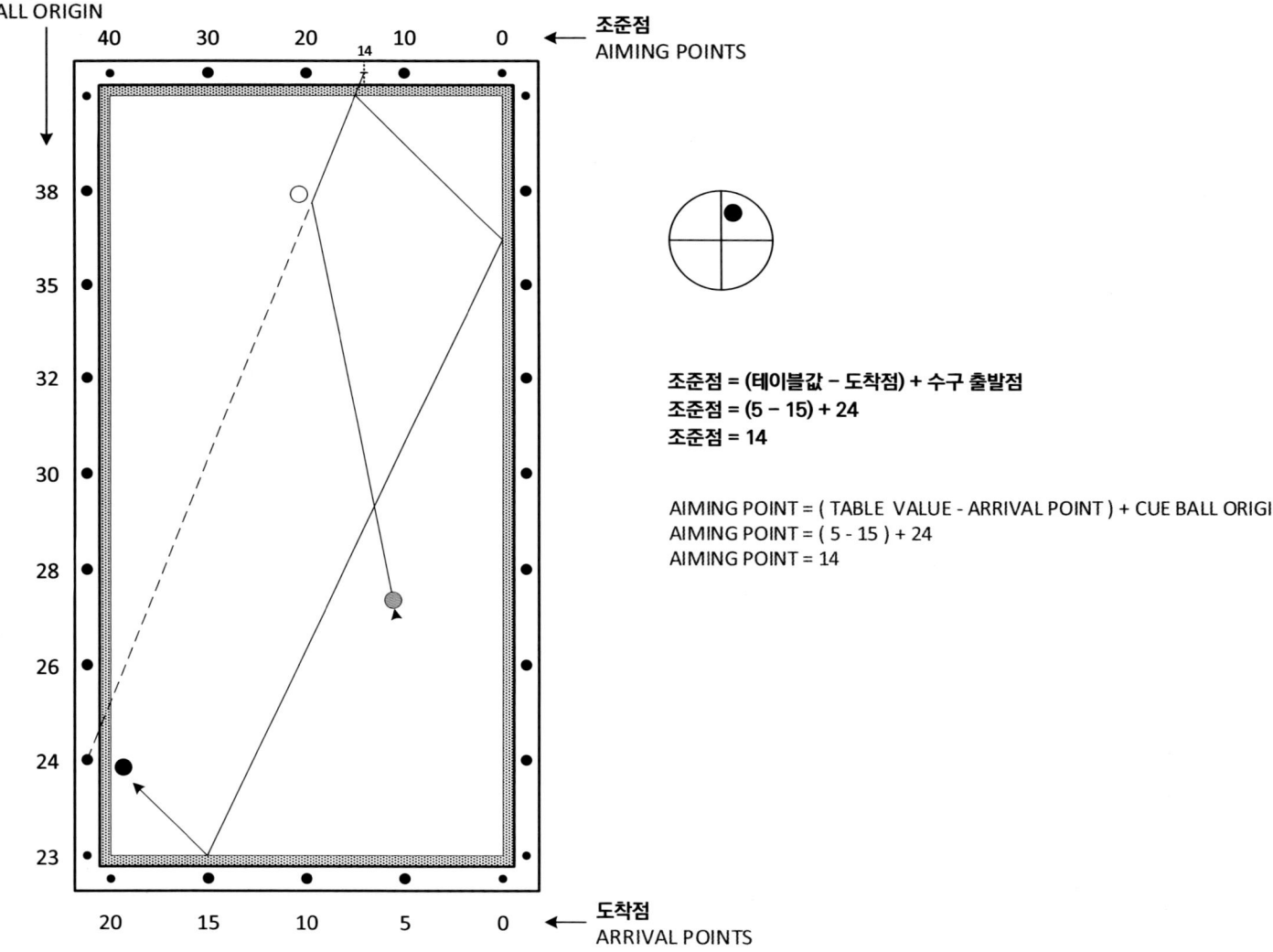

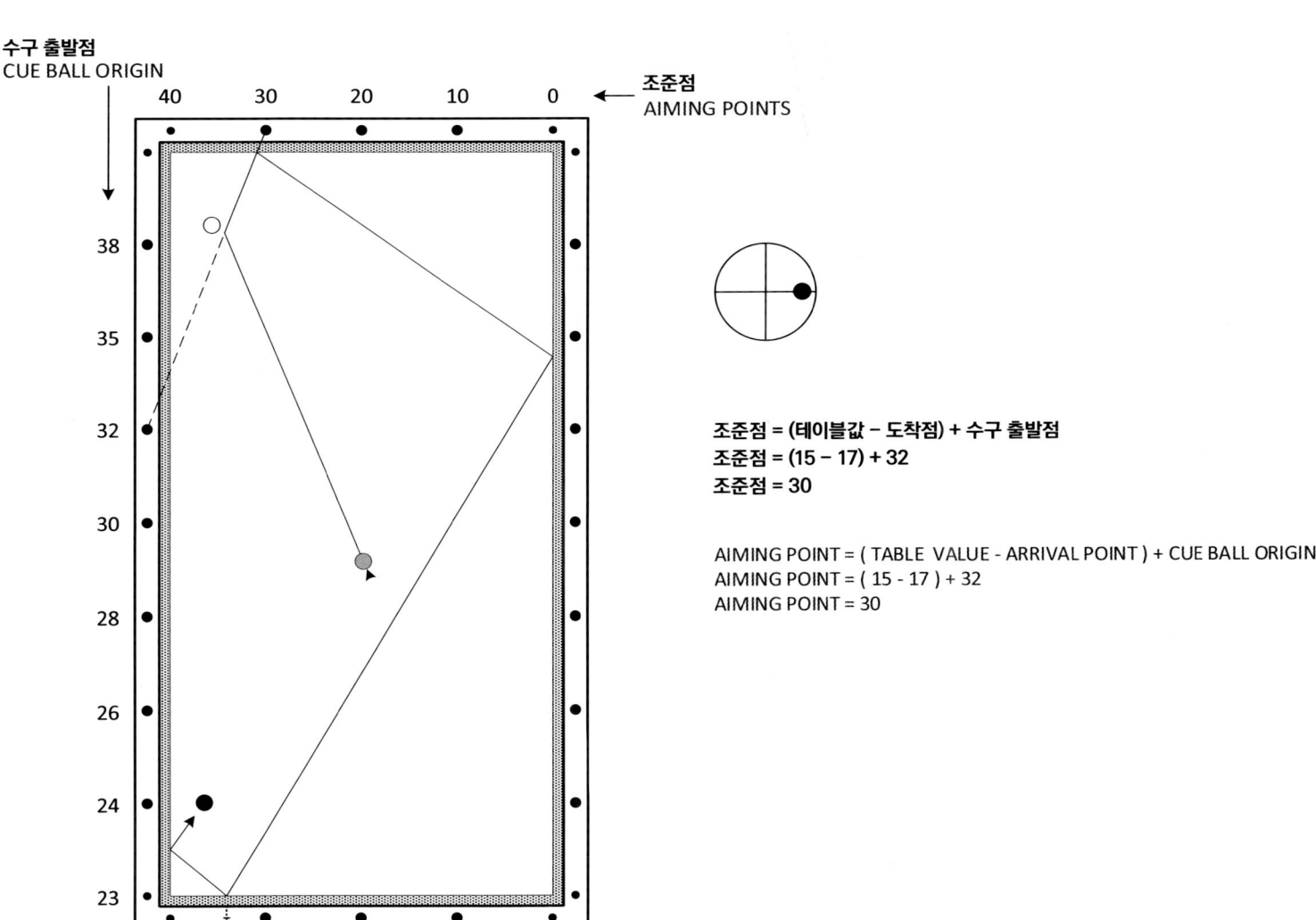

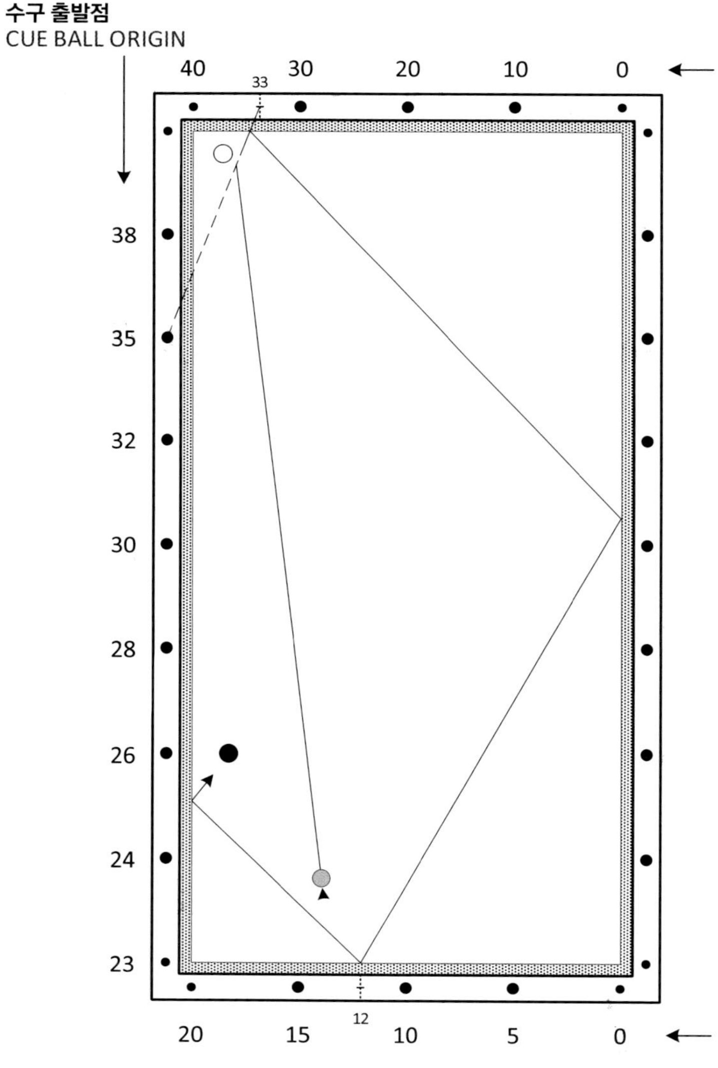

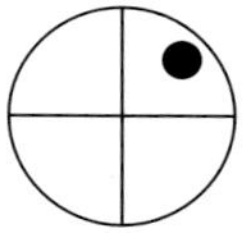

수구 출발점
CUE BALL ORIGIN

조준점
AIMING POINTS

조준점 = (테이블값 − 도착점) + 수구 출발점
조준점 = (10 − 12) + 35
조준점 = 33

AIMING POINT = (TABLE VALUE − ARRIVAL POINT) + CUE BALL ORIGIN
AIMING POINT = (10 − 12) + 35
AIMING POINT = 33

도착점
ARRIVAL POINTS

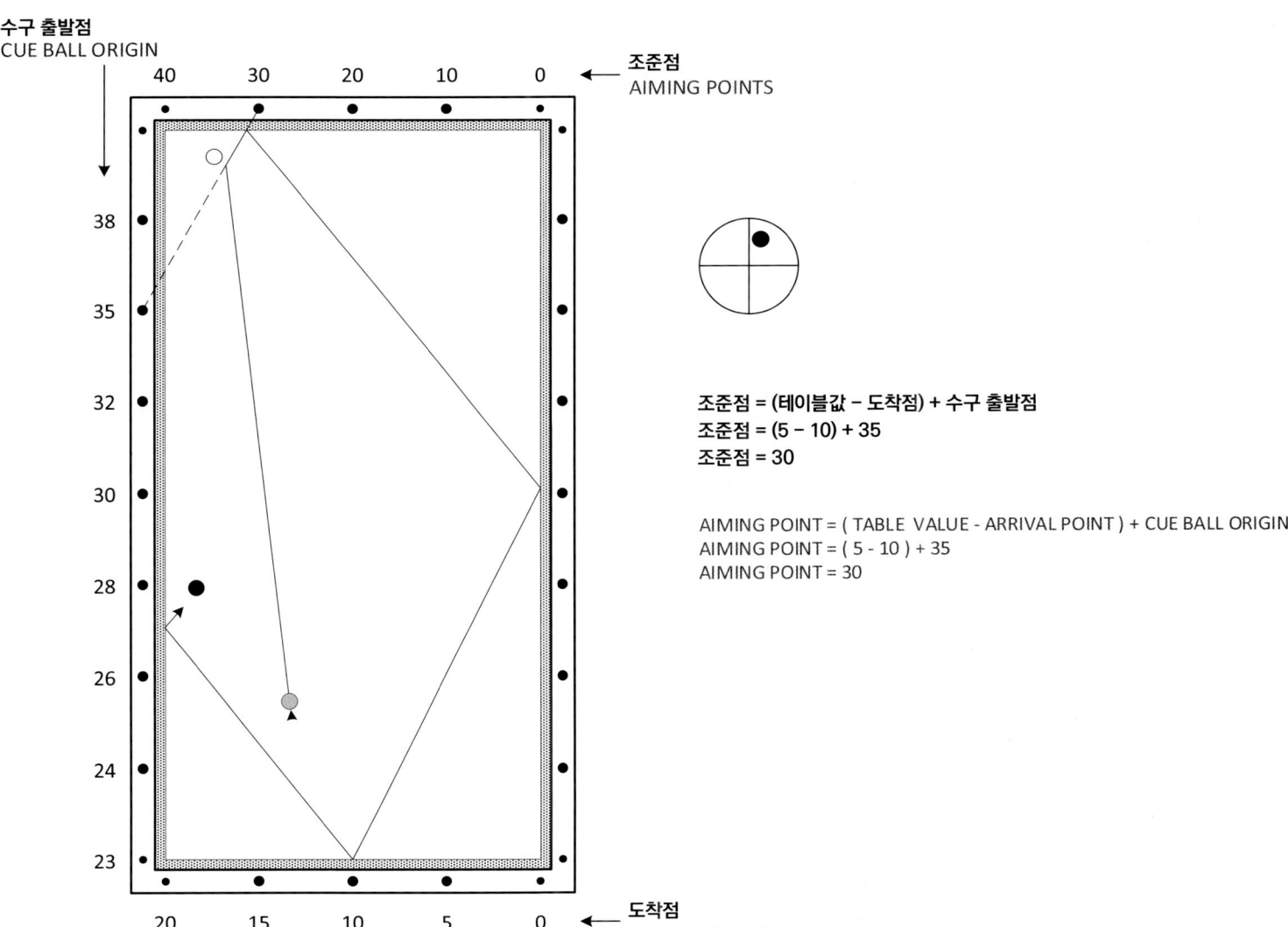

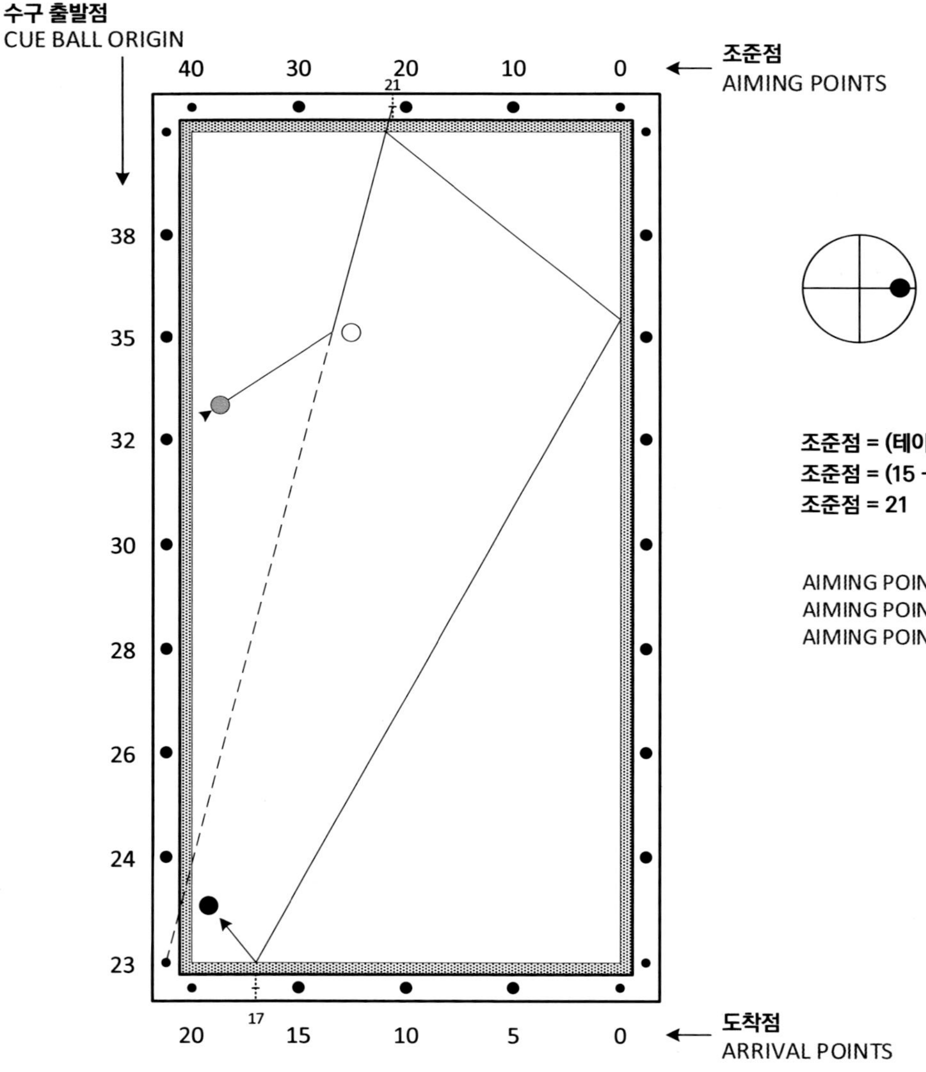

수구 출발점
CUE BALL ORIGIN

조준점
AIMING POINTS

도착점
ARRIVAL POINTS

조준점 = (테이블값 − 도착점) + 수구 출발점
조준점 = (15 − 17) + 23
조준점 = 21

AIMING POINT = (TABLE VALUE − ARRIVAL POINT) + CUE BALL ORIGIN
AIMING POINT = (15 − 17) + 23
AIMING POINT = 21

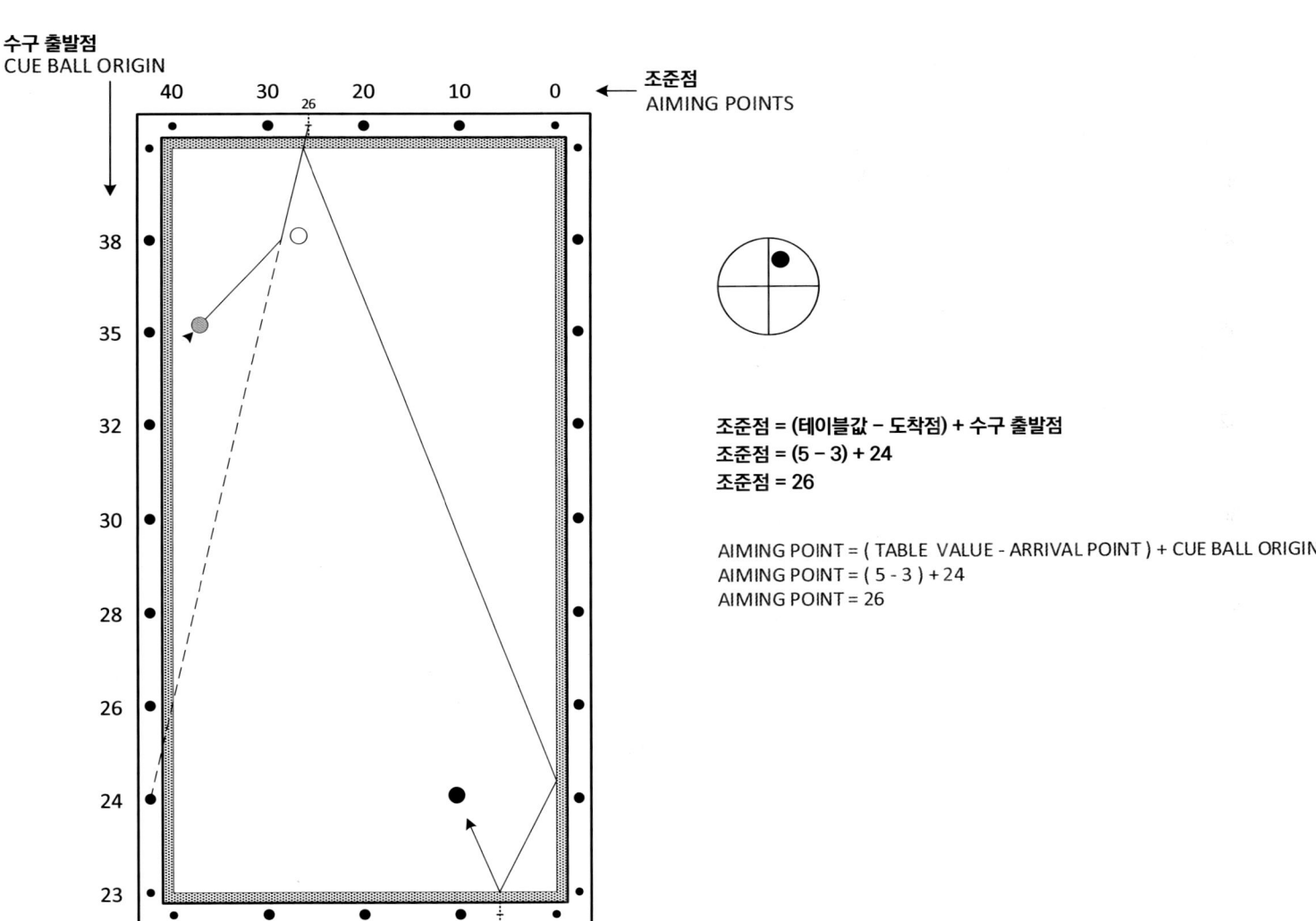

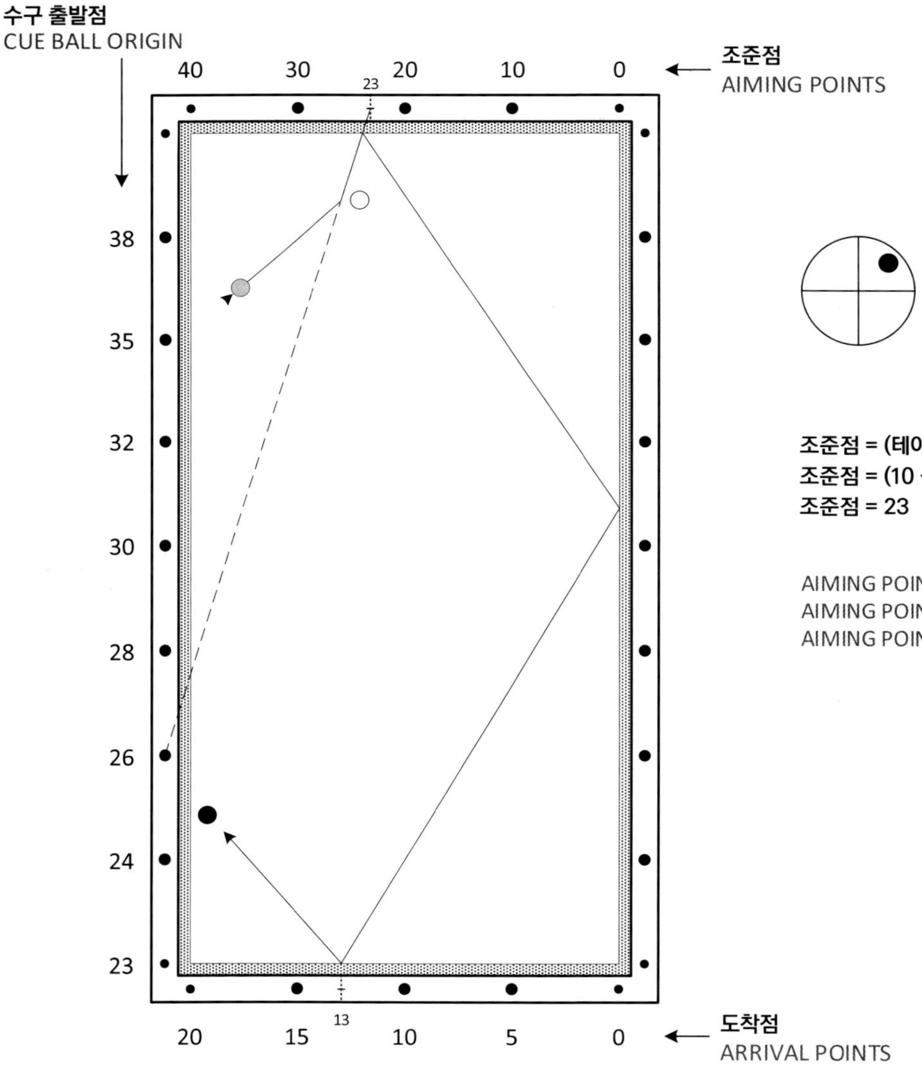

수구 출발점
CUE BALL ORIGIN

조준점
AIMING POINTS

도착점
ARRIVAL POINTS

조준점 = (테이블값 − 도착점) + 수구 출발점
조준점 = (10 − 13) + 26
조준점 = 23

AIMING POINT = (TABLE VALUE - ARRIVAL POINT) + CUE BALL ORIGIN
AIMING POINT = (10 - 13) + 26
AIMING POINT = 23

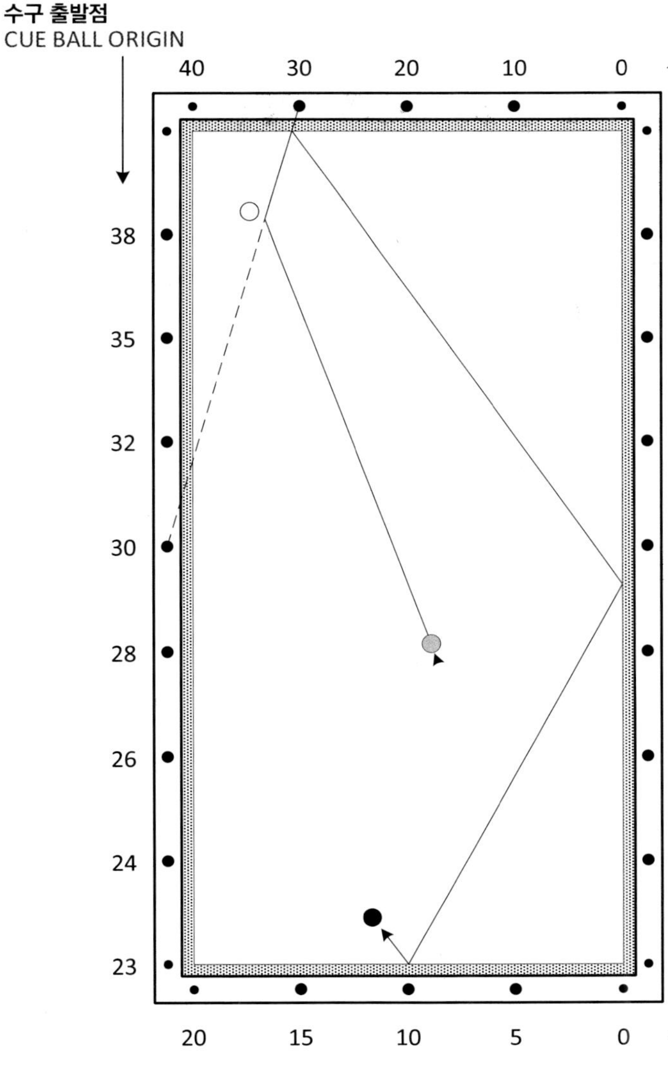

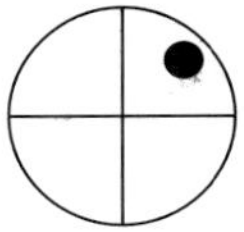

수구 출발점
CUE BALL ORIGIN

조준점
AIMING POINTS

조준점 = (테이블값 − 도착점) + 수구 출발점
조준점 = (10 − 10) + 30
조준점 = 30

AIMING POINT = (TABLE VALUE − ARRIVAL POINT) + CUE BALL ORIGIN
AIMING POINT = (10 − 10) + 30
AIMING POINT = 30

도착점
ARRIVAL POINTS

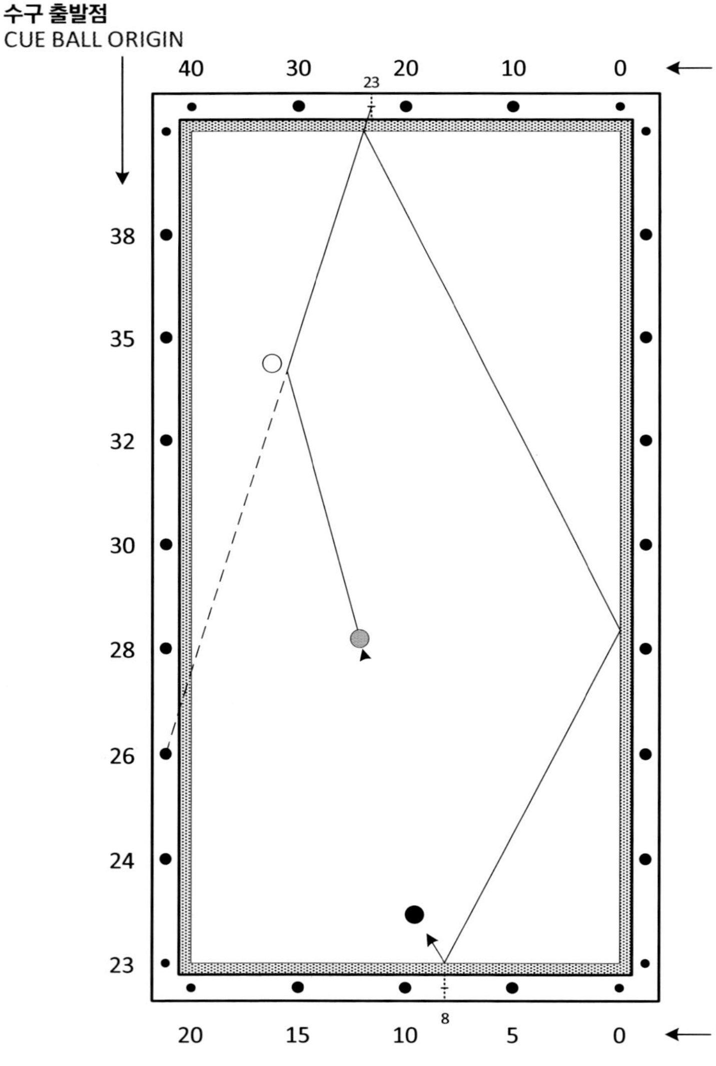

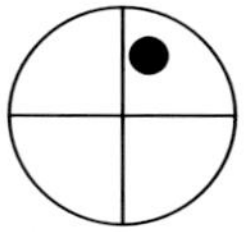

수구 출발점
CUE BALL ORIGIN

조준점
AIMING POINTS

도착점
ARRIVAL POINTS

조준점 = (테이블값 − 도착점) + 수구 출발점
조준점 = (5 − 8) + 26
조준점 = 23

AIMING POINT = (TABLE VALUE − ARRIVAL POINT) + CUE BALL ORIGIN
AIMING POINT = (5 − 8) + 26
AIMING POINT = 23

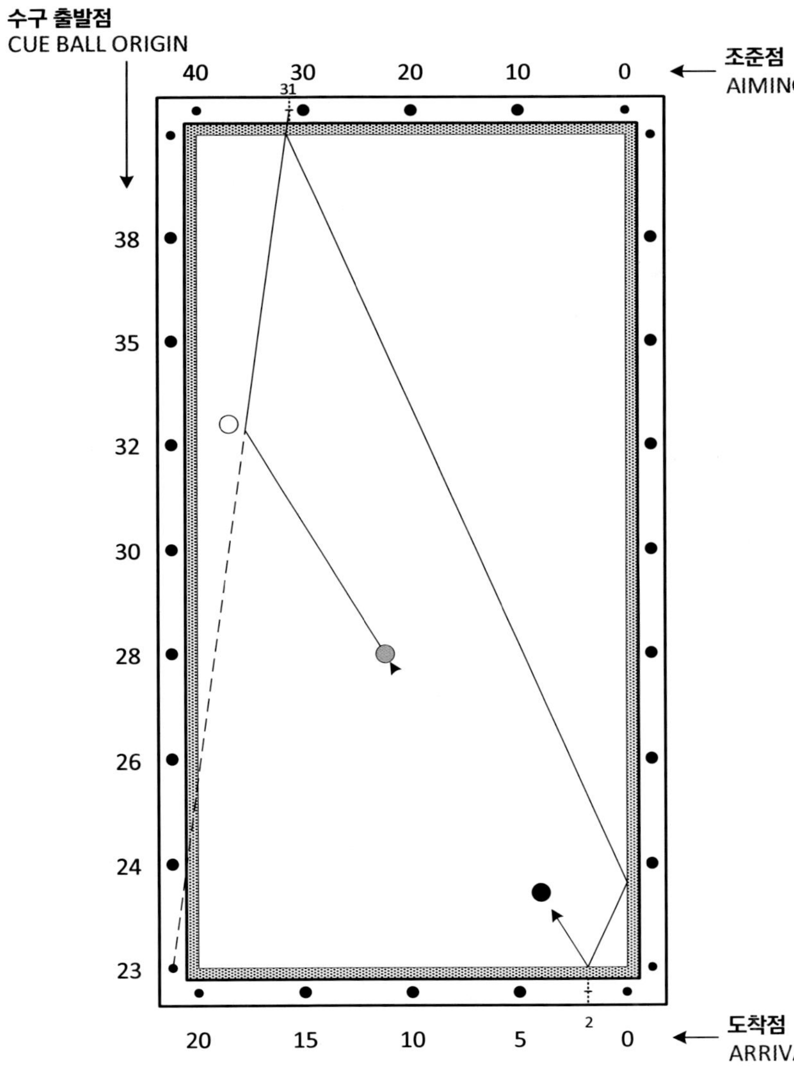

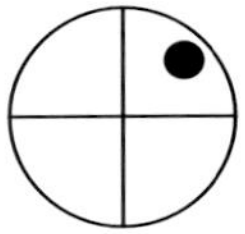

수구 출발점
CUE BALL ORIGIN

조준점
AIMING POINTS

도착점
ARRIVAL POINTS

조준점 = (테이블값 − 도착점) + 수구 출발점
조준점 = (10 − 2) + 23
조준점 = 31

AIMING POINT = (TABLE VALUE − ARRIVAL POINT) + CUE BALL ORIGIN
AIMING POINT = (10 − 2) + 23
AIMING POINT = 31

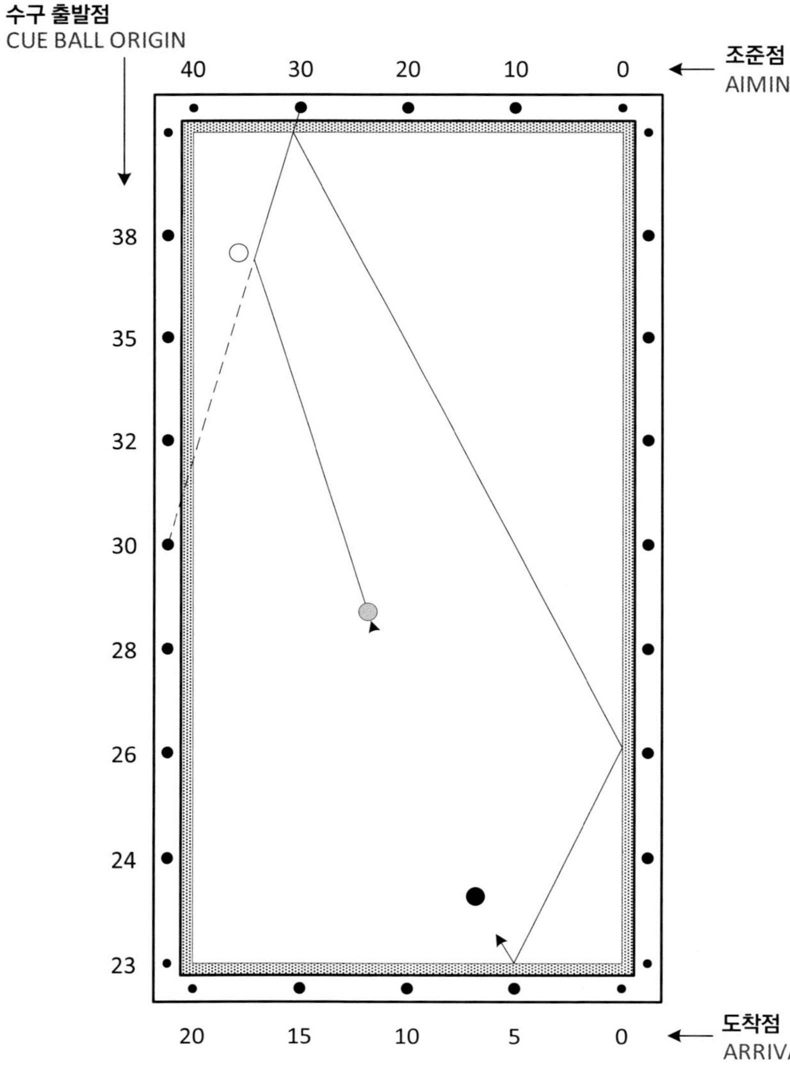

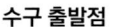

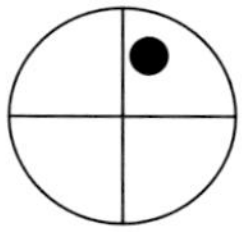

수구 출발점
CUE BALL ORIGIN

조준점
AIMING POINTS

도착점
ARRIVAL POINTS

조준점 = (테이블값 − 도착점) + 수구 출발점
조준점 = (5 − 5) + 30
조준점 = 30

AIMING POINT = (TABLE VALUE − ARRIVAL POINT) + CUE BALL ORIGIN
AIMING POINT = (5 − 5) + 30
AIMING POINT = 30

3. 튜즐 시스템 – ¼ 테이블 응용

당구 테이블은 두 개의 동일한 정사각형으로 이루어져 있다. 장쿠션의 두 번째 포인트에서 출발하는 단쿠션에 평행한 가상선을 그려 테이블을 나누면, 정확하게 당구 테이블의 4분의 1 크기의 작은 테이블이 된다. 이 ¼ 크기의 테이블에서도 모든 수학적 이론이 유효하다. 이 ¼ 테이블에서 부여되는 숫자는 튜즐 시스템 – 단쿠션 출발에서와 동일하다. ¼ 테이블이어서 당구공이 상대적으로 큰 크기가 되므로, 시스템의 적용에 이점이 있다는 것을 느낄 것이다. 항상 그렇듯이, 이 시스템의 효과적인 적용하는 데 있어서 가장 중요한 것은 테이블값을 보장하는 일관된 회전량으로 샷을 구사하는 능력이다.

3. SYSTEM TÜZÜL -1/4 TABLE APPLICATION

As you know, the billiard table consists of two identical squares. When we divide the table by a hypothetical line departing from the second diamond on the long cushion and parallel to the short cushion, we obtain a small table exactly equal to a quarter of the table. All the mathematical theories are valid within this small table. The numbering obtained within this small table behaves parallel to the System Tüzül -Starting From Short Cushion. You will realize that big balls in a small table will provide you an advantage in your system applications. As always, the most important factor in the effective use of the system is the capability of making shots that verify the Table Value.

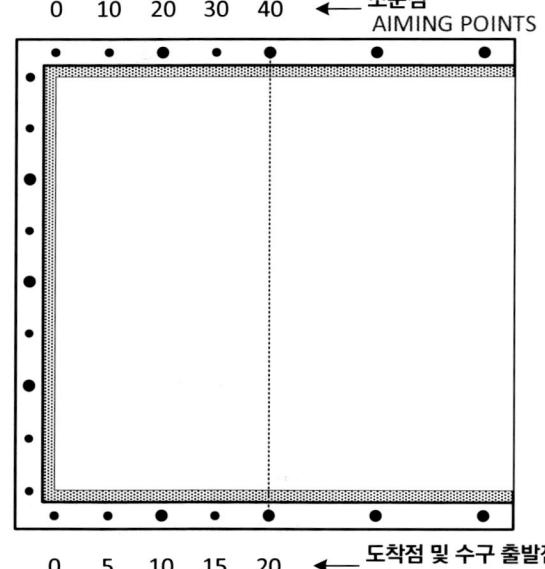

조준점 = (테이블값 − 도착점) + 수구 출발점

AIMING POINT = (TABLE VALUE - ARRIVAL POINT) + CUE BALL ORIGIN

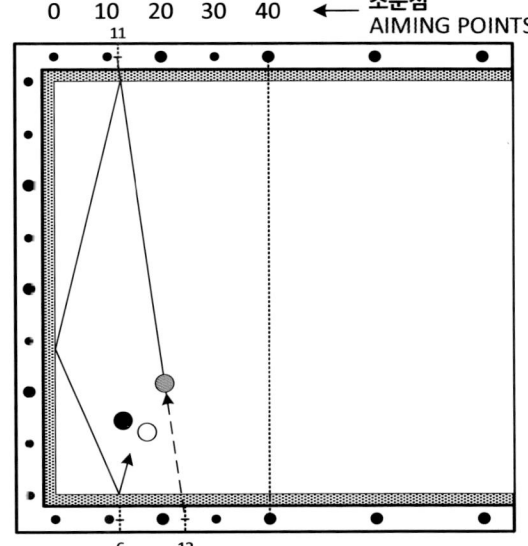

조준점
AIMING POINTS

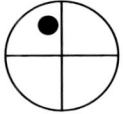

조준점 = (테이블값 − 도착점) + 수구 출발점
조준점 = (5 − 6) + 12
조준점 = 11

AIMING POINT = (TABLE VALUE − ARRIVAL POINT) + CUE BALL ORIGIN
AIMING POINT = (5 − 6) + 12
AIMING POINT = 11

도착점 및 수구 출발점
ARRIVAL POINTS AND CUE BALL ORIGIN

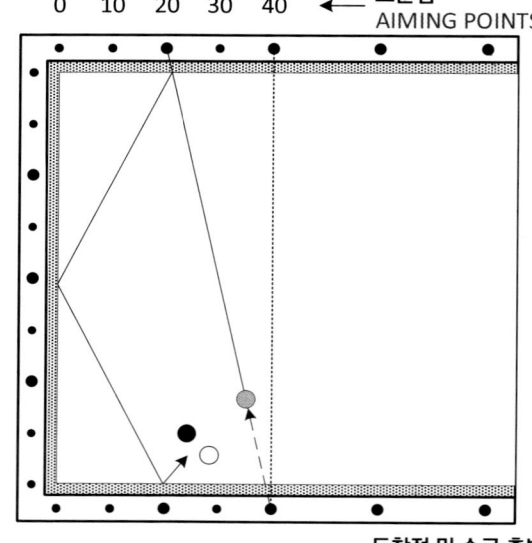

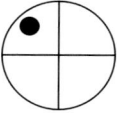

조준점 = (테이블값 − 도착점) + 수구 출발점
조준점 = (10 − 10) + 20
조준점 = 20

AIMING POINT = (TABLE VALUE - ARRIVAL POINT) + CUE BALL ORIGIN
AIMING POINT = (10 - 10) + 20
AIMING POINT = 20

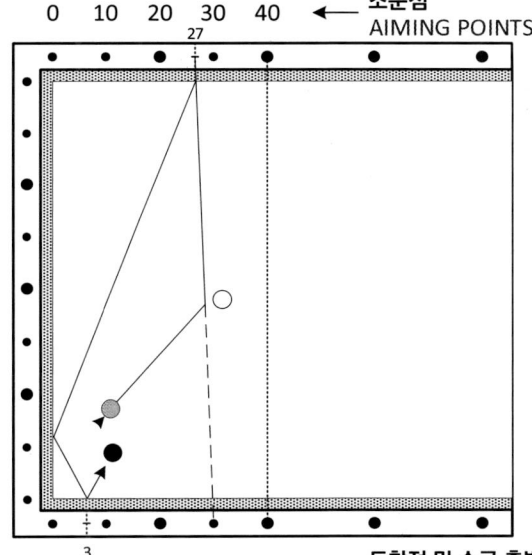

조준점 AIMING POINTS

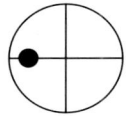

조준점 = (테이블값 - 도착점) + 수구 출발점
조준점 = (15 - 3) + 15
조준점 = 27

AIMING POINT = (TABLE VALUE - ARRIVAL POINT) + CUE BALL ORIGIN
AIMING POINT = (15 - 3) + 15
AIMING POINT = 27

도착점 및 수구 출발점
ARRIVAL POINTS AND CUE BALL ORIGIN

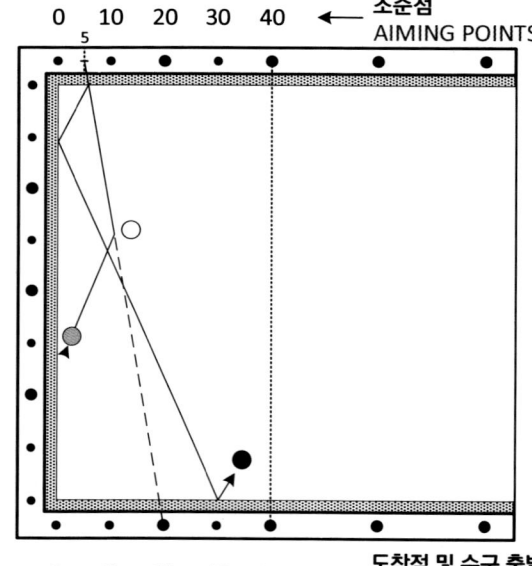
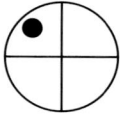

조준점 = (테이블값 − 도착점) + 수구 출발점
조준점 = (10 − 15) + 10
조준점 = 5

AIMING POINT = (TABLE VALUE − ARRIVAL POINT) + CUE BALL ORIGIN
AIMING POINT = (10 − 15) + 10
AIMING POINT = 5

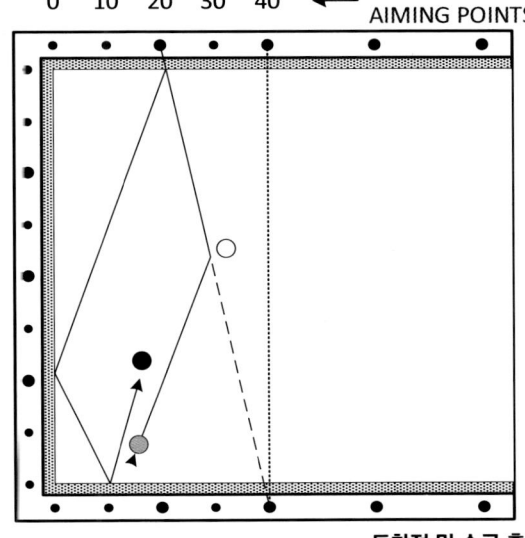
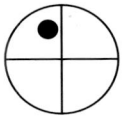

조준점 = (테이블값 - 도착점) + 수구 출발점
조준점 = (5 - 5) + 20
조준점 = 20

AIMING POINT = (TABLE VALUE - ARRIVAL POINT) + CUE BALL ORIGIN
AIMING POINT = (5 - 5) + 20
AIMING POINT = 20

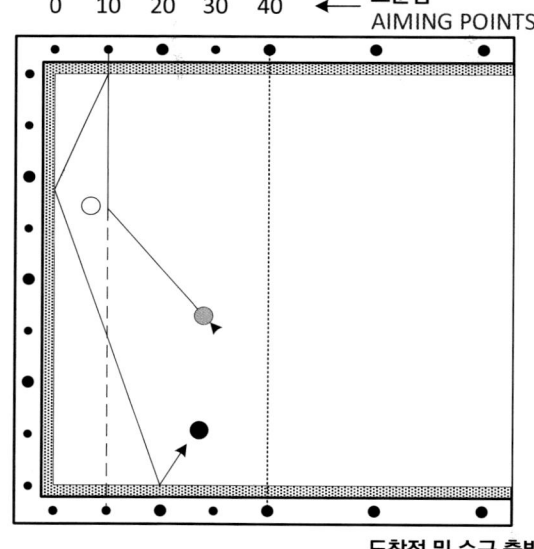

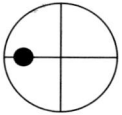

조준점 = (테이블값 − 도착점) + 수구 출발점
조준점 = (15 − 10) + 5
조준점 = 10

AIMING POINT = (TABLE VALUE - ARRIVAL POINT) + CUE BALL ORIGIN
AIMING POINT = (15 - 10) + 5
AIMING POINT = 10

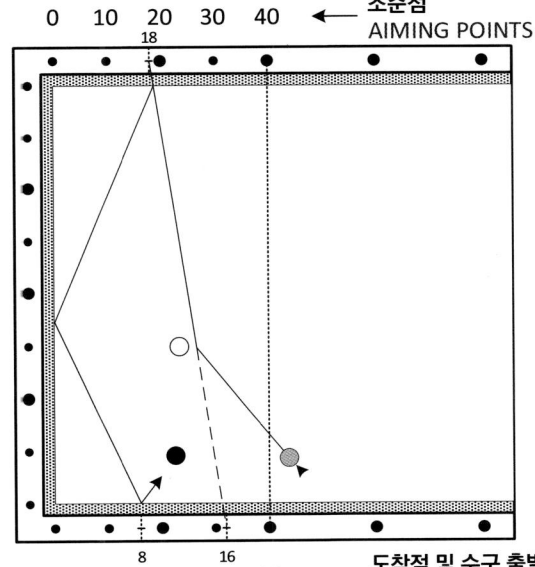
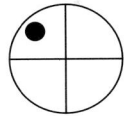

조준점 = (테이블값 − 도착점) + 수구 출발점
조준점 = (10 − 8) + 16
조준점 = 18

AIMING POINT = (TABLE VALUE − ARRIVAL POINT) + CUE BALL ORIGIN
AIMING POINT = (10 − 8) + 16
AIMING POINT = 18

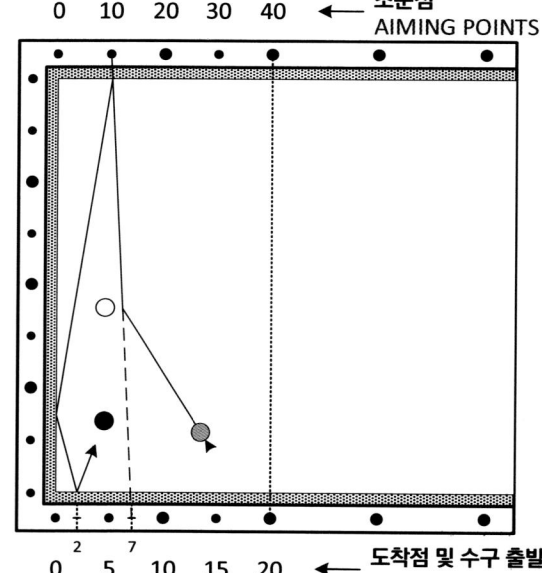
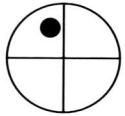

조준점 = (테이블값 – 도착점) + 수구 출발점
조준점 = (5 – 2) + 7
조준점 = 10

AIMING POINT = (TABLE VALUE - ARRIVAL POINT) + CUE BALL ORIGIN
AIMING POINT = (5 - 2) + 7
AIMING POINT = 10

4. 튜즐 더블레일 시스템

전체 튜즐 시스템(회전)에서와 마찬가지로, 이 시스템의 수학적 토대는 테이블값에 기초한다. 그러나, 이번에는 테이블값의 2배를 사용하여 계산한다. 이 값은 또한 수치화한 그림에서 테이블의 더블레일 한계 각도를 나타낸다. 이 시스템의 수치화는 차트에서 알 수 있는 바와 같이 매우 쉽다. 항상 그렇듯이 테이블값을 보장하는 샷이 구사되어야 한다. 3번째 쿠션에서는 수구의 회전이 현저하게 감소되어야 한다. 속도감 있는 방식보다는 팔로우스루(follow-through) 스트로크 기법이 바람직하다. 해결되어야 하는 포지션의 각도에 따라 사용될 테이블값과 큐팁의 접점은 플레이어의 감각에 따른다.

4. TÜZÜL DOUBLE RAIL SYSTEM

As in entire Tüzül System (english), the mathematical base of this system relies also on the Table Value. But this time, the double of the Table Value will be used in the calculations. This value shows at the same time the extreme limit double rail angle of the table according to the figures on the numbering graph. The numbering of the system is very easy as can be seen in the chart. As always, the stroke technique that verifies the Table Value should be chosen. The spin of the cue ball has to be saved effectively at the third cushion. My proposal is to use the follow-through stroke technique in a rather speedy manner. The cue-tip contact point and the related Table Value that will be used according to the angles of the position to be solved is at the player's initiative.

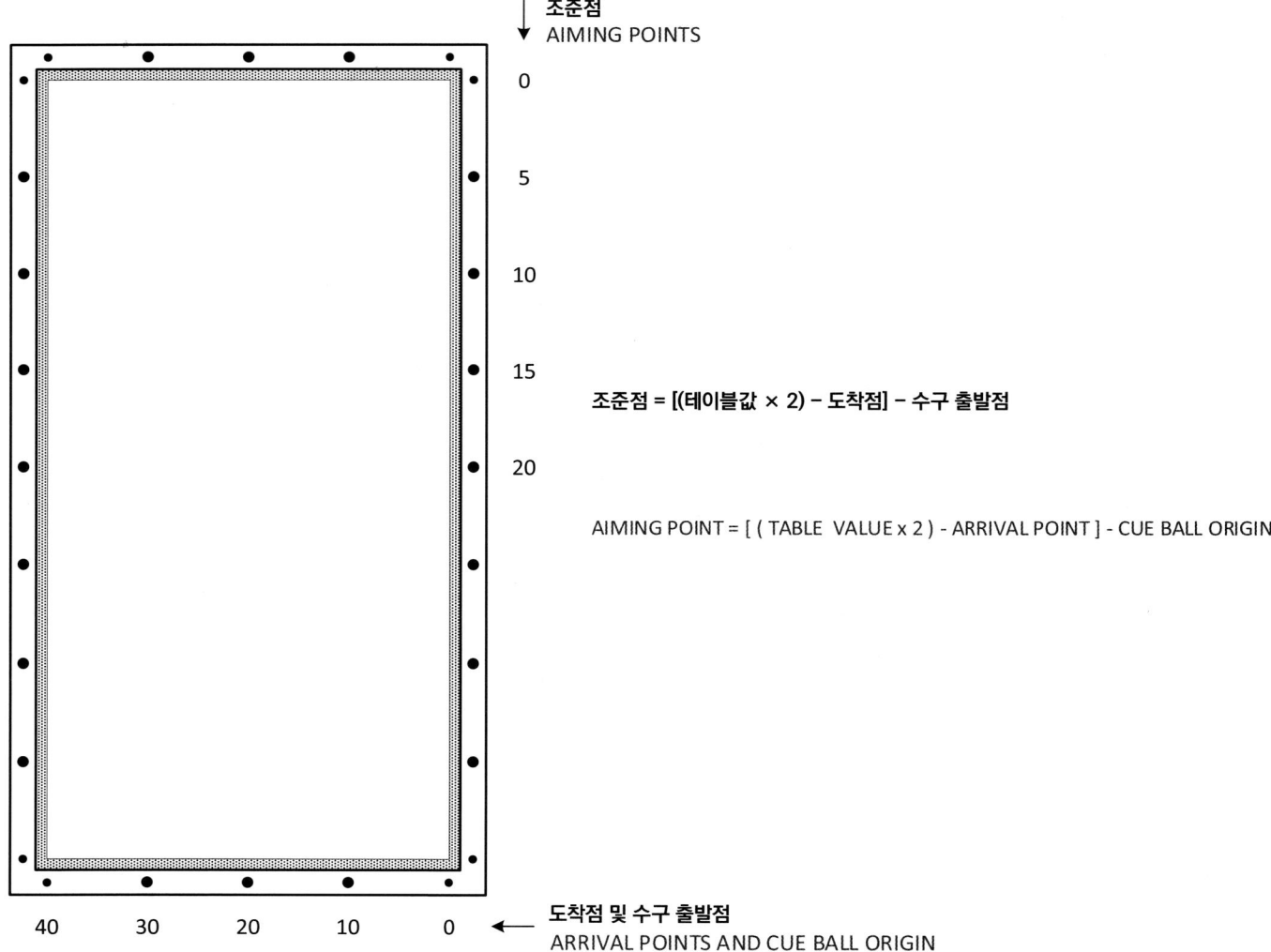

조준점 = [(테이블값 × 2) − 도착점] − 수구 출발점

AIMING POINT = [(TABLE VALUE x 2) - ARRIVAL POINT] - CUE BALL ORIGIN

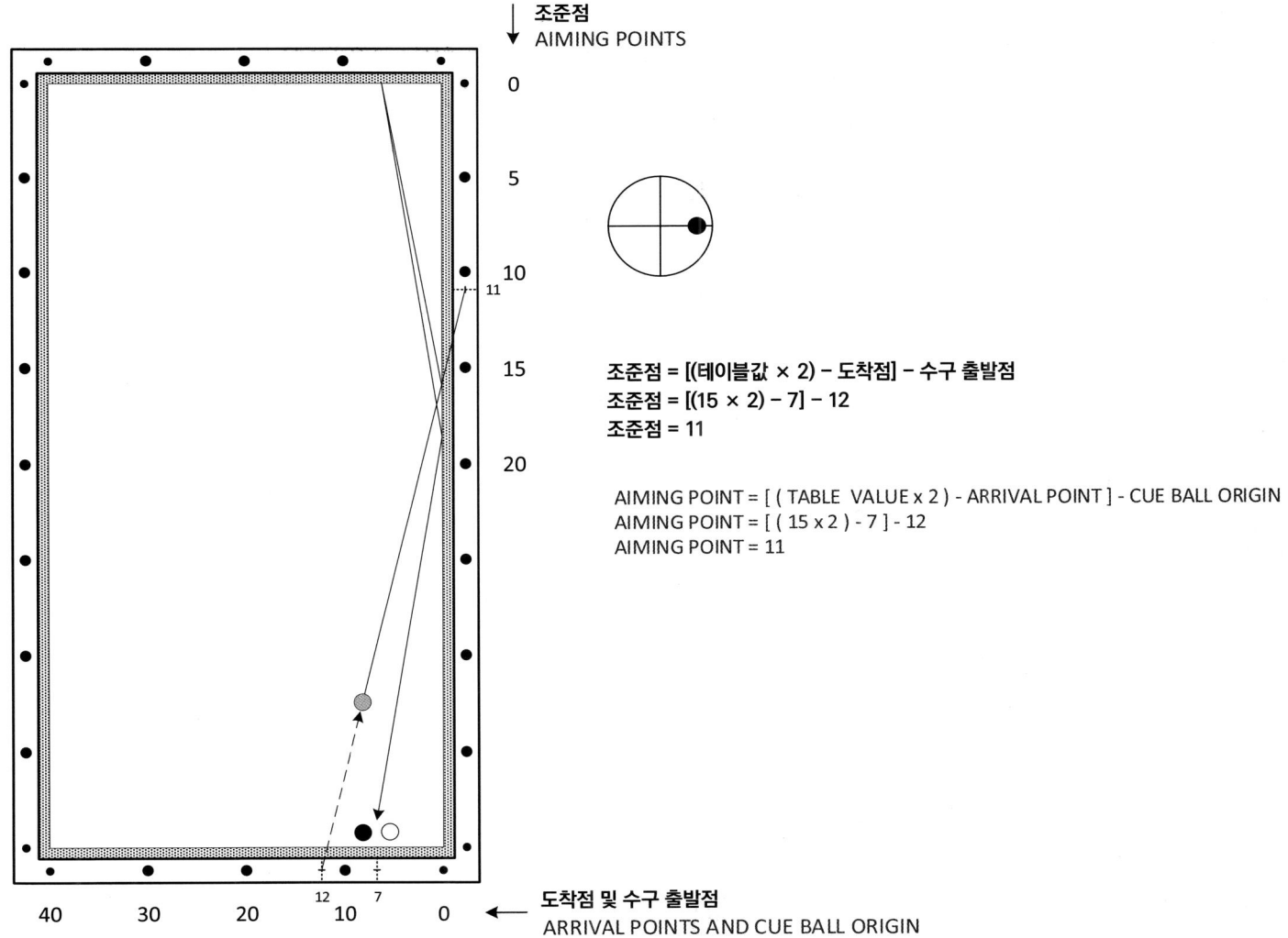

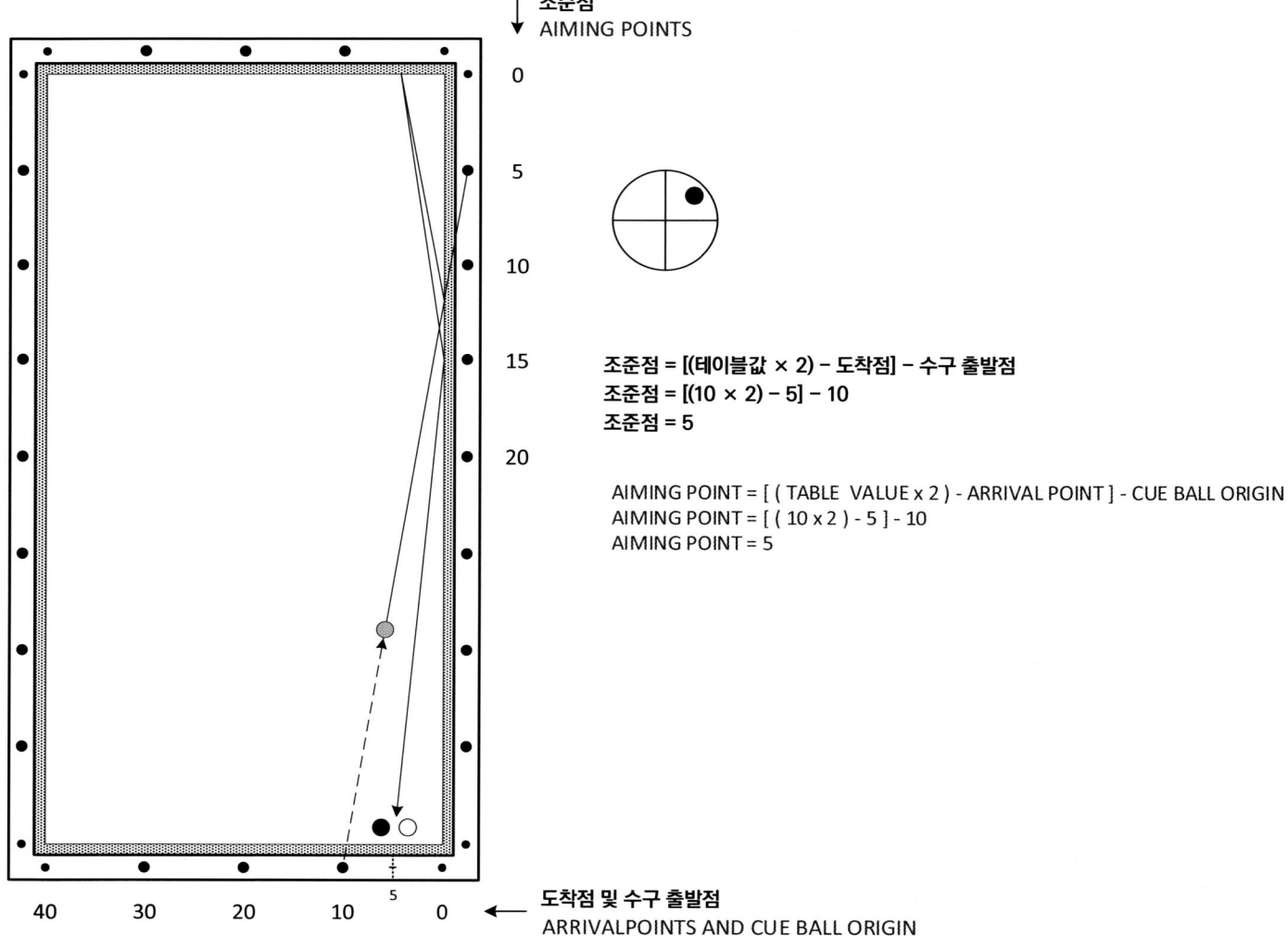

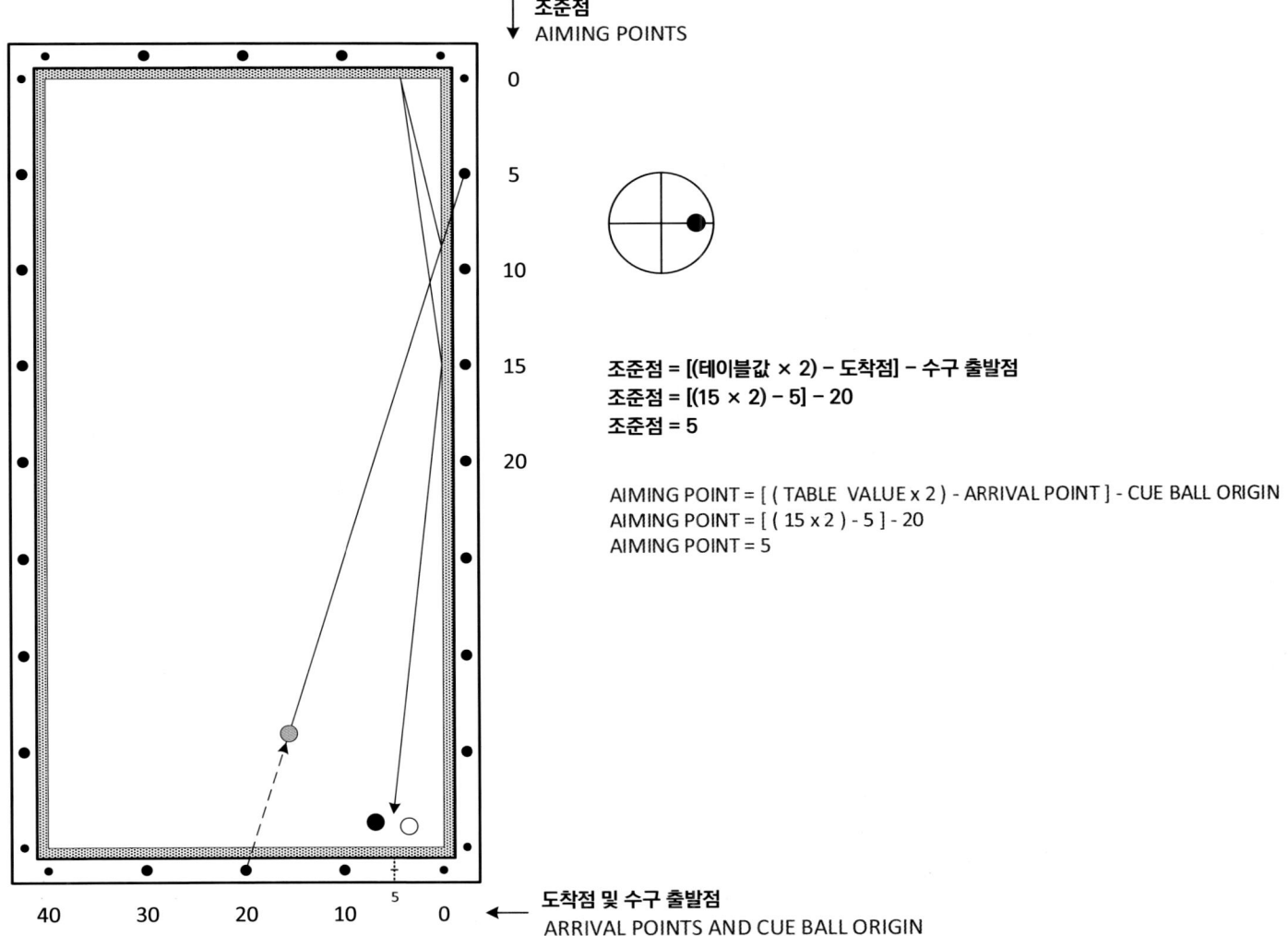

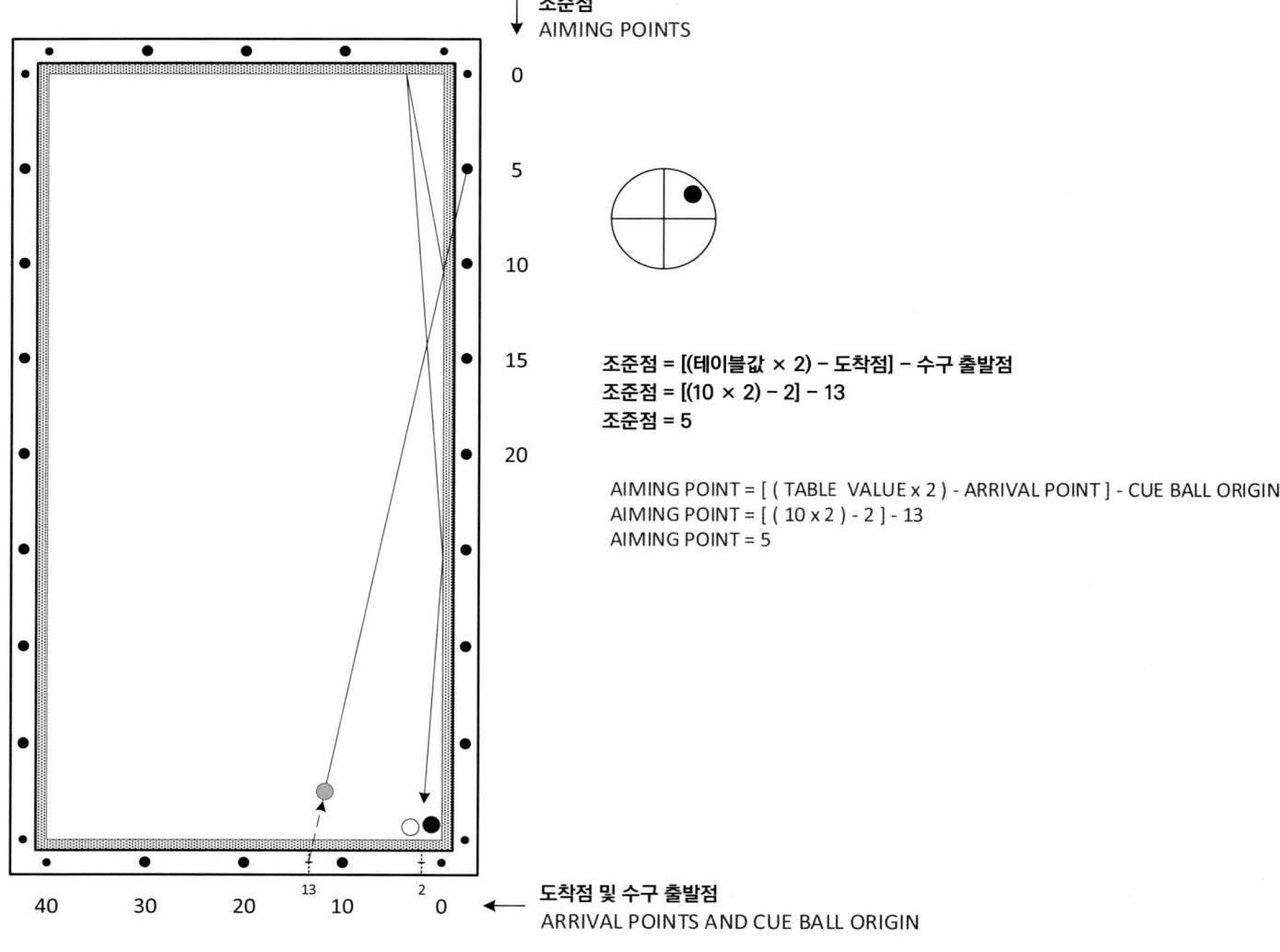

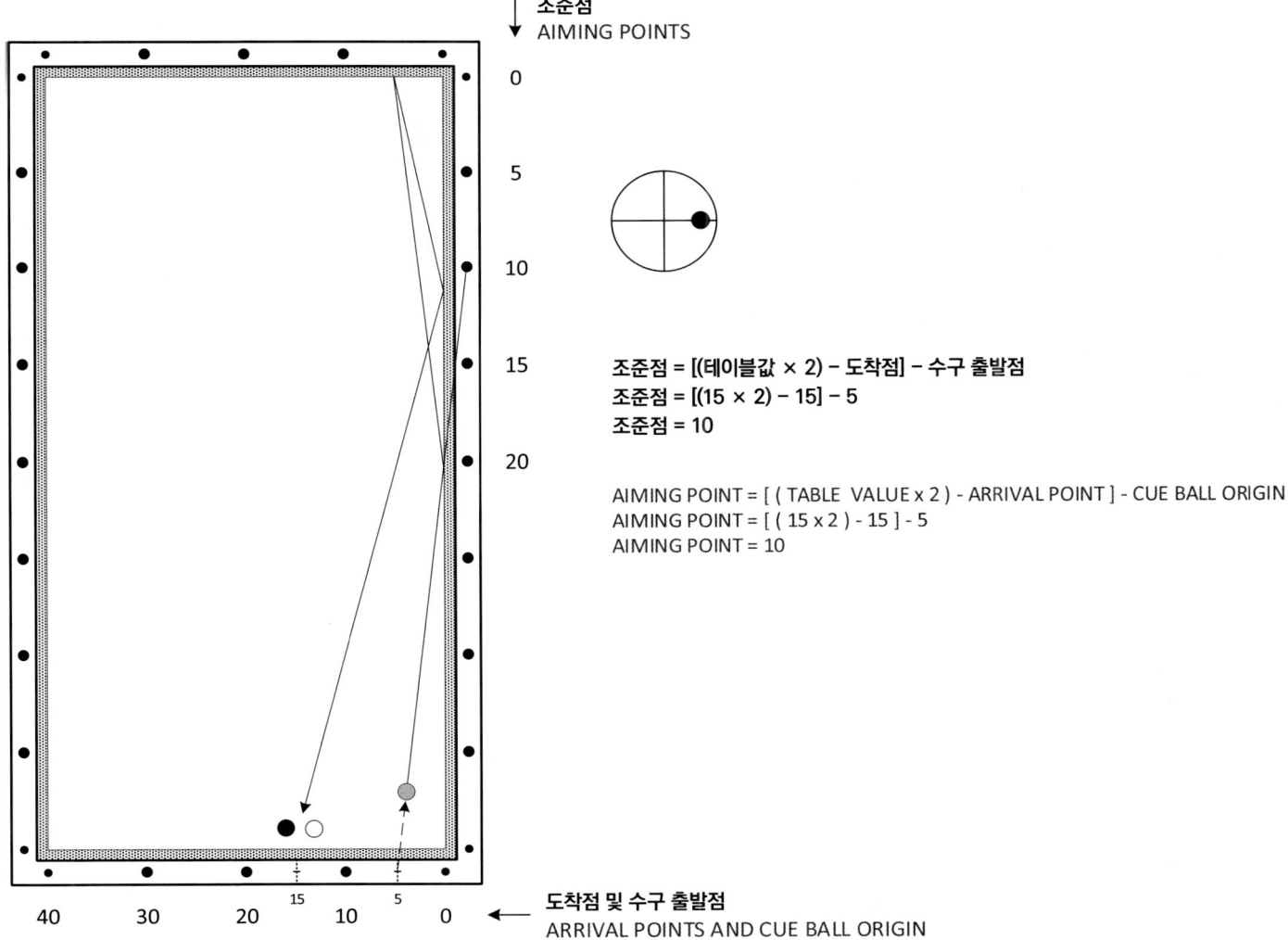

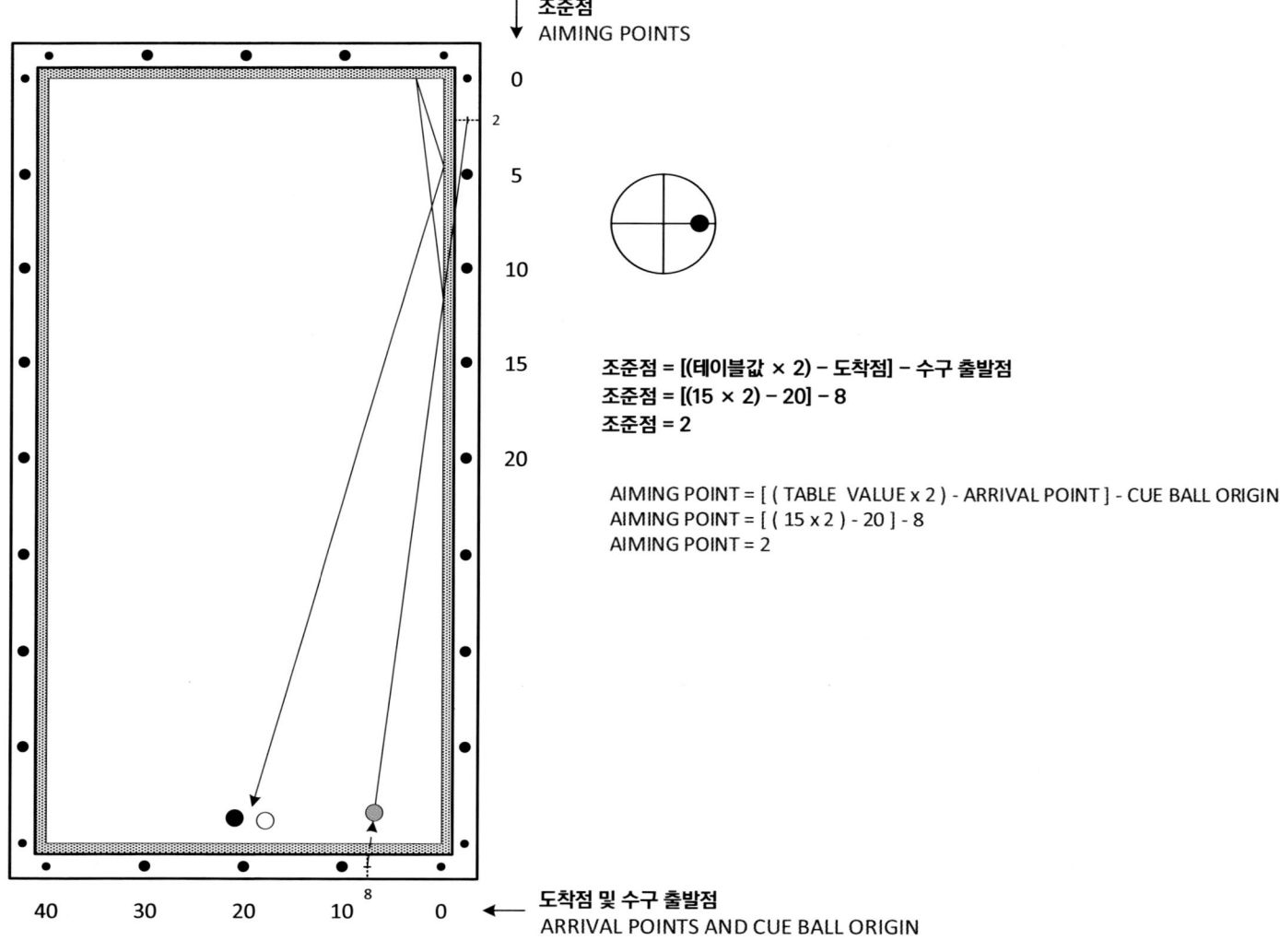

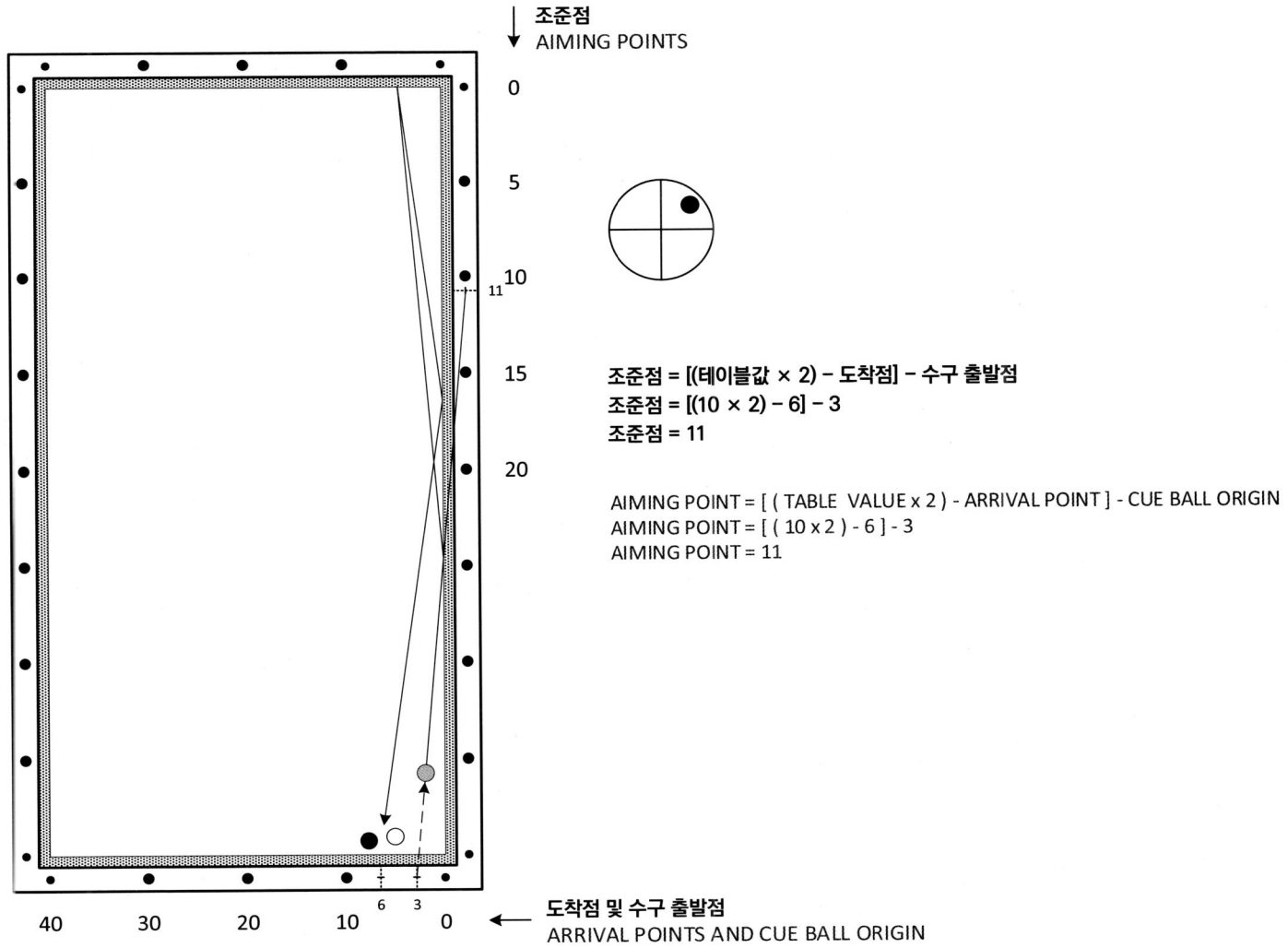

5. 튜즐 더블레일 시스템 – ¼ 테이블 응용

튜즐 더블레일 시스템에서는 테이블값의 2배가 사용된다는 점과 이 값이 테이블의 더블레일 한계 각도를 나타낸다는 점을 설명하였다. 그러나 ¼ 테이블에서는 테이블값의 2배는 더 이상 사용되지 않는다. 수치화된 그림의 테이블값은 단쿠션에서 더블레일을 통해 구사할 수 있는 한계 각도를 보여준다. ¼ 테이블에 적용할 때는 수구가 짧아진 경로를 진행하므로 다소 부드러운 샷을 구사하는 것이 이상적인 회전량을 보장할 것이다.

5. TÜZÜL DOUBLE RAIL SYSTEM -1/4 TABLE APPLICATION

As in other small table applications, the big table numbering is replicated exactly in the small table in this system. Remember that in Tüzül Double Rail System's calculations, the double of the Table Value is used and this also shows the extreme limit double rail angle of the table. In the small table application, the double of the Table Value is no longer used. The Table Value on the numbering graph shows the ultimate angle that could make a double rail at the short cushion. In small table applications, a rather soft shot will ensure the cue ball that moves with an ideal rotation due to the fact that it is covering a shorter path.

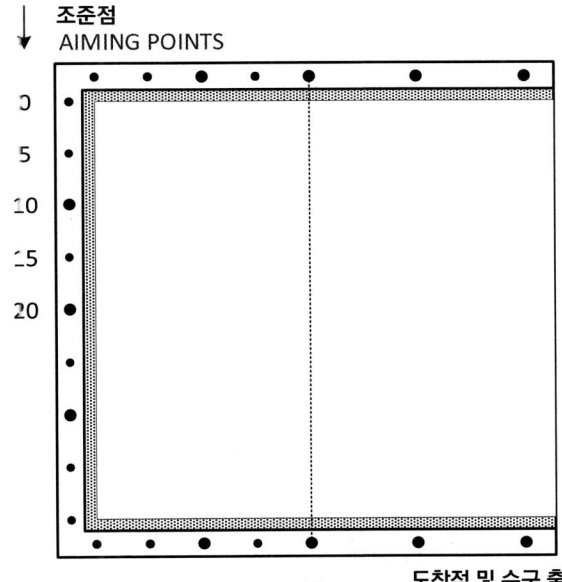

조준점 = (테이블값 - 도착점) - 수구 출발점

AIMING POINT = (TABLE VALUE - ARRIVAL POINT) - CUE BALL ORIGIN

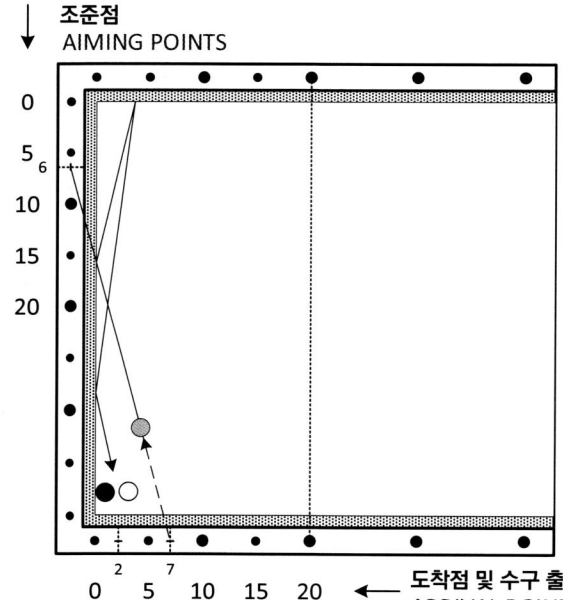

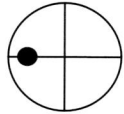

조준점 = (테이블값 - 도착점) - 수구 출발점
조준점 = (15 - 2) - 7
조준점 = 6

AIMING POINT = (TABLE VALUE - ARRIVAL POINT) - CUE BALL ORIGIN
AIMING POINT = (15 - 2) - 7
AIMING POINT = 6

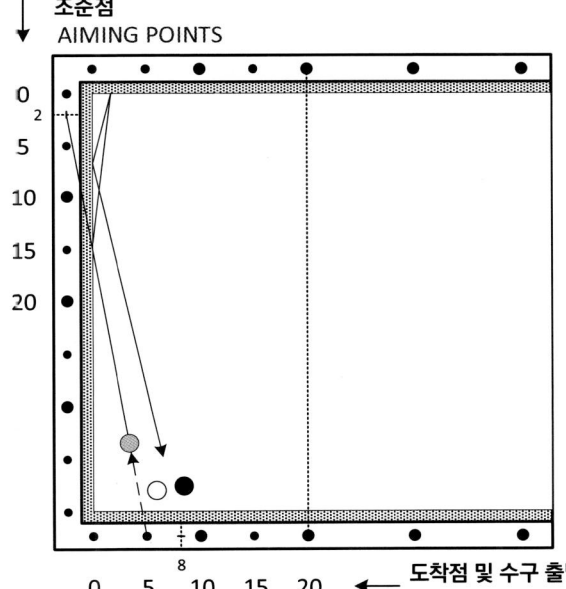

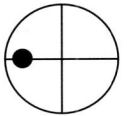

조준점 = (테이블값 - 도착점) - 수구 출발점
조준점 = (15 - 8) - 5
조준점 = 2

AIMING POINT = (TABLE VALUE - ARRIVAL POINT) - CUE BALL ORIGIN
AIMING POINT = (15 - 8) - 5
AIMING POINT = 2

조준점
AIMING POINTS

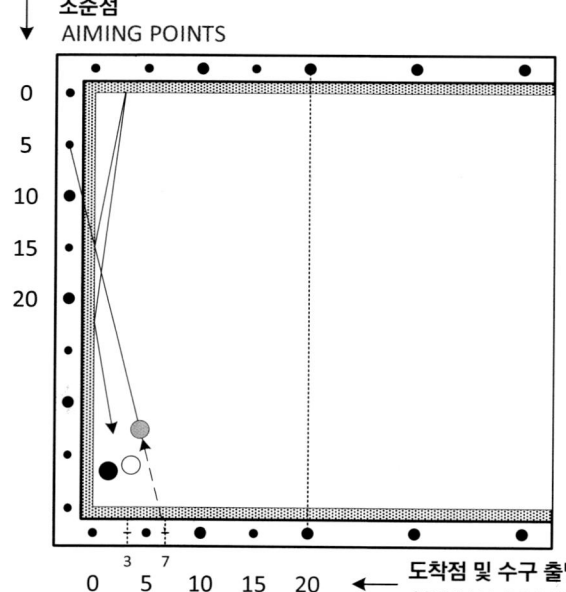

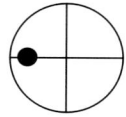

조준점 = (테이블값 − 도착점) − 수구 출발점
조준점 = (15 − 3) − 7
조준점 = 5

AIMING POINT = (TABLE VALUE − ARRIVAL POINT) − CUE BALL ORIGIN
AIMING POINT = (15 − 3) − 7
AIMING POINT = 5

도착점 및 수구 출발점
ARRIVAL POINTS AND CUE BALL ORIGIN

조준점
AIMING POINTS

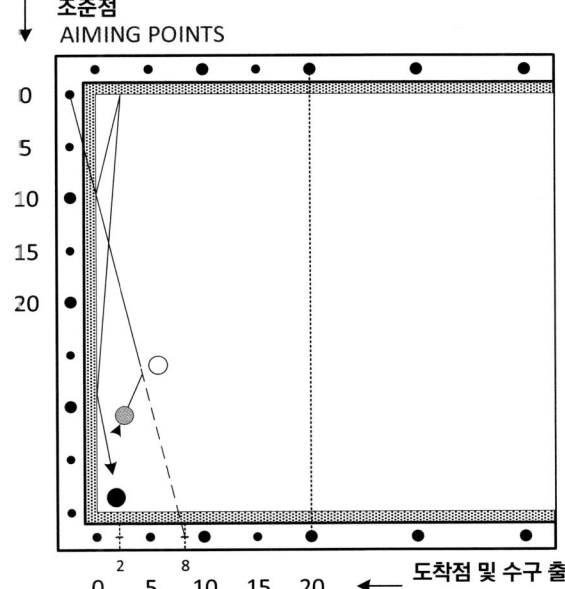

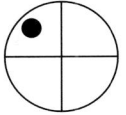

조준점 = (테이블값 - 도착점) - 수구 출발점
조준점 = (10 - 2) - 8
조준점 = 0

AIMING POINT = (TABLE VALUE - ARRIVAL POINT) - CUE BALL ORIGIN
AIMING POINT = (10 - 2) - 8
AIMING POINT = 0

도착점 및 수구 출발점
ARRIVAL POINTS AND CUE BALL ORIGIN

6. "튜즐 – 몰" 시스템

이 시스템은 당구 선수이자 연구가인 나의 친구 누리 몰과 합작의 결과물이다.

이 시스템은 스핀샷으로 단쿠션-장쿠션-장쿠션 경로에 대해 테이블값을 적용하는 것이다. 테이블값의 개념은 모든 종류의 테이블에 대해 이 시스템을 효과적으로 적용할 수 있게 한다. 테이블값을 사용하는 데에 있어서는 수구가 첫 번째 쿠션에 이르기까지 커브를 그리지 않도록 샷을 구사할 것을 권한다.

정상적인 각도와 평균적인 샷 기법으로 반응하는 테이블에서는 이 값은 약 25이다. 오래되었거나 꺾이는 특성의 라사지의 테이블에서는 이 값은 27~28 정도로 증가될 수 있다. 새로 교체하였거나 미끄러운 라사지의 테이블에서는 이 값은 약 23 정도일 수 있다.

단쿠션-장쿠션-장쿠션 경로에서는 샷 또는 첫 번째 쿠션의 조준점에 대해 조금만 실수를 하여도 도착 쿠션에서는 큰 차이가 발생한다. 연습 시 이 점에 대해 유의할 것을 권한다.

6. "TÜZÜL- MOL" SYSTEM

This system is the result of collaborative work with my friend NURİ MOL who is a billiards player-researcher.

This solves the short cushion - long cushion - long cushion line with a spin shot by considering the Table Value. The Table Value notion enables the effective application of the system to all kind of tables. The technique that I would propose while calculating the Table Value is to make a shot which prevents the cue ball from making a curve while reaching the first cushion.

For a table which reacts with normal angles and with an average shooting technique, this value will be about 25. This may increase to 27-28 in a table with an old or right-angled cloth. It will be about 23 in a table with a new and slippery cloth.

Short cushion - long cushion - long cushion lines may cause big variances in the reach cushion in case of small mistakes in the shot or in the first cushion target point. I would advise you to consider this point in your practicing.

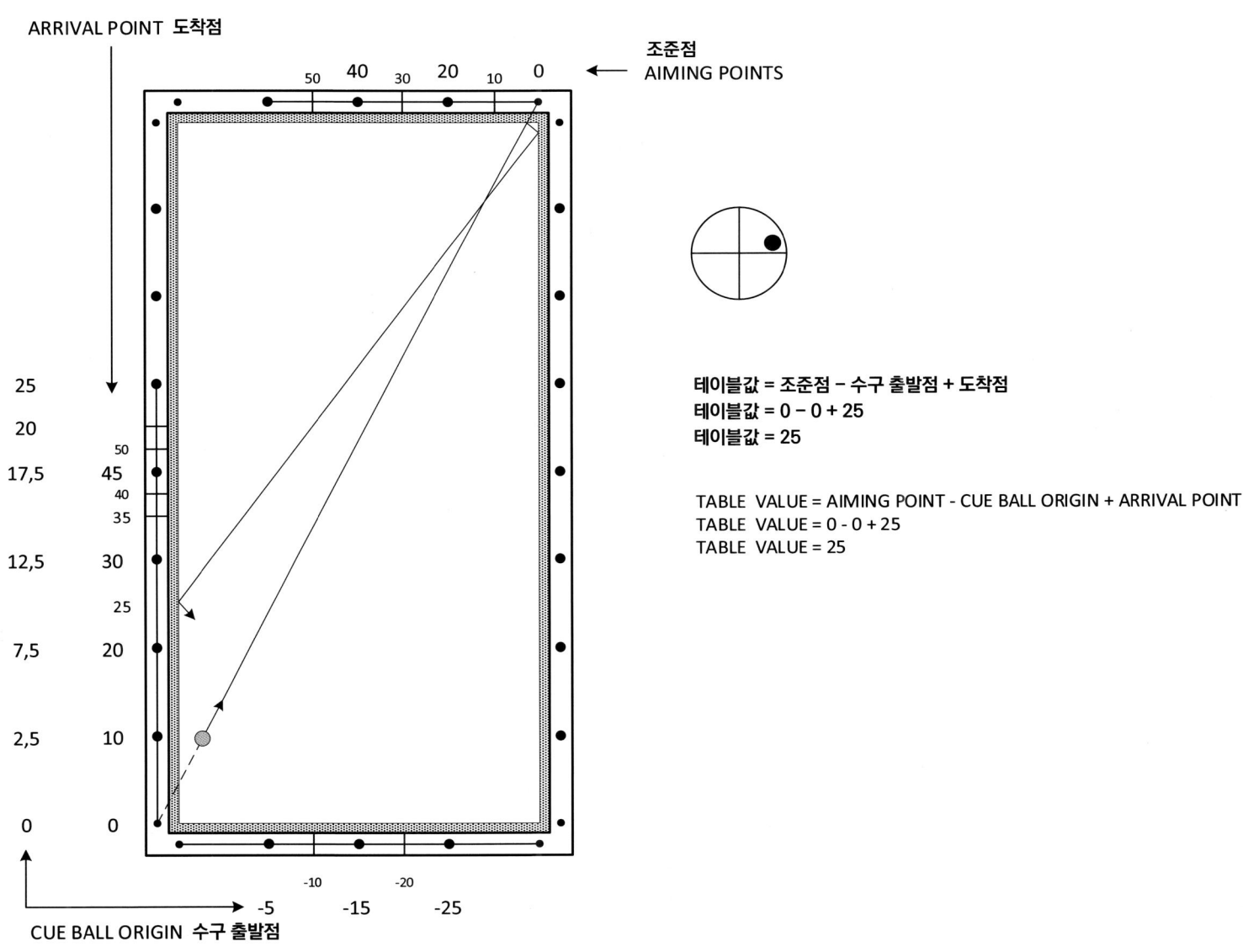

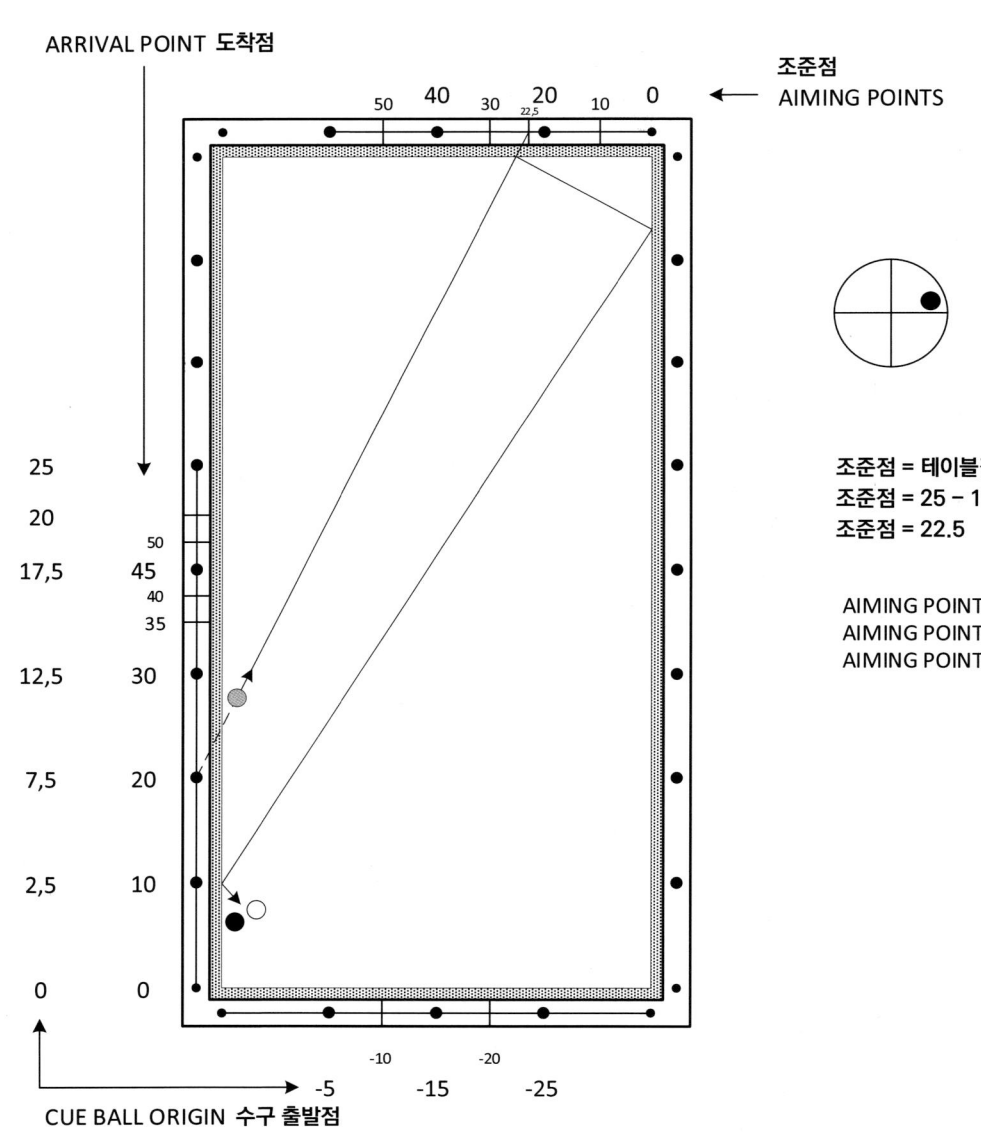

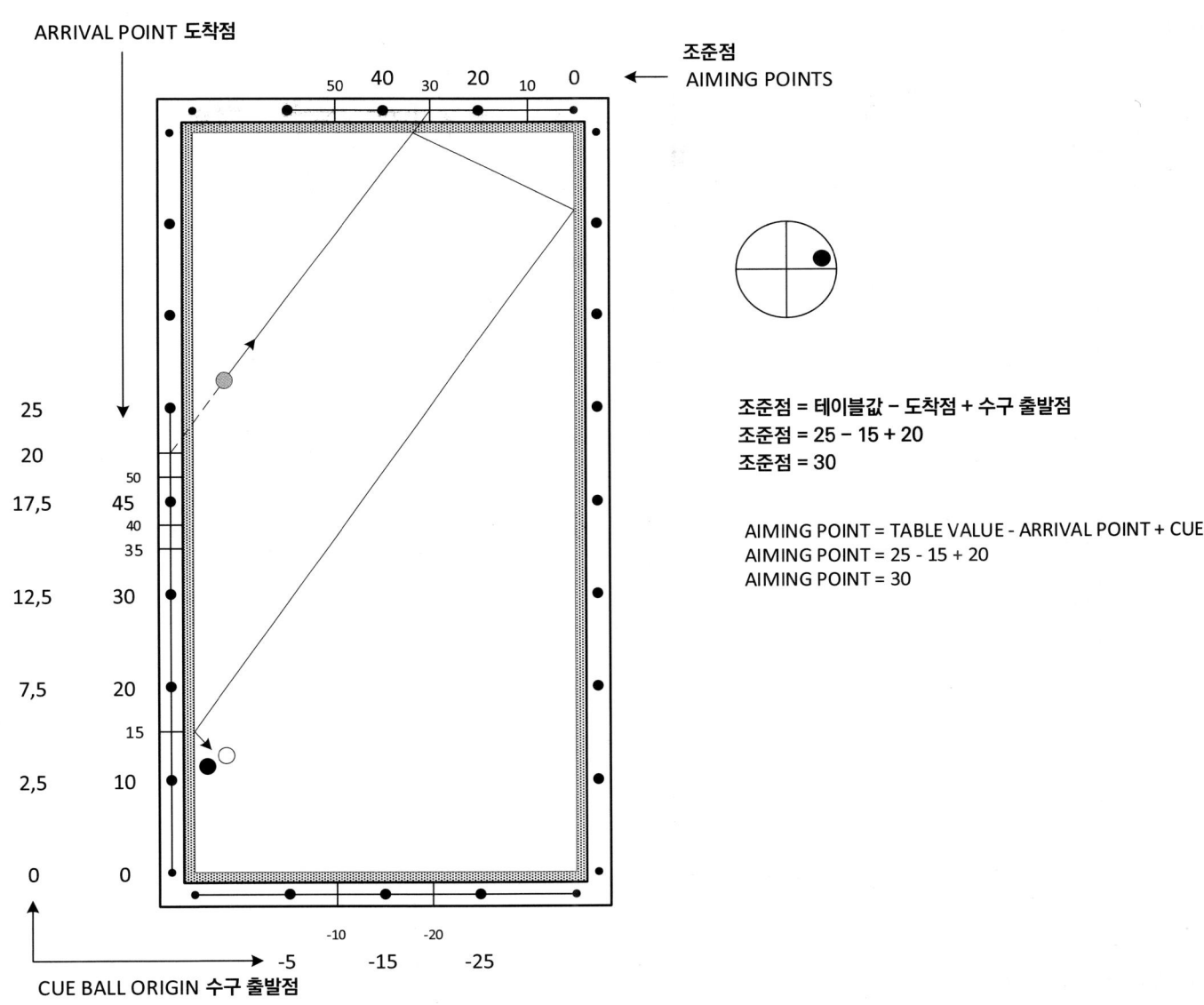

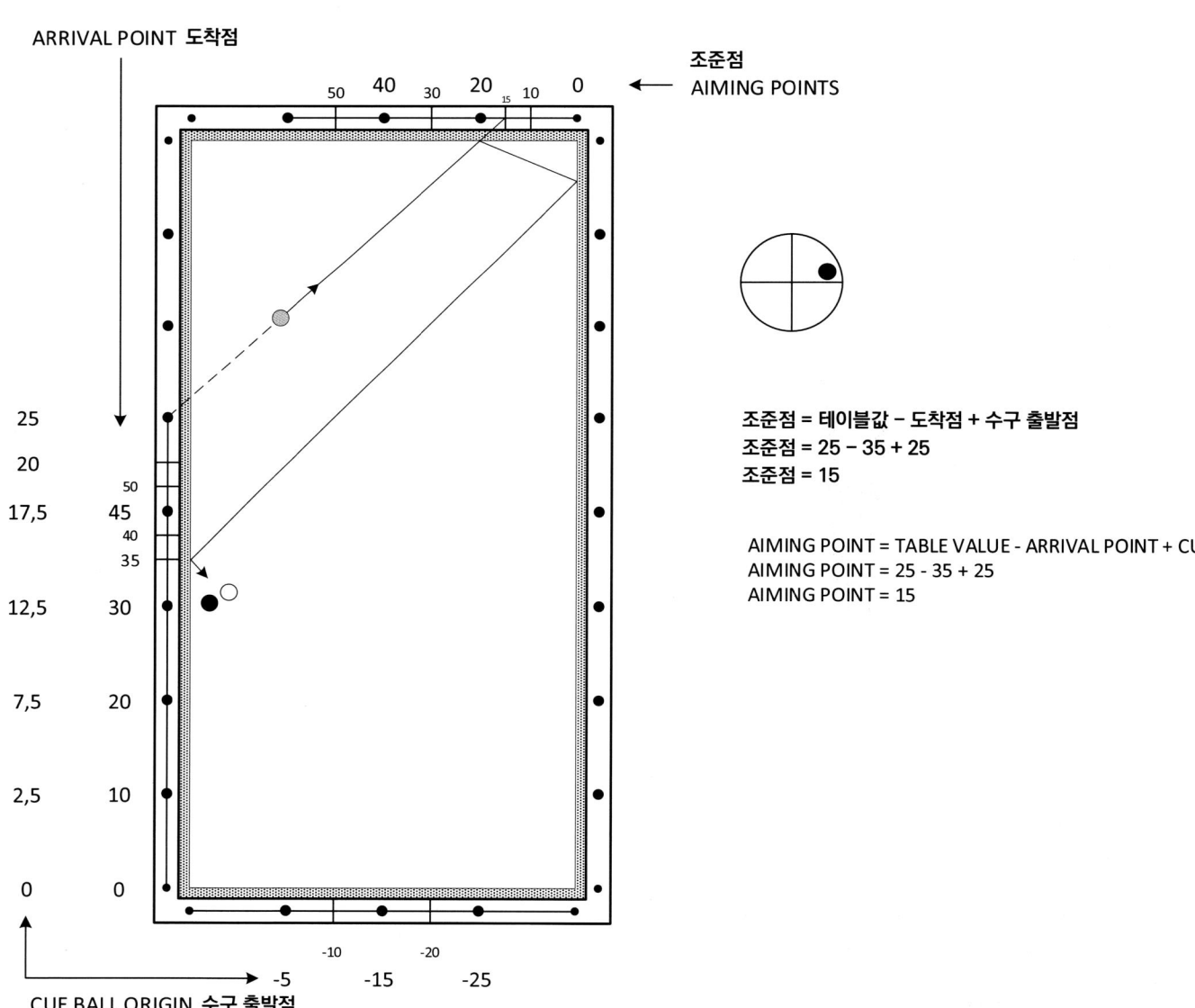

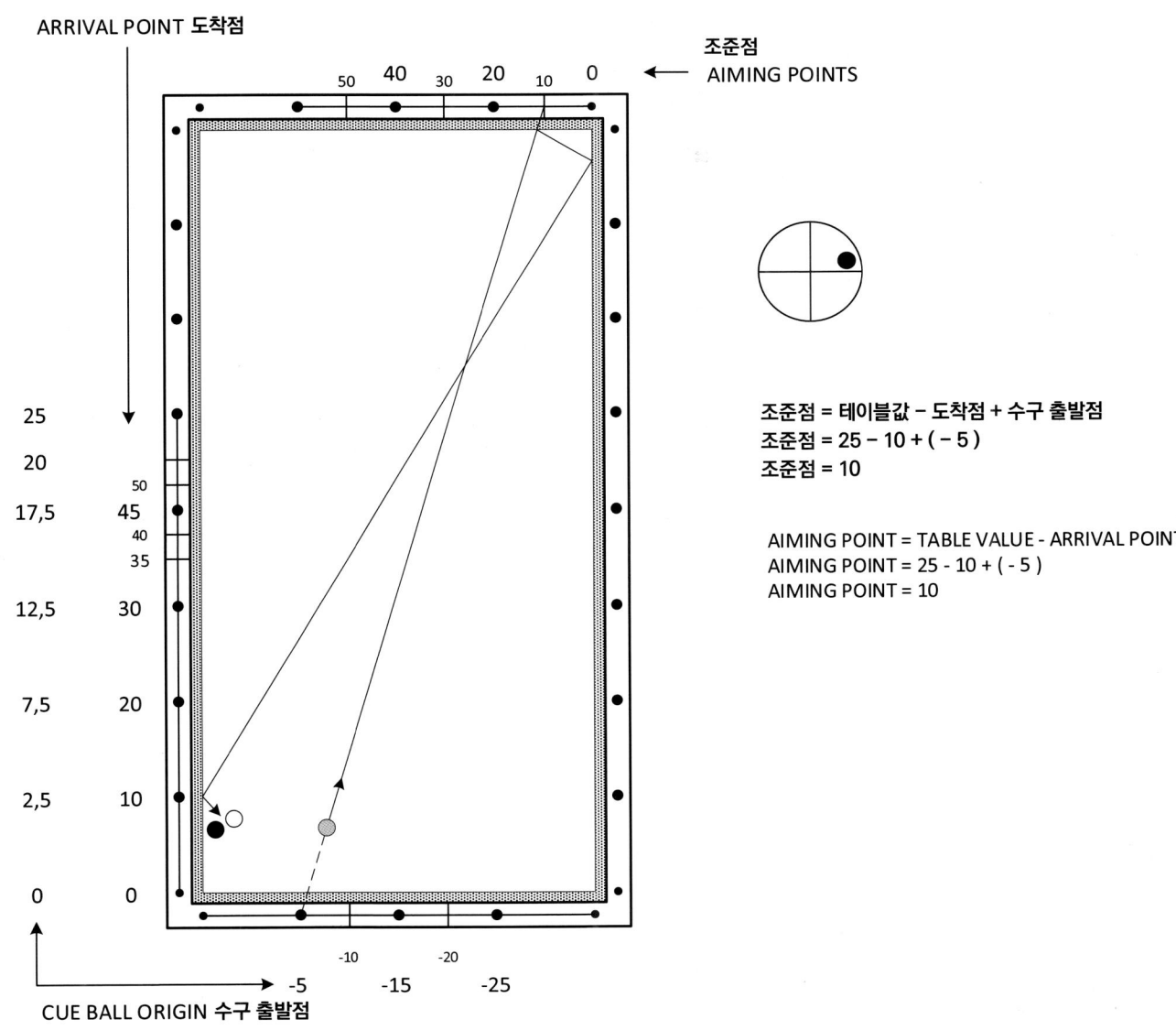

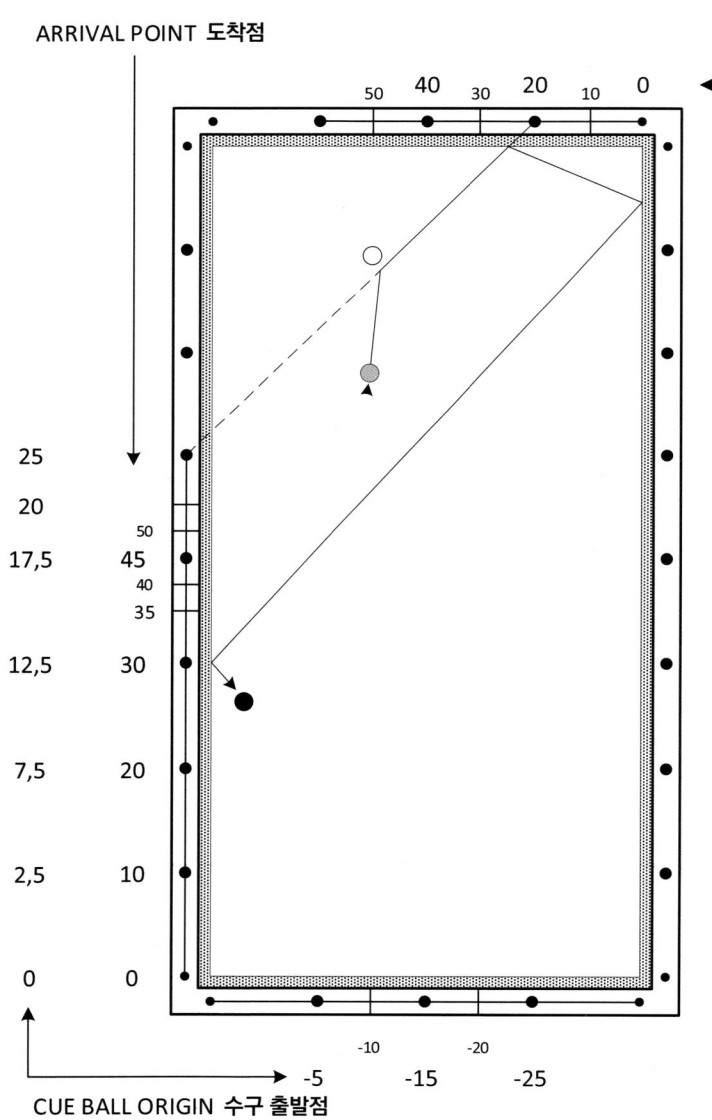
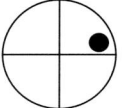

조준점 = 테이블값 − 도착점 + 수구 출발점
조준점 = 25 − 30 + 25
조준점 = 20

AIMING POINT = TABLE VALUE − ARRIVAL POINT + CUE BALL ORIGIN
AIMING POINT = 25 − 30 + 25
AIMING POINT = 20

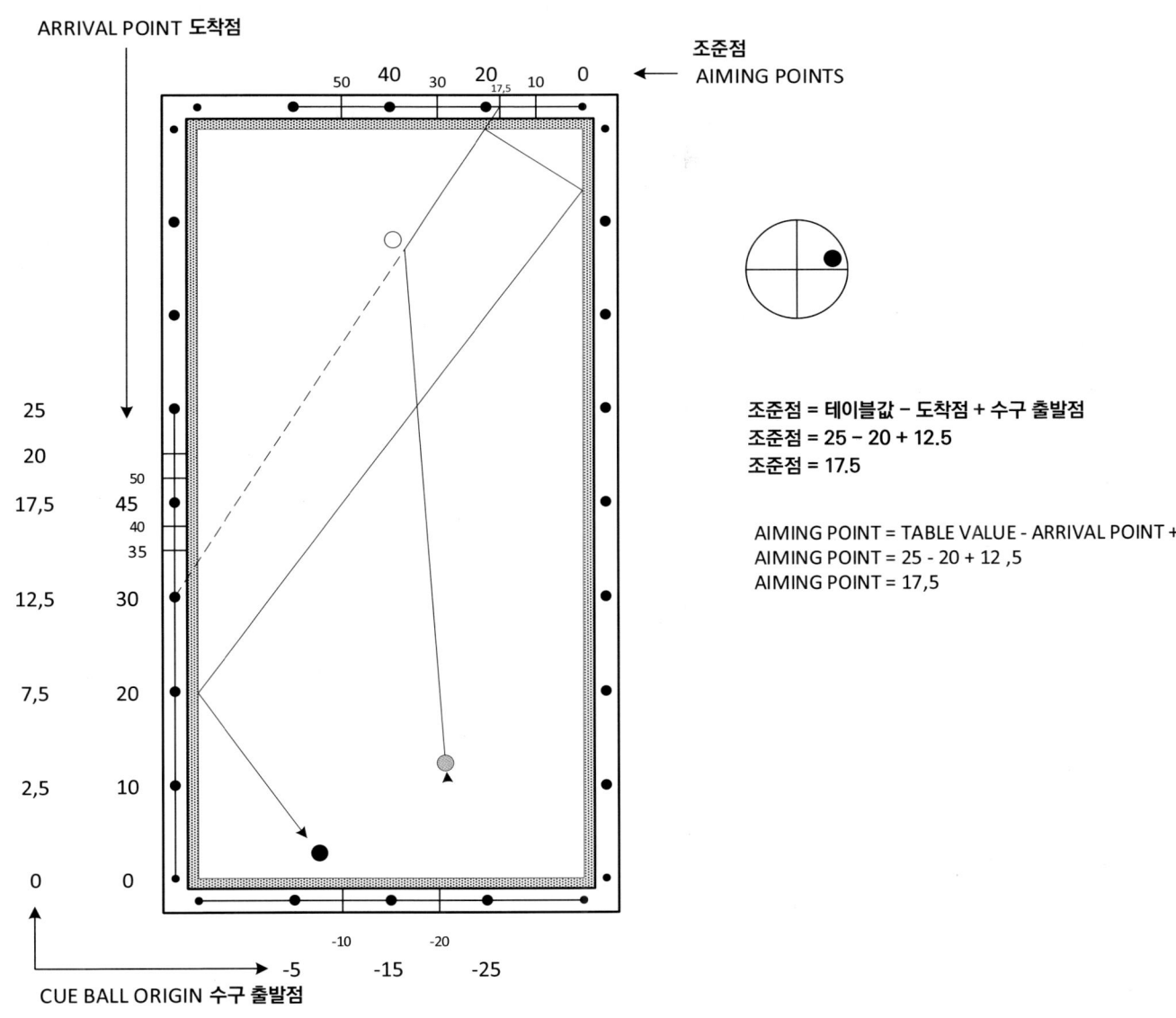

조준점 = 테이블값 − 도착점 + 수구 출발점
조준점 = 25 − 20 + 12.5
조준점 = 17.5

AIMING POINT = TABLE VALUE − ARRIVAL POINT + CUE BALL ORIGIN
AIMING POINT = 25 − 20 + 12 ,5
AIMING POINT = 17,5

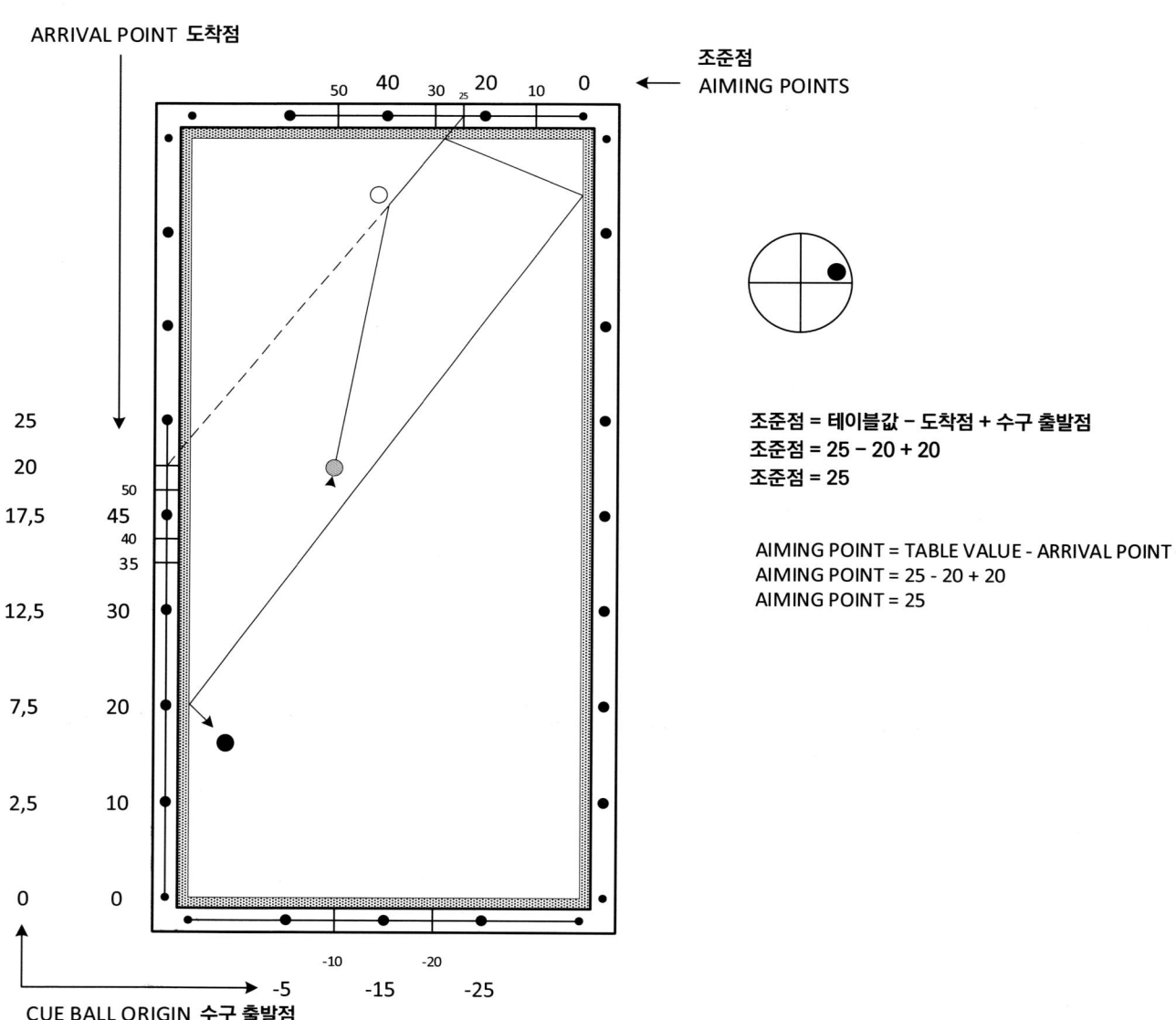

part 02

튜즐 시스템
무회전

1. 튜즐 무회전 시스템

반사 법칙은 모든 무회전 시스템의 기본을 이룬다. 튜즐 무회전 시스템 또한 이 반사 법칙과 함께 당구 테이블은 두 개의 정사각형으로 구성되어 있다는 점에 기초하고 있다. 이 시스템은 매우 광범위하게 사용되며, 수학적 측면에서는 간단하다. 염두에 두어야 할 것은 무회전 공의 샷을 구사하는 것이 쉽지 않다는 점이다. 연습에 있어서 이 점을 고려하기를 바란다. 추천하는 스트로크 기법은 강하지 않고 팔로우스루(follow-through)도 아닌 타법이다. 이 방식은 플레이어의 수구에 대한 지배력을 높이고 무회전 샷을 구사하는 능력을 향상시킬 것이다.

1. TÜZÜL DEAD BALL SYSTEM

For all the dead ball systems, reflection rules are the base. Tüzül Dead Ball Systems are also based on the reflection rules and the fact that the billiard table consists of two squares. The use of these systems is very wide and their mathematical side is easy. The point to bear in mind is that making a dead ball shot is not so easy. I suggest you to take this into account during your practices. The stroke technique that I would recommend is not to make a hard and follow-through stroke. This technique will increase your dominance over the cue ball and will improve your ability to make dead ball shots.

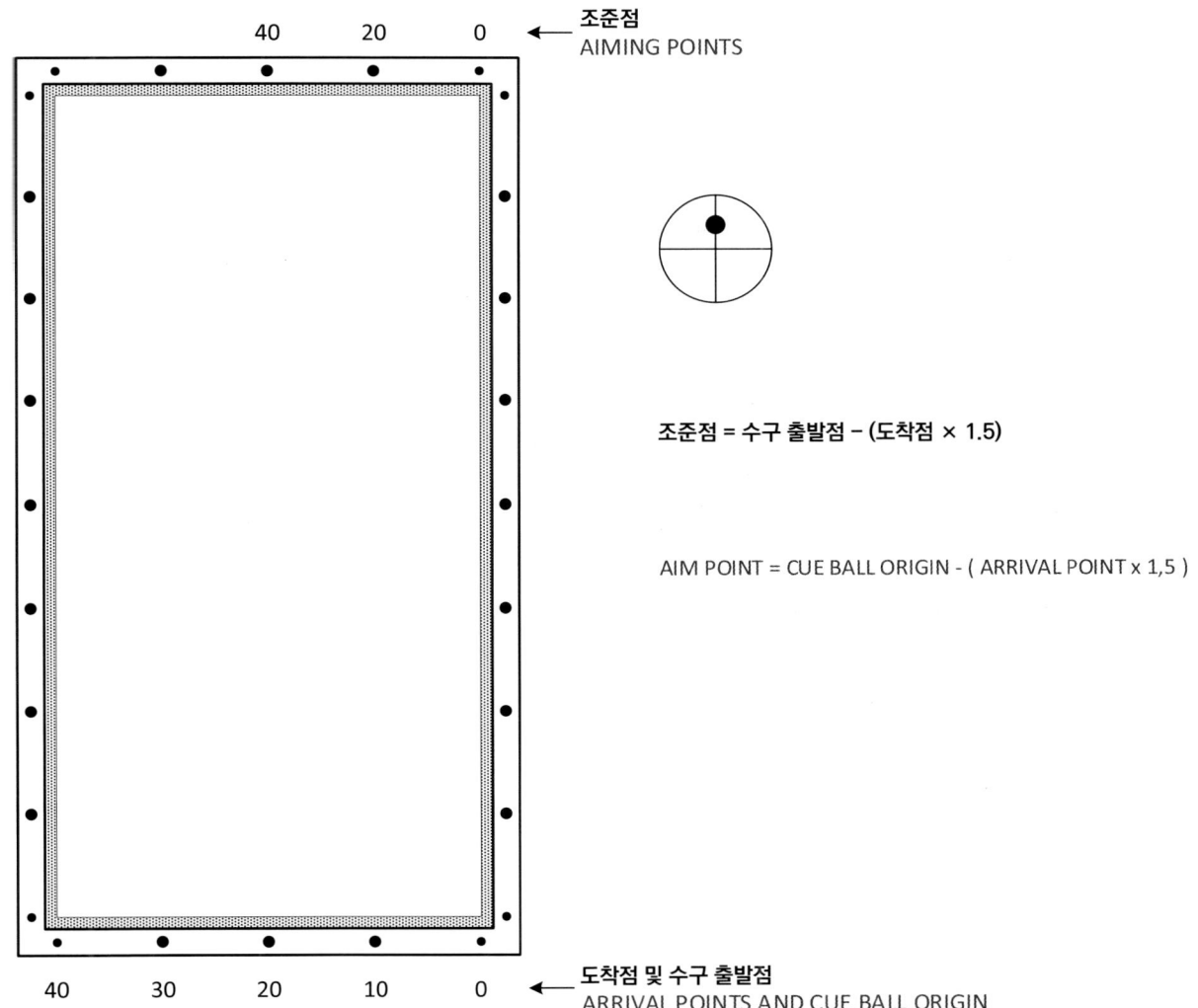

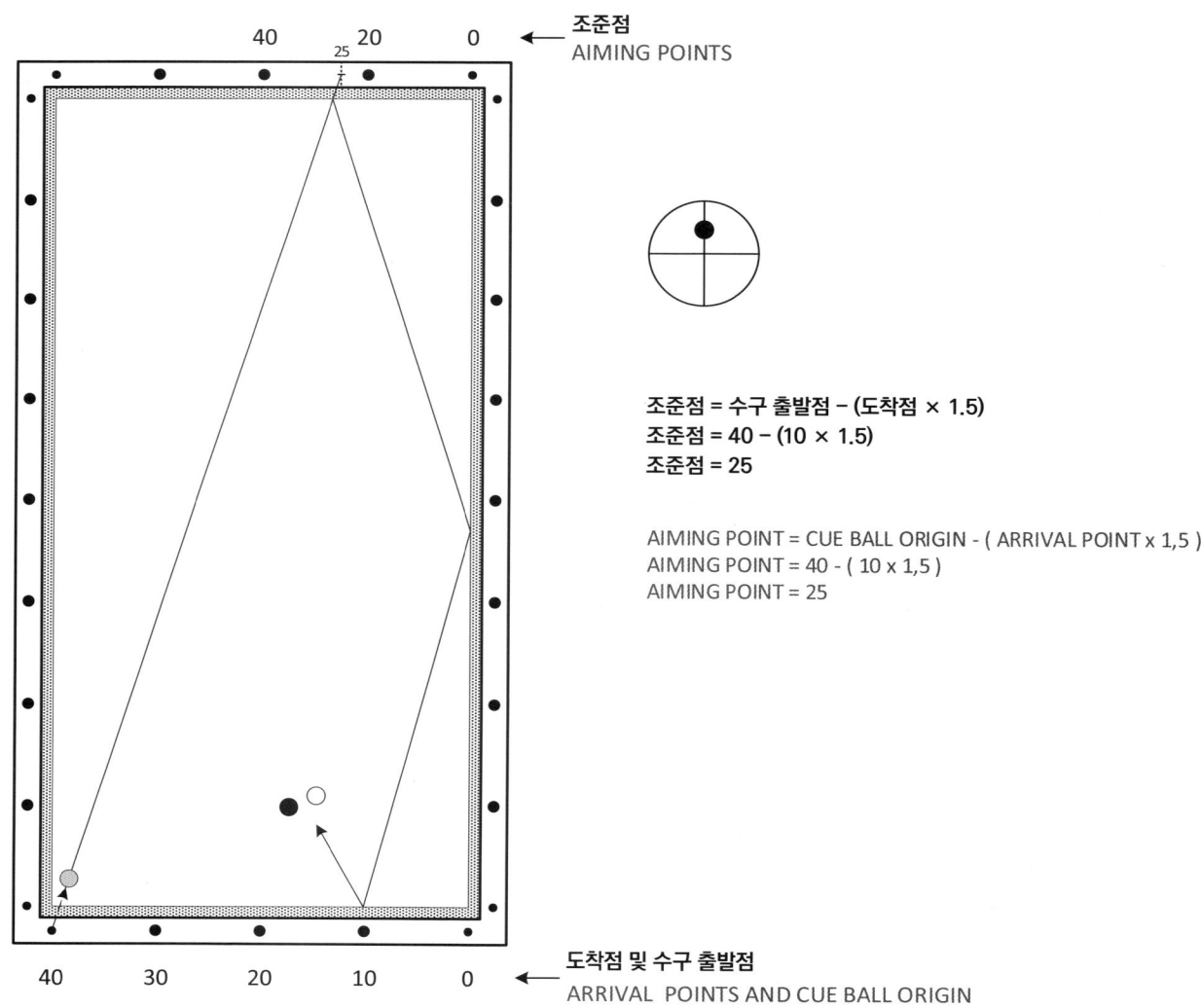

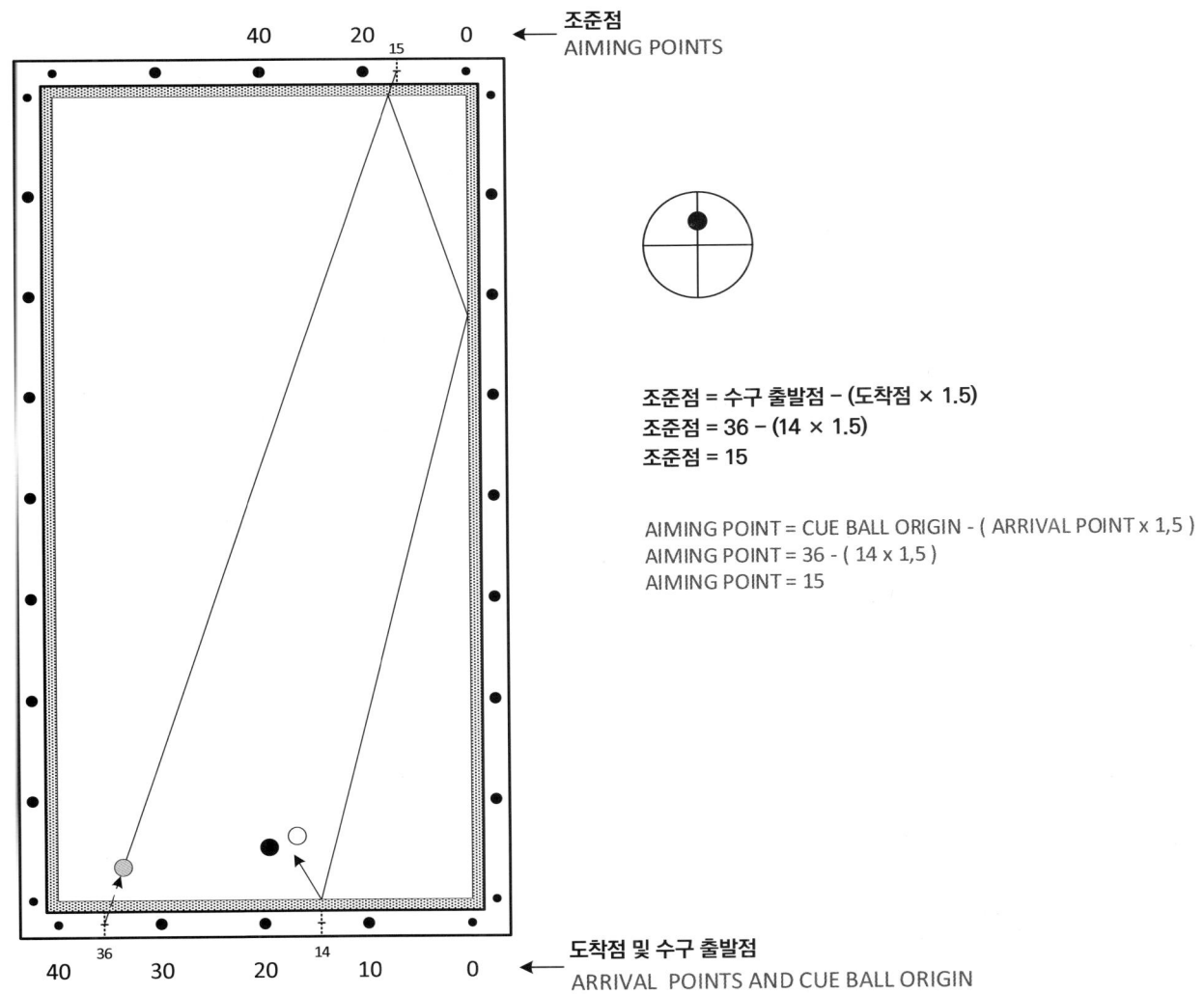

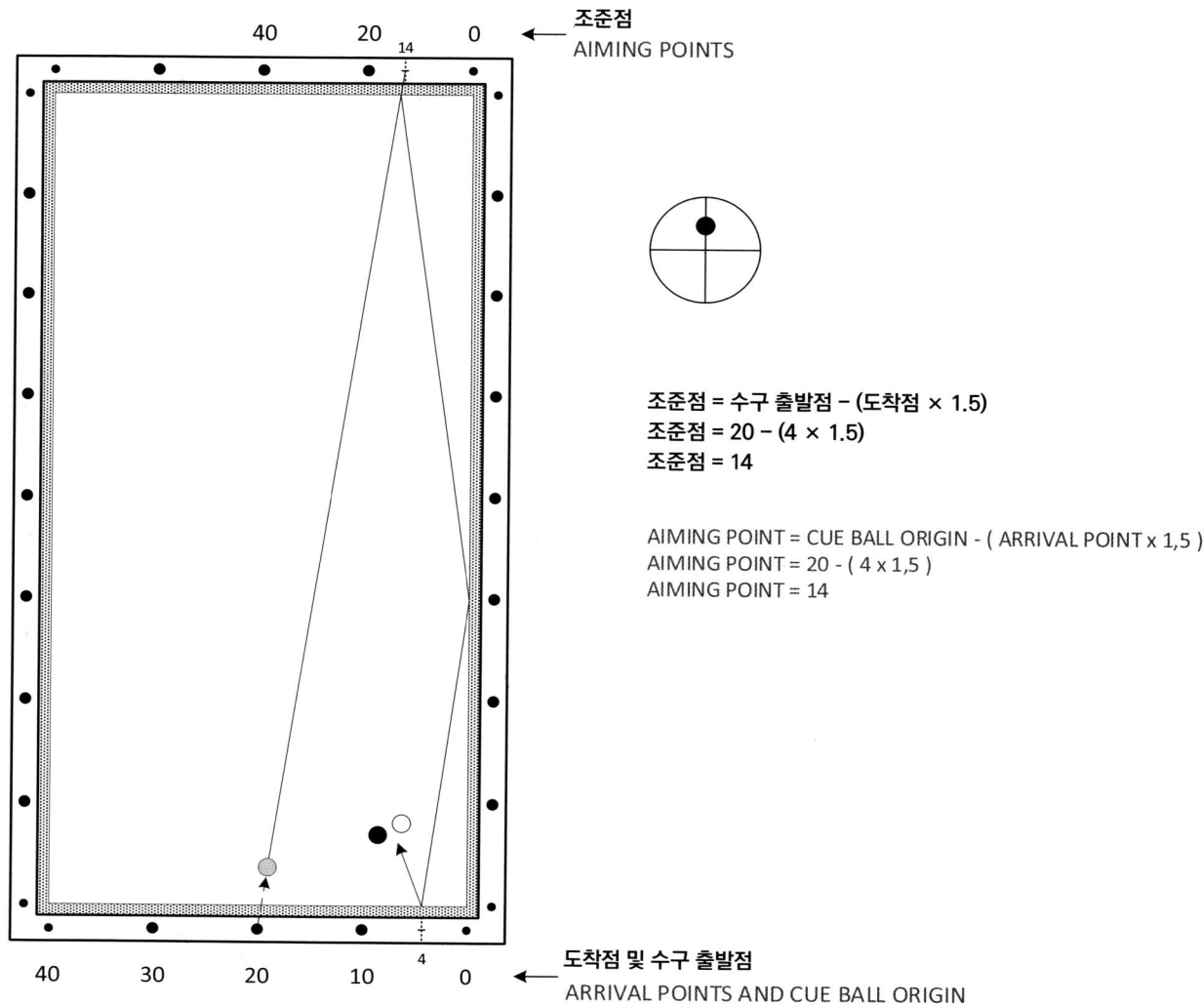

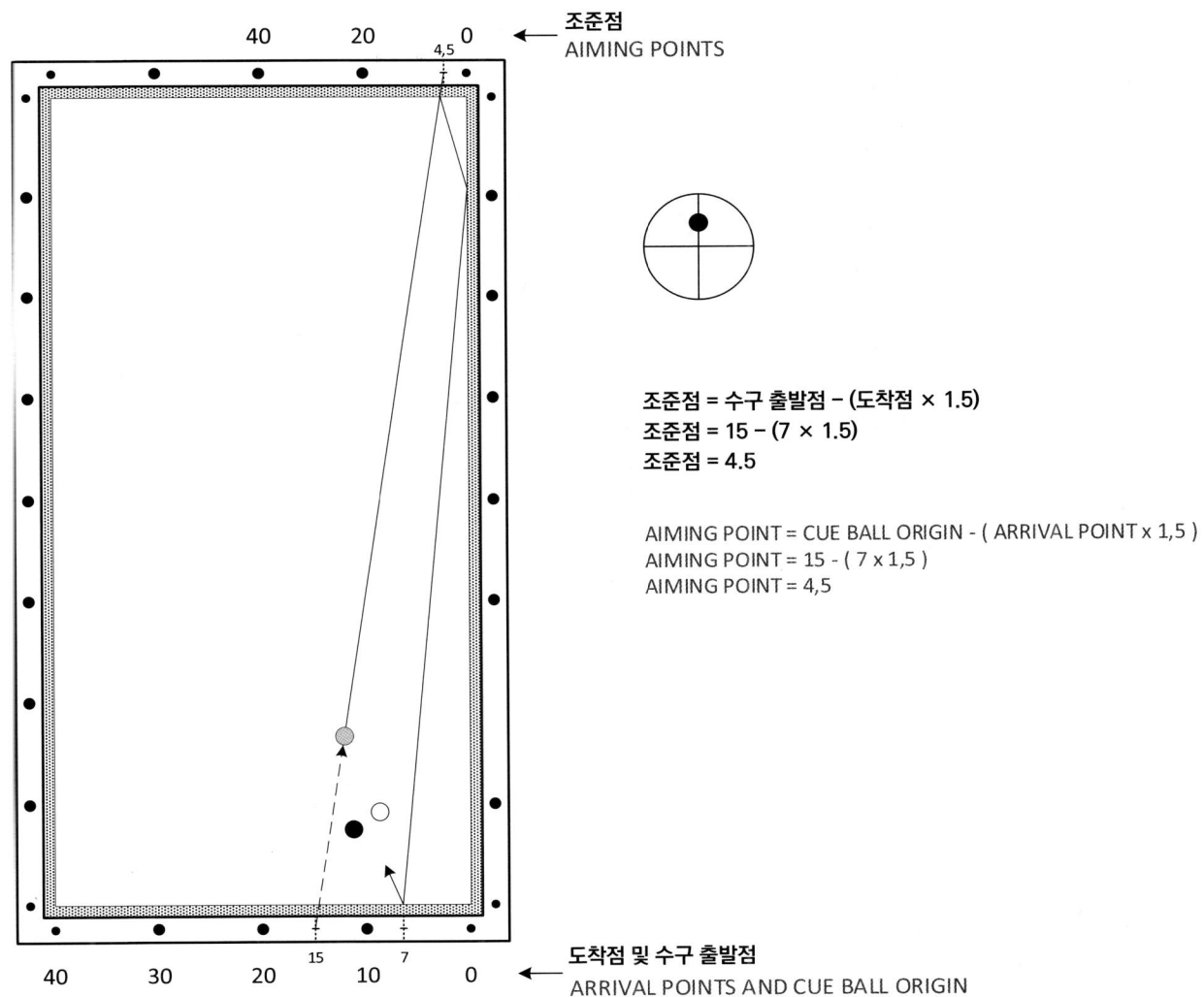

조준점 = 수구 출발점 − (도착점 × 1.5)
조준점 = 15 − (7 × 1.5)
조준점 = 4.5

AIMING POINT = CUE BALL ORIGIN − (ARRIVAL POINT x 1,5)
AIMING POINT = 15 − (7 x 1,5)
AIMING POINT = 4,5

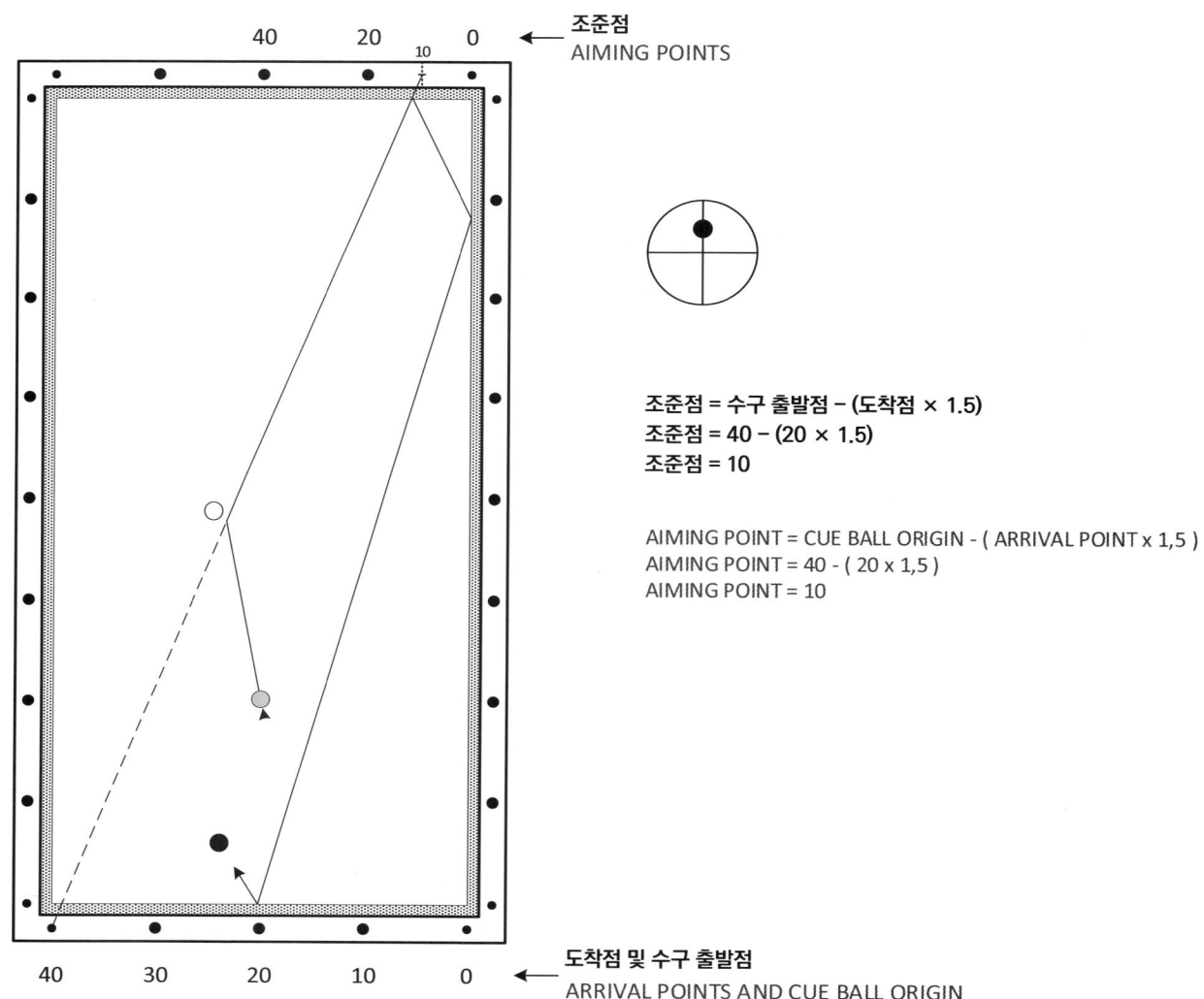

조준점
AIMING POINTS

조준점 = 수구 출발점 − (도착점 × 1.5)
조준점 = 40 − (20 × 1.5)
조준점 = 10

AIMING POINT = CUE BALL ORIGIN − (ARRIVAL POINT x 1,5)
AIMING POINT = 40 − (20 x 1,5)
AIMING POINT = 10

도착점 및 수구 출발점
ARRIVAL POINTS AND CUE BALL ORIGIN

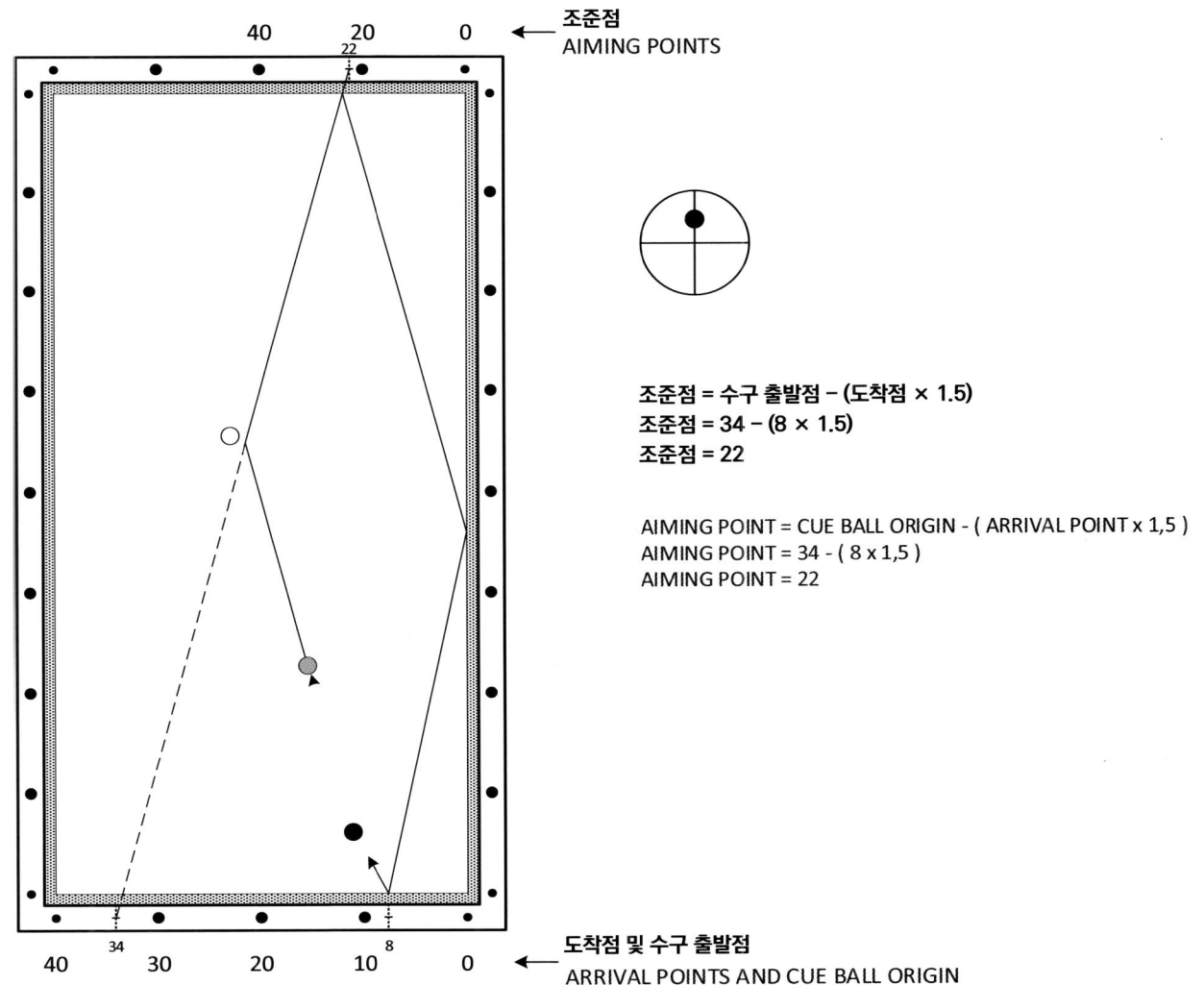

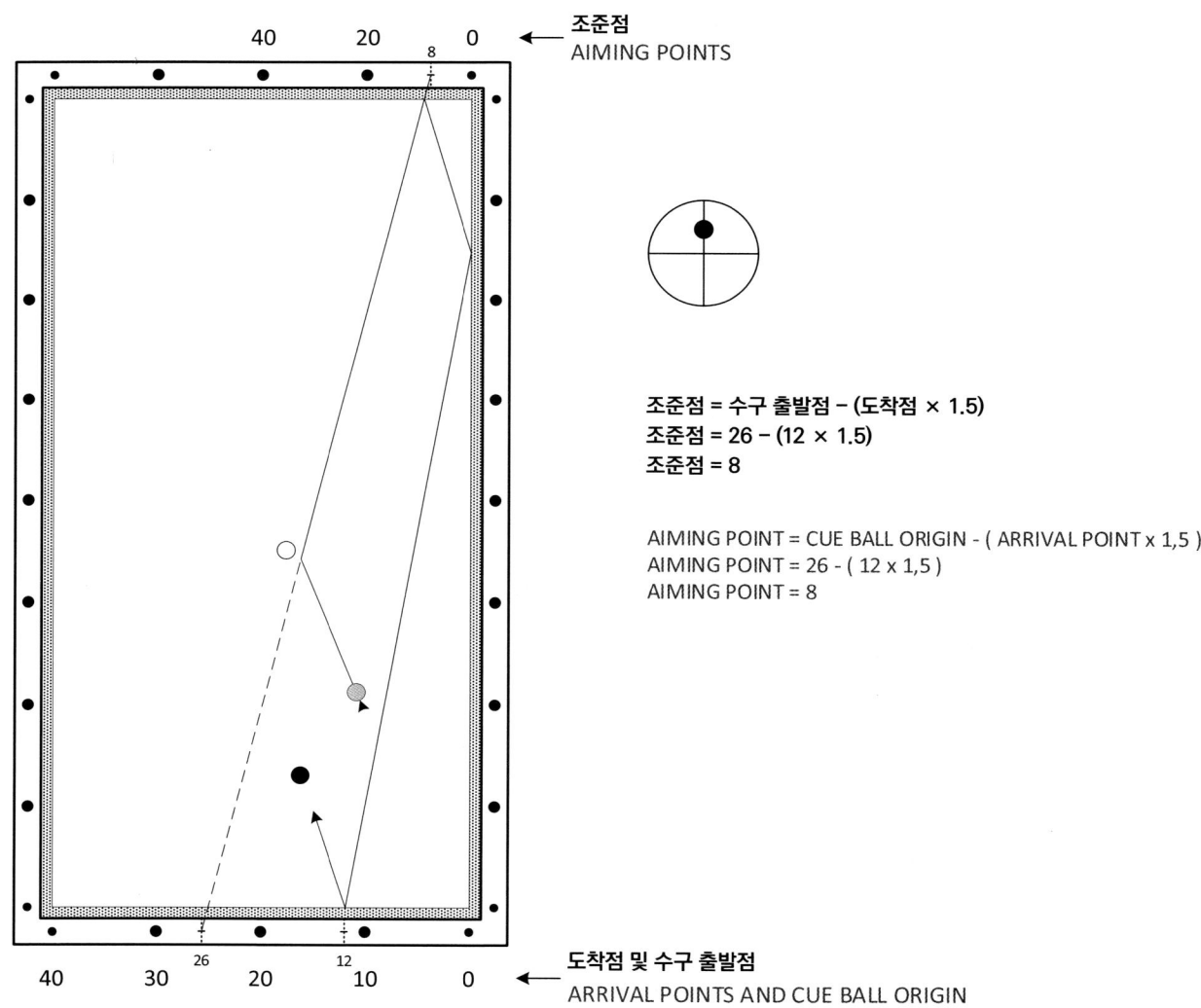

조준점 = 수구 출발점 − (도착점 × 1.5)
조준점 = 26 − (12 × 1.5)
조준점 = 8

AIMING POINT = CUE BALL ORIGIN - (ARRIVAL POINT x 1,5)
AIMING POINT = 26 - (12 x 1,5)
AIMING POINT = 8

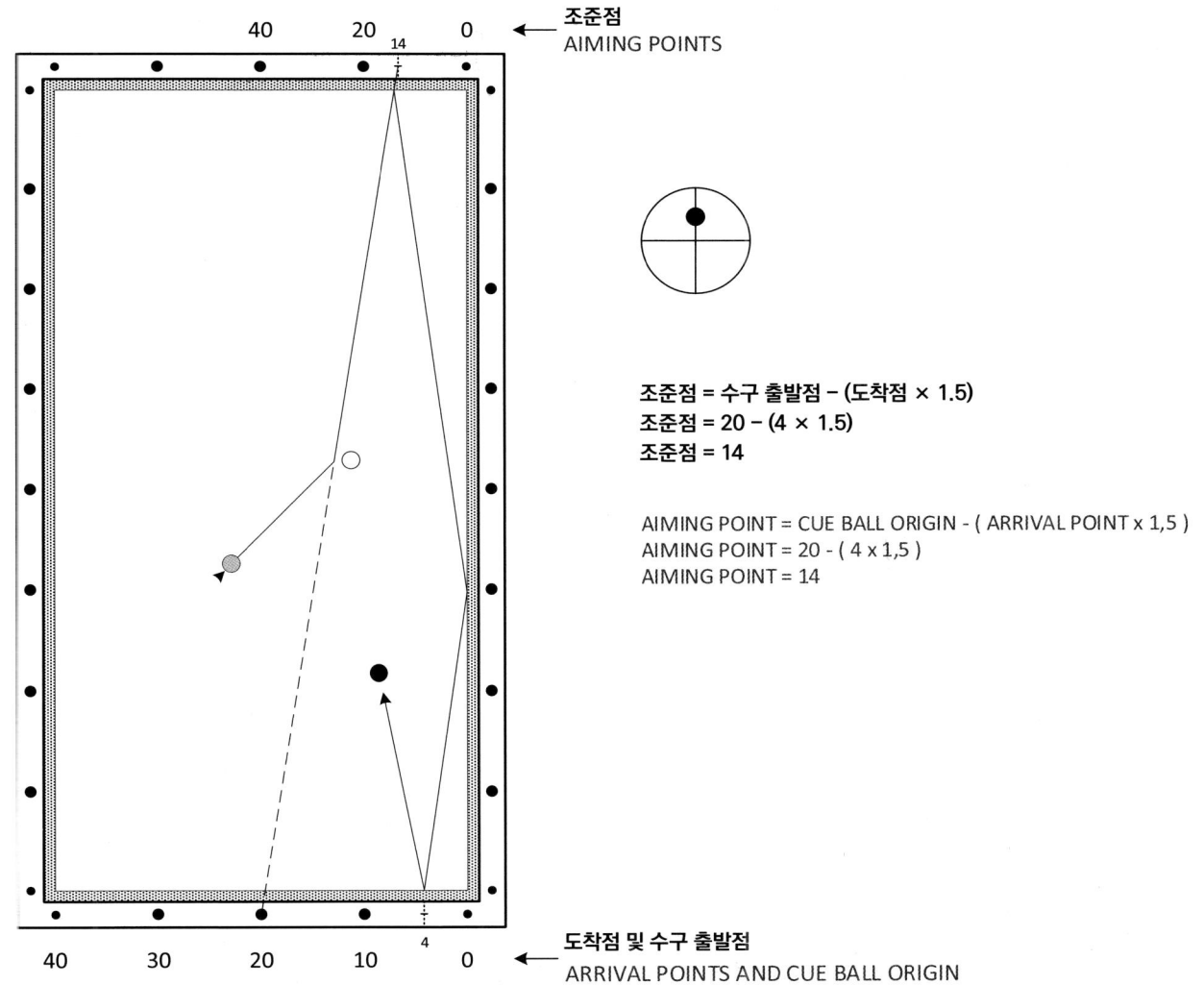

조준점 = 수구 출발점 − (도착점 × 1.5)
조준점 = 20 − (4 × 1.5)
조준점 = 14

AIMING POINT = CUE BALL ORIGIN − (ARRIVAL POINT x 1,5)
AIMING POINT = 20 − (4 x 1,5)
AIMING POINT = 14

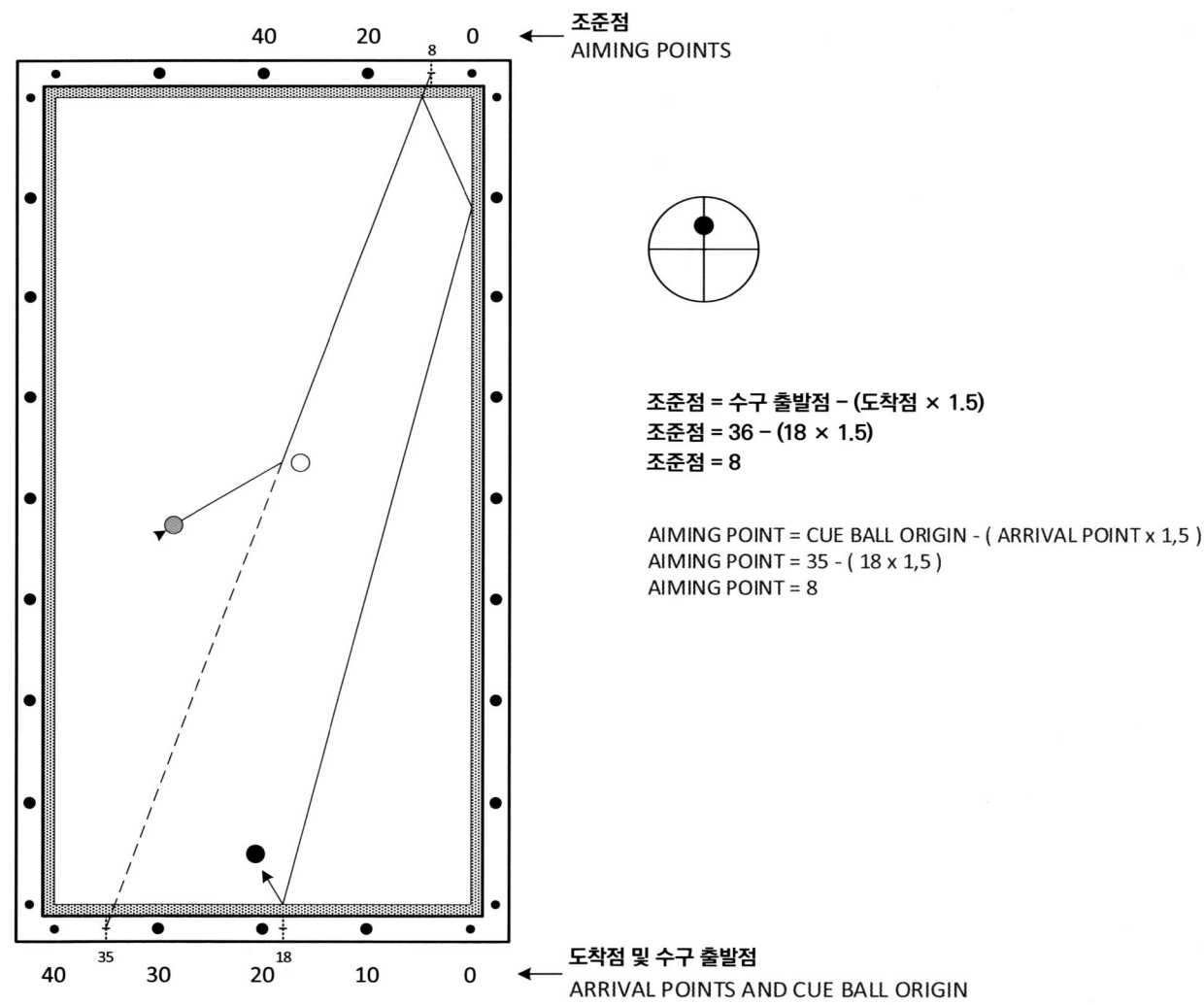

조준점 = 수구 출발점 − (도착점 × 1.5)
조준점 = 36 − (18 × 1.5)
조준점 = 8

AIMING POINT = CUE BALL ORIGIN - (ARRIVAL POINT x 1,5)
AIMING POINT = 35 - (18 x 1,5)
AIMING POINT = 8

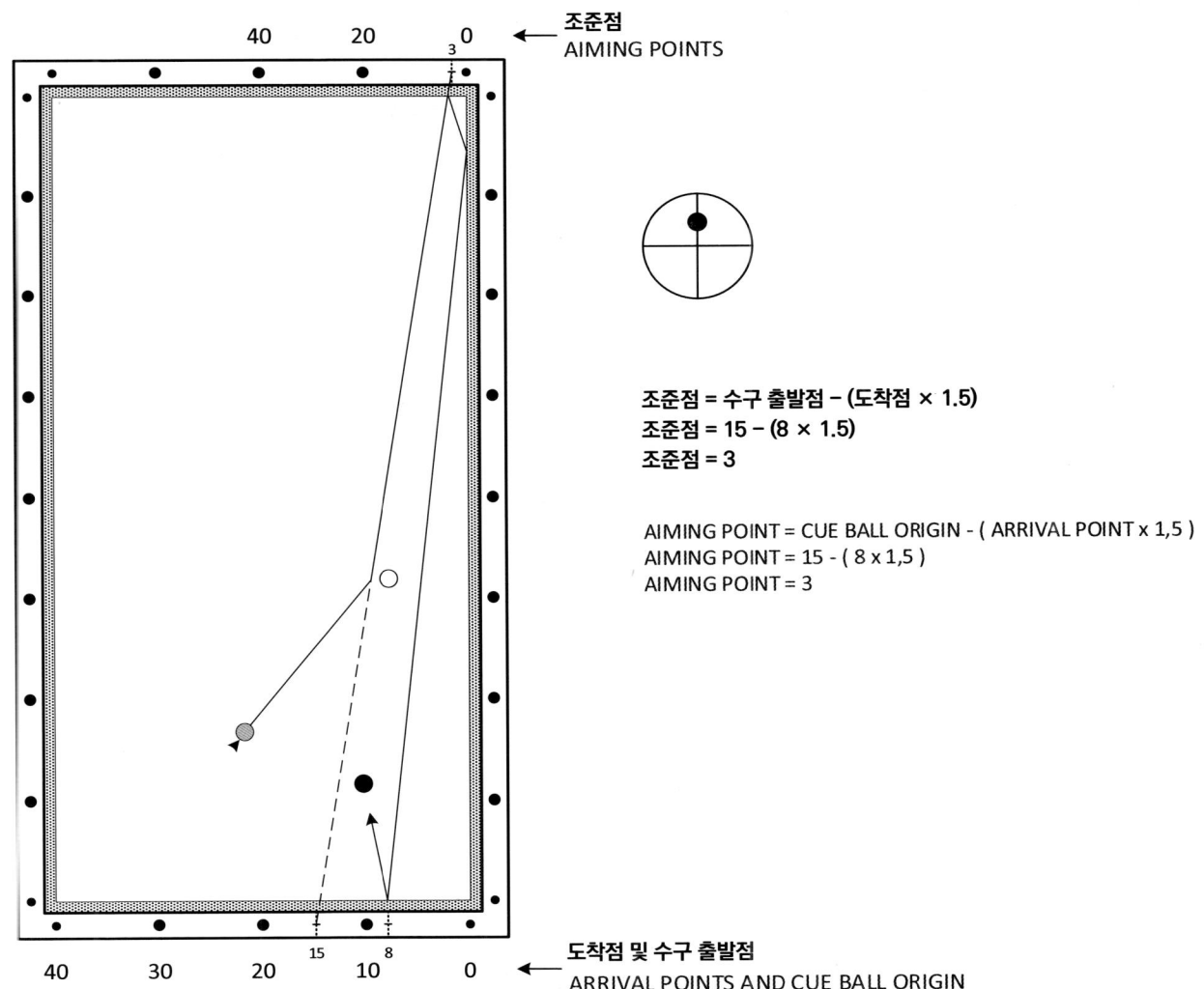

조준점 = 수구 출발점 − (도착점 × 1.5)
조준점 = 15 − (8 × 1.5)
조준점 = 3

AIMING POINT = CUE BALL ORIGIN − (ARRIVAL POINT x 1,5)
AIMING POINT = 15 − (8 x 1,5)
AIMING POINT = 3

2. 튜즐 무회전 시스템 – ¼ 테이블 응용

수치를 부여하는 방식이 그림에 표시되어 있다. 스트로크 기법과 공식은 전체 테이블에 적용할 때와 동일하다. 그림에서 볼 수 있듯이, 이 시스템을 통해 ¼ 테이블의 경계 내에서 유리한 각도를 이용하여 득점할 수 있게 된다. 다른 ¼ 테이블 응용에서와 마찬가지로, 작은 테이블 범위 내에서는 당구공이 상대적으로 커지므로 더욱 이점이 있다.

2. TÜZÜL DEAD BALL SYSTEM -1/4 TABLE APPLICATION

The numbering system is shown in the chart. The stroke technique and the formulization are the same as in the big table application. As you will see in the graphs, this system enables you to make points with advantageous angles within the small table boundaries. Big balls within small table frontiers provide an advantage as in other small table applications.

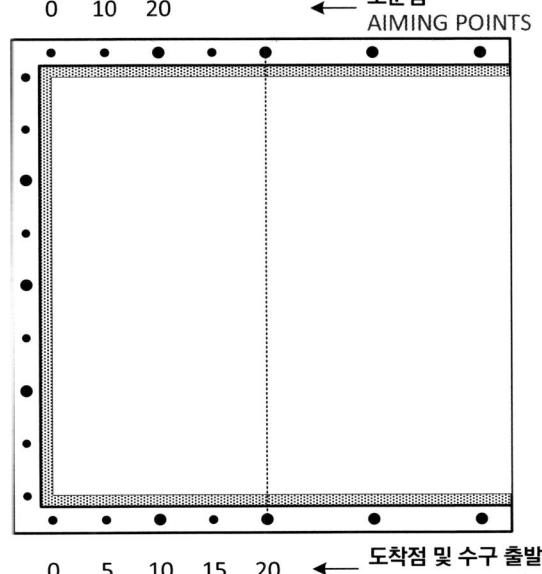

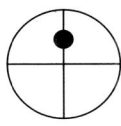

조준점 = 수구 출발점 − (도착점 × 1.5)

AIMING POINT = CUE BALL ORIGIN − (ARRIVAL POINT x 1,5)

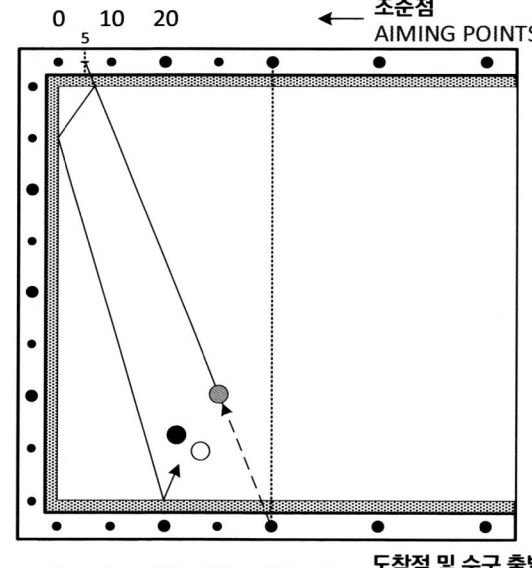

조준점
AIMING POINTS

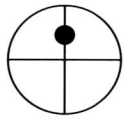

조준점 = 수구 출발점 − (도착점 × 1.5)
조준점 = 20 − (10 × 1.5)
조준점 = 5

AIMING POINT = CUE BALL ORIGIN − (ARRIVAL POINT x 1,5)
AIMING POINT = 20 − (10 x 1,5)
AIMING POINT = 5

도착점 및 수구 출발점
ARRIVAL POINTS AND CUE BALL ORIGIN

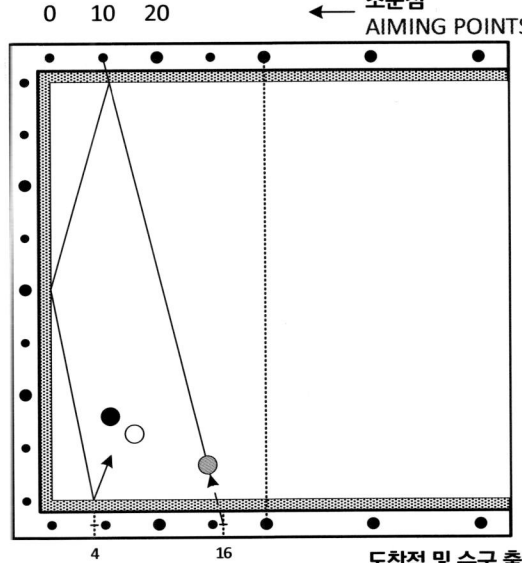
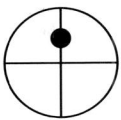

조준점 = 수구 출발점 − (도착점 × 1.5)
조준점 = 16 − (4 × 1.5)
조준점 = 10

AIMING POINT = CUE BALL ORIGIN - (ARRIVAL POINT x 1,5)
AIMING POINT = 16 - (4 x 1,5)
AIMING POINT = 10

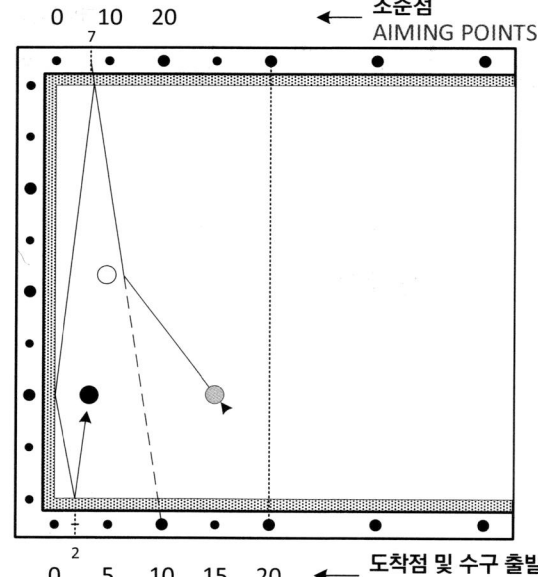
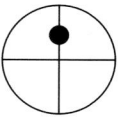

조준점 = 수구 출발점 − (도착점 × 1.5)
조준점 = 10 − (2 × 1.5)
조준점 = 7

AIMING POINT = CUE BALL ORIGIN − (ARRIVAL POINT x 1,5)
AIMING POINT = 10 − (2 x 1,5)
AIMING POINT = 7

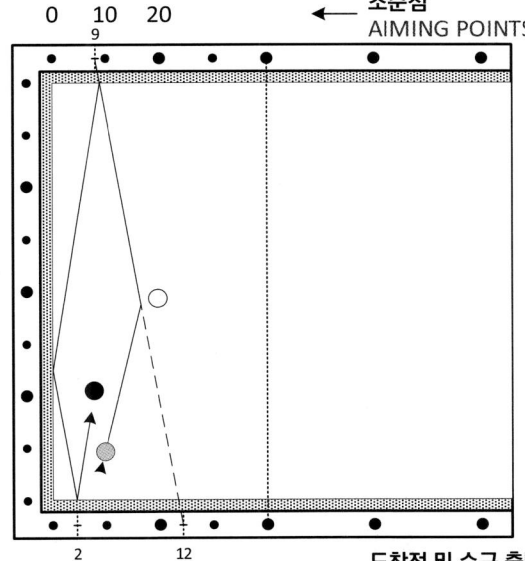
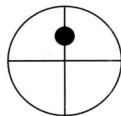

조준점 = 수구 출발점 − (도착점 × 1.5)
조준점 = 12 − (2 × 1.5)
조준점 = 9

AIMING POINT = CUE BALL ORIGIN − (ARRIVAL POINT x 1,5)
AIMING POINT = 12 − (2 x 1,5)
AIMING POINT = 9

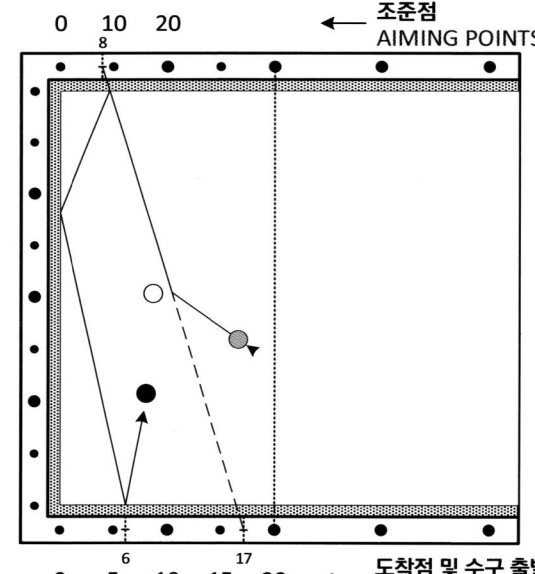
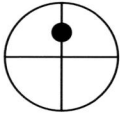

조준점 = 수구 출발점 - (도착점 × 1.5)
조준점 = 17 - (6 × 1.5)
조준점 = 8

AIMING POINT = CUE BALL ORIGIN - (ARRIVAL POINT x 1,5)
AIMING POINT = 17 - (6 x 1,5)
AIMING POINT = 8

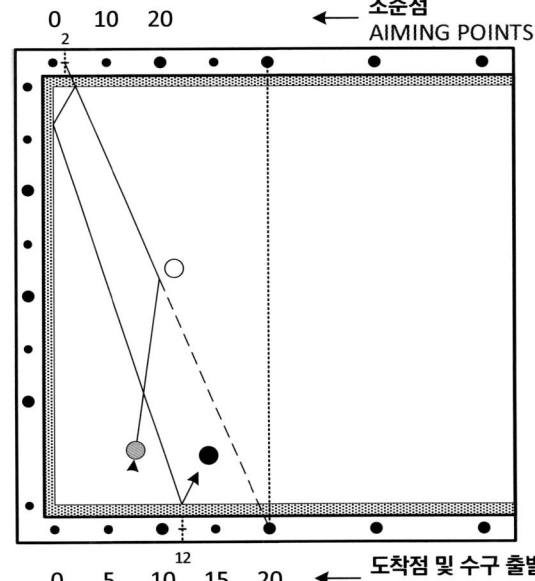

조준점
AIMING POINTS

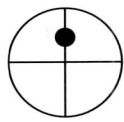

도착점 및 수구 출발점
ARRIVAL POINTS AND CUE BALL ORIGIN

조준점 = 수구 출발점 − (도착점 × 1.5)
조준점 = 20 − (12 × 1.5)
조준점 = 2

AIMING POINT = CUE BALL ORIGIN − (ARRIVAL POINT x 1,5)
AIMING POINT = 20 − (12 x 1,5)
AIMING POINT = 2

3. 튜즐 부가점 시스템

만약 큐의 뒤쪽이 단쿠션을 향하고 있다면, 이 시스템의 사용은 무회전으로 단쿠션-단쿠션-장쿠션 경로에 대해 원하는 결과를 만들어낼 것이다. 단쿠션측에 배치된 수구 출발점들에 각각 대응되는 부가점들의 값이 수치화된 그림에 표시되어 있다. 그림에서 보는 바와 같이 각 출발점에 대한 부가점의 값은 상이하다. 이 시스템의 적용에 있어서, 특정의 수구 출발점에 대응되는 부가점의 값은 3쿠션에 해당되는 장쿠션에 대해 동등하게 할당되어야 한다. 3쿠션 도착점은 부가점의 할당 후에 결정된다. 수구 출발점에 부가점의 값을 더하면 첫 번째 쿠션의 조준점이 얻어진다. 다른 모든 튜즐 시스템(무회전)에서와 마찬가지로 다소 부드럽고 짧은 스트로크 기법이 권고된다. 항상 그렇듯이, 이 시스템을 사용하기 위해 가장 중요한 것은 무회전 샷을 구사하는 능력이다.

3. TÜZÜL ADD POINT SYSTEM

If the back of the cue is towards the short cushion, the use of this system will produce the required result through the short cushion-long cushion-short cushion line without english. The additional points belonging to the cue ball origin points aligned on the short cushion may be seen in the numbering graph. The additional point value for each start point is different. In the application of the system, the value of the additional point belonging to a specific cue ball origin point should be distributed equally on the long cushion equivalent to the third cushion. The third cushion arrival point is determined after the distribution of the additional points. After adding the cue ball origin point on this value, the aiming points on the first cushion is reached.

I propose to use a rather soft and short-stroke technique as in all other Tüzül Systems (dead ball). As always, the most important factor in the effective use of the system is the capability of making dead ball shots.

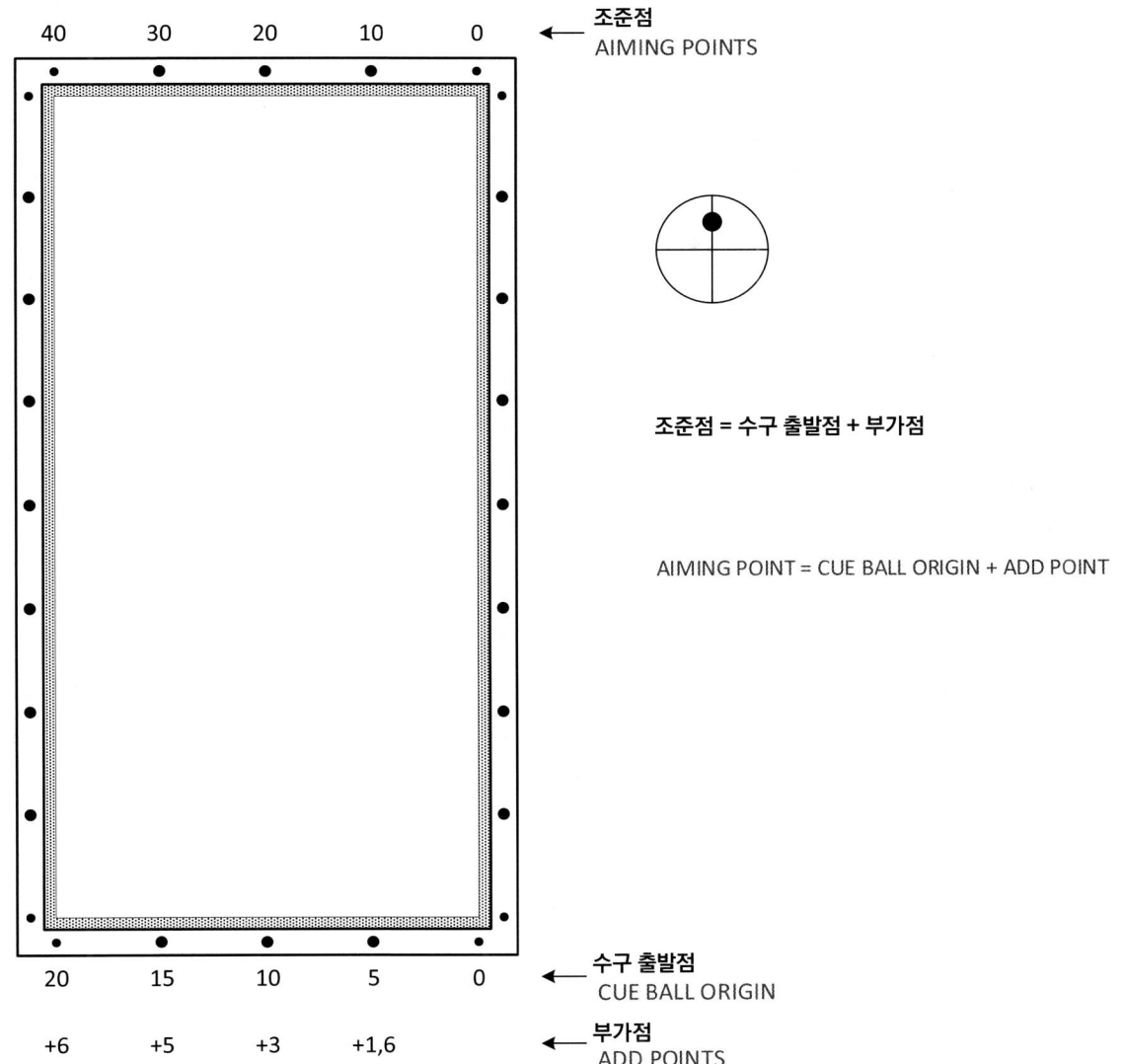

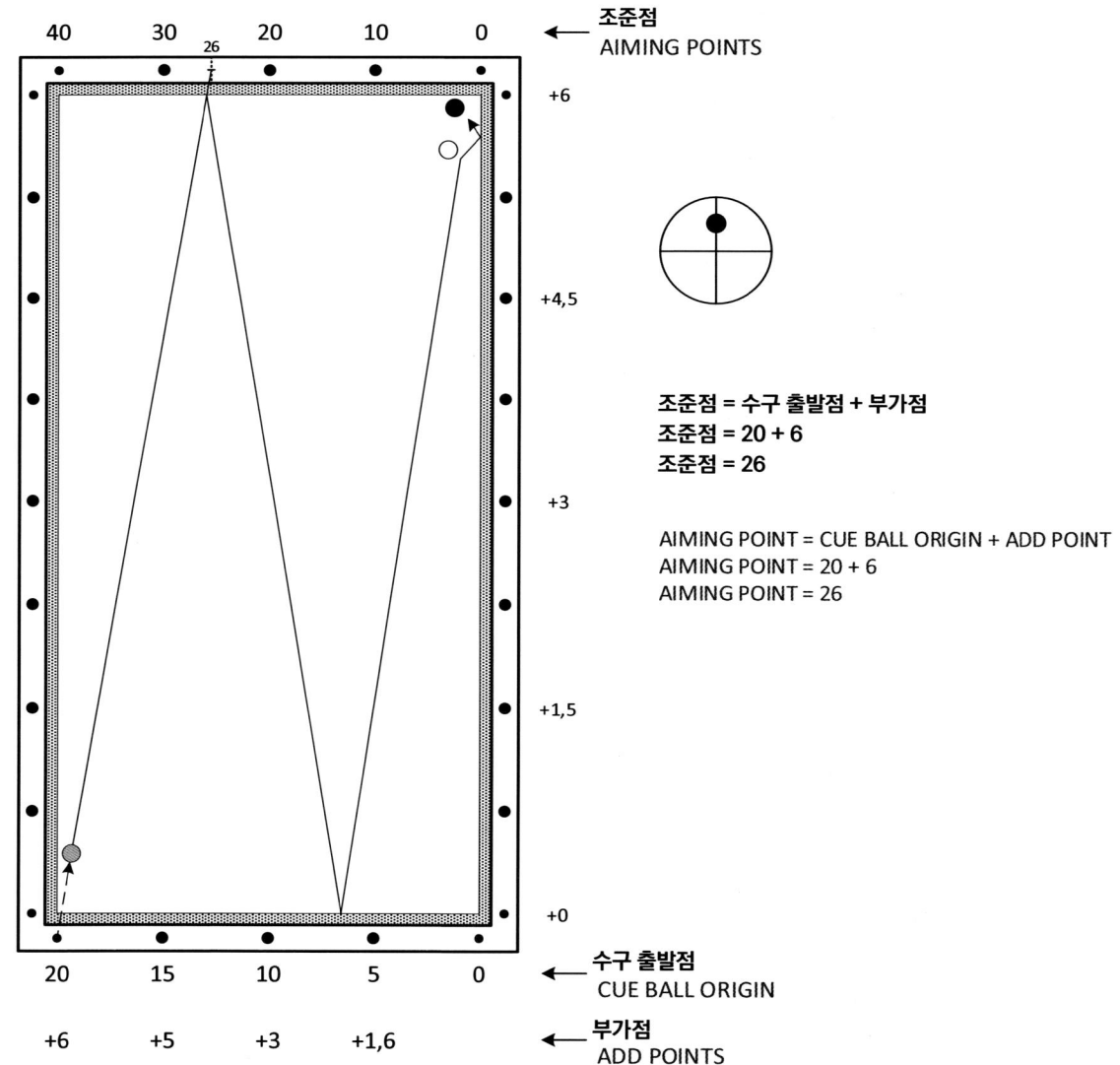

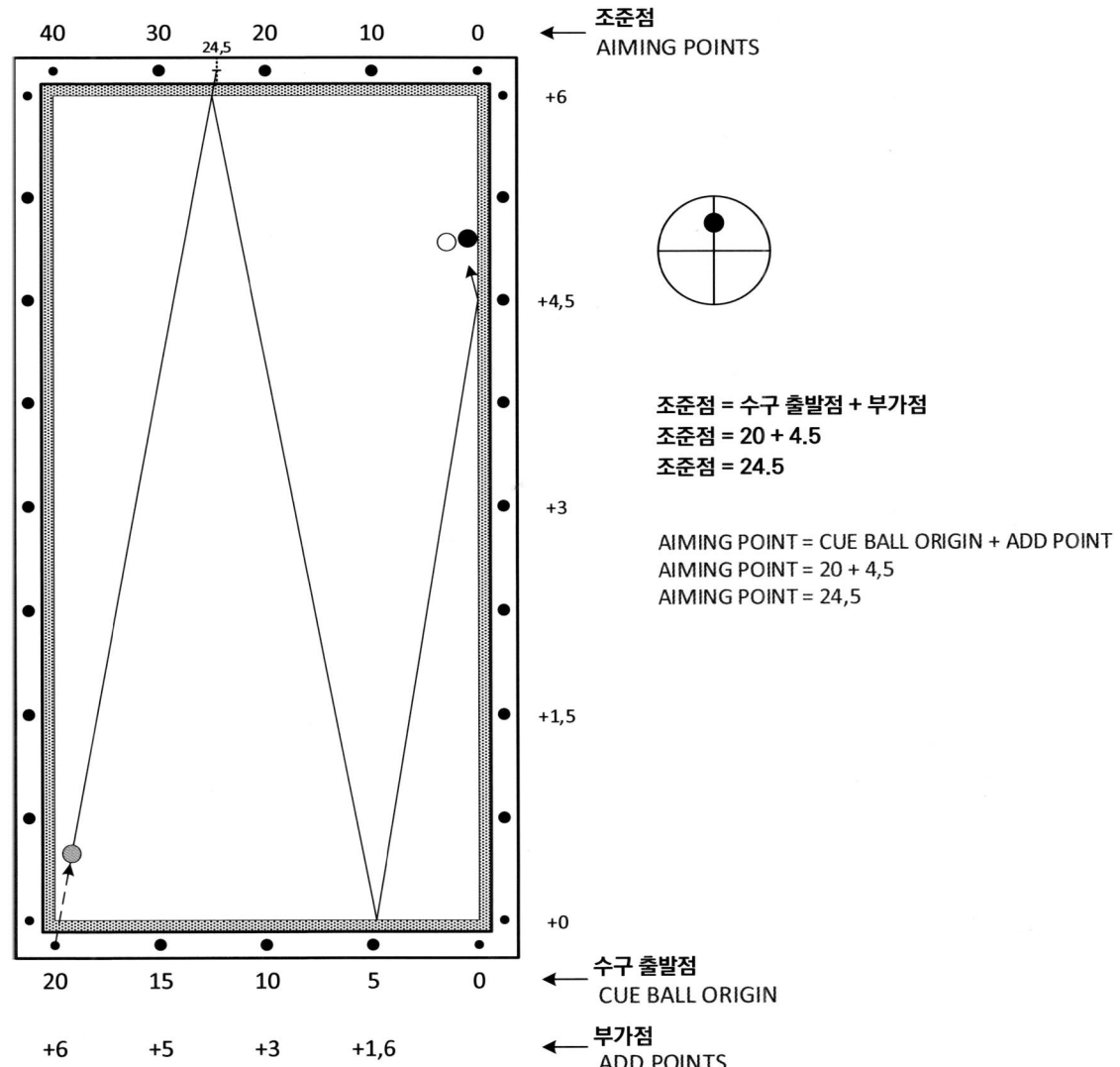

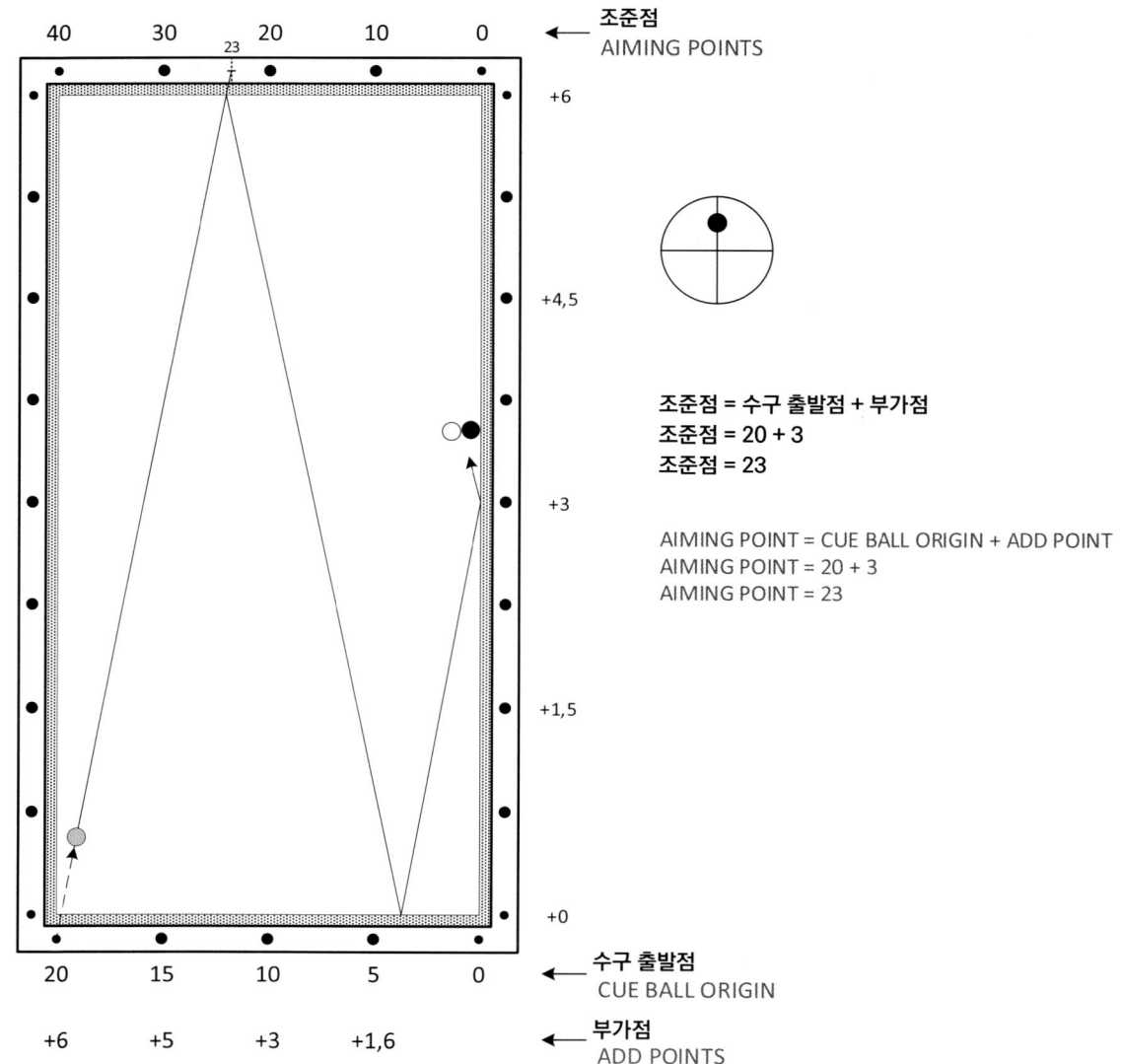

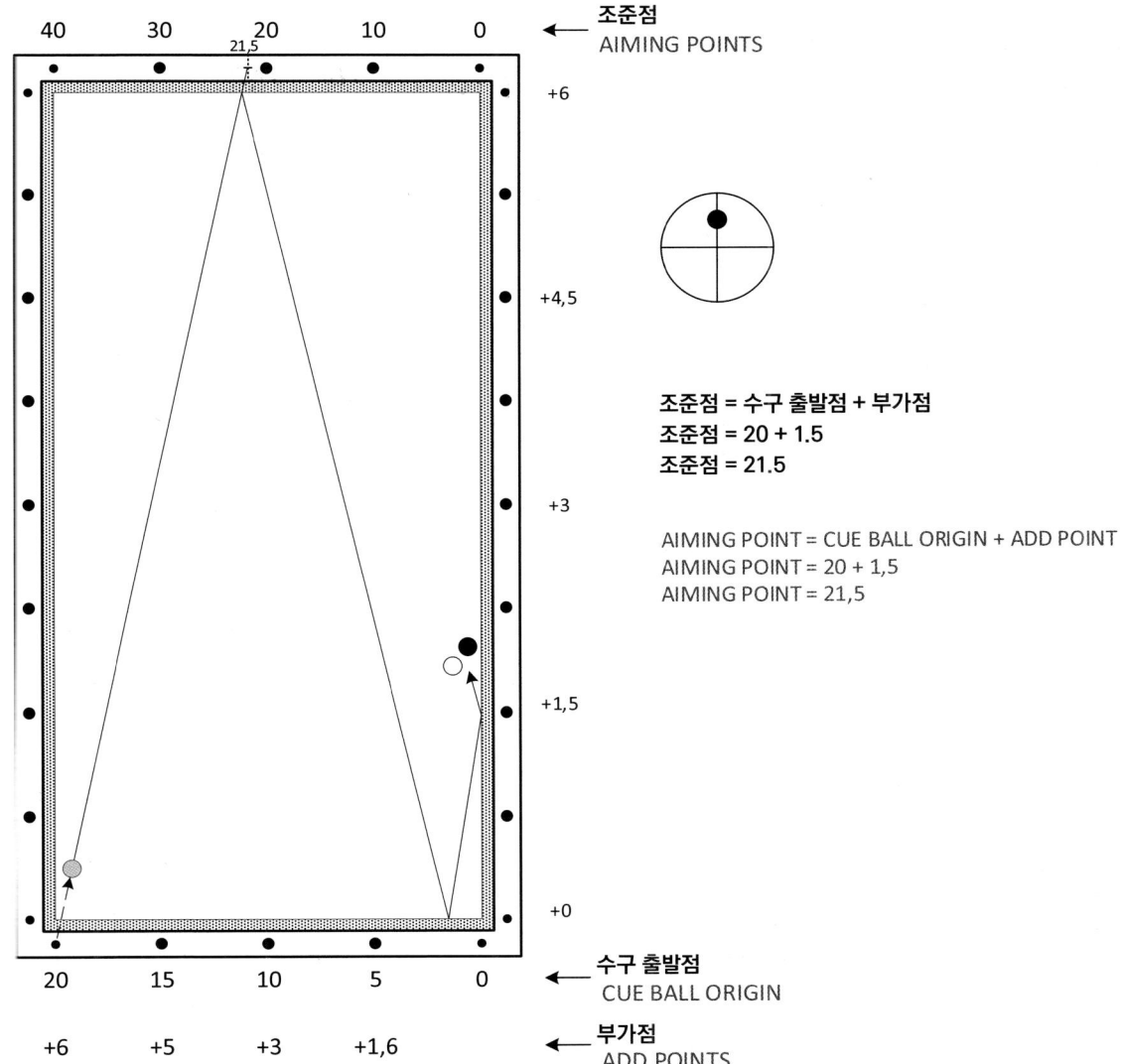

조준점 = 수구 출발점 + 부가점
조준점 = 20 + 1.5
조준점 = 21.5

AIMING POINT = CUE BALL ORIGIN + ADD POINT
AIMING POINT = 20 + 1,5
AIMING POINT = 21,5

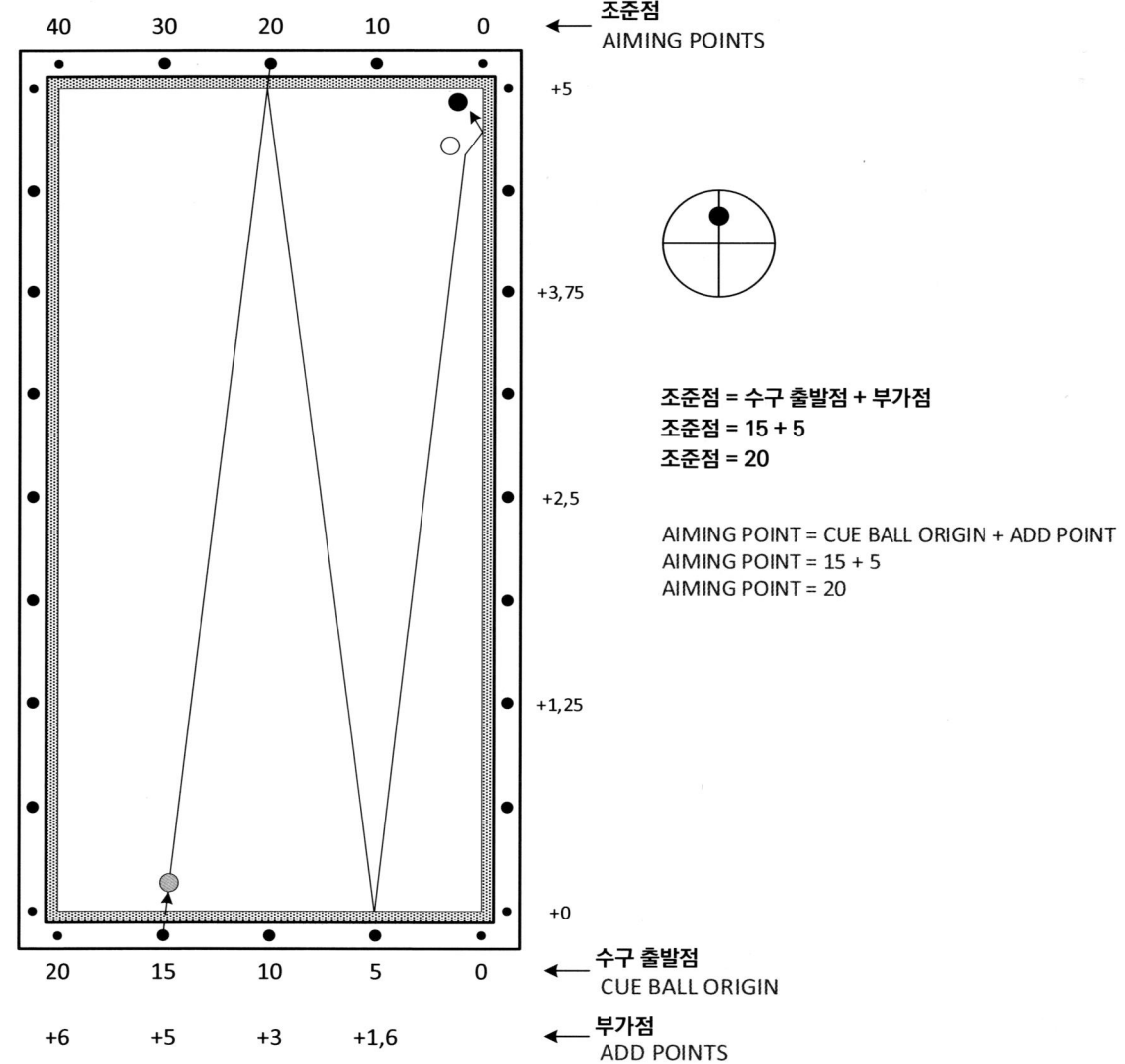

조준점 = 수구 출발점 + 부가점
조준점 = 15 + 5
조준점 = 20

AIMING POINT = CUE BALL ORIGIN + ADD POINT
AIMING POINT = 15 + 5
AIMING POINT = 20

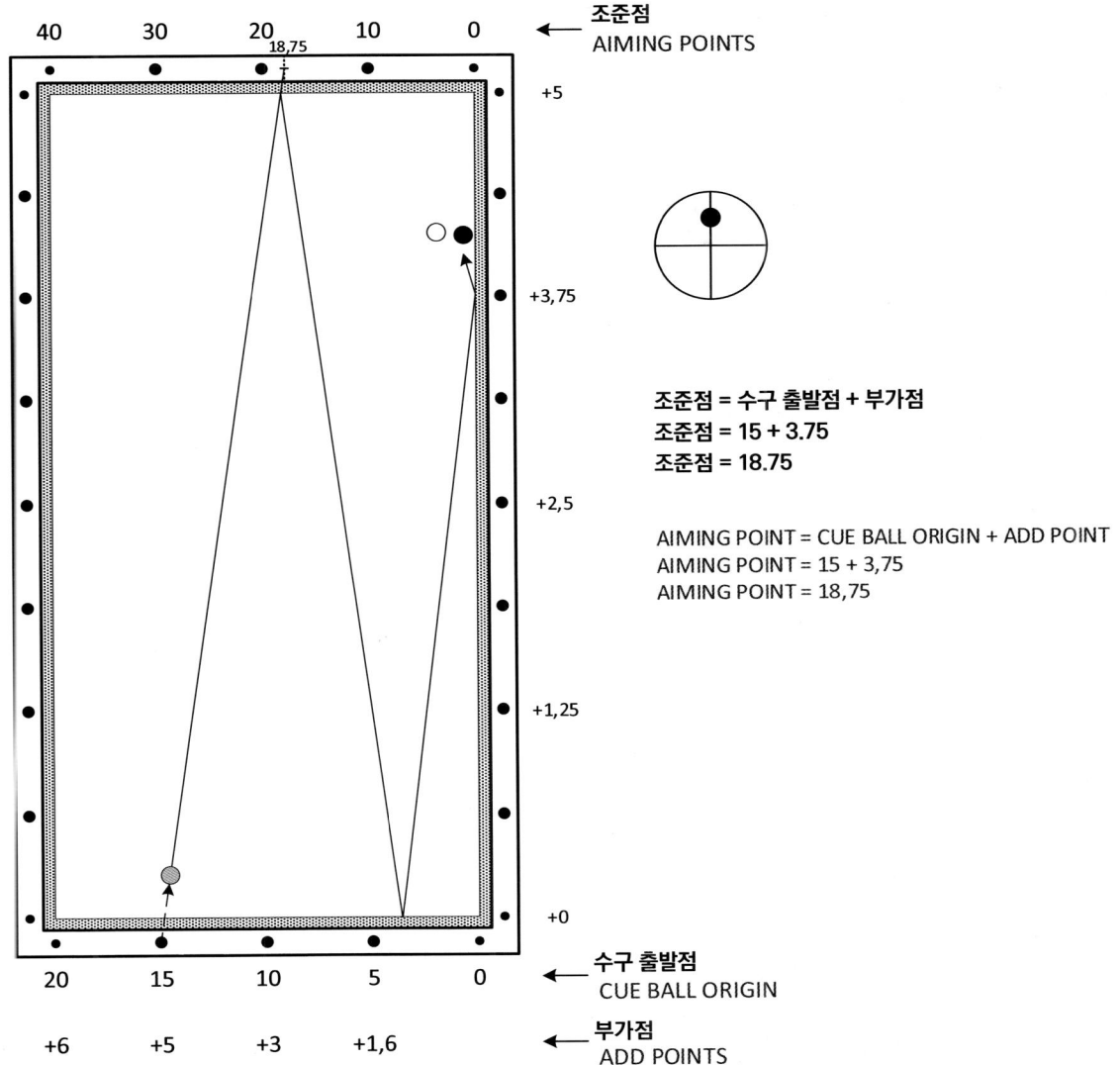

조준점 = 수구 출발점 + 부가점
조준점 = 15 + 3.75
조준점 = 18.75

AIMING POINT = CUE BALL ORIGIN + ADD POINT
AIMING POINT = 15 + 3,75
AIMING POINT = 18,75

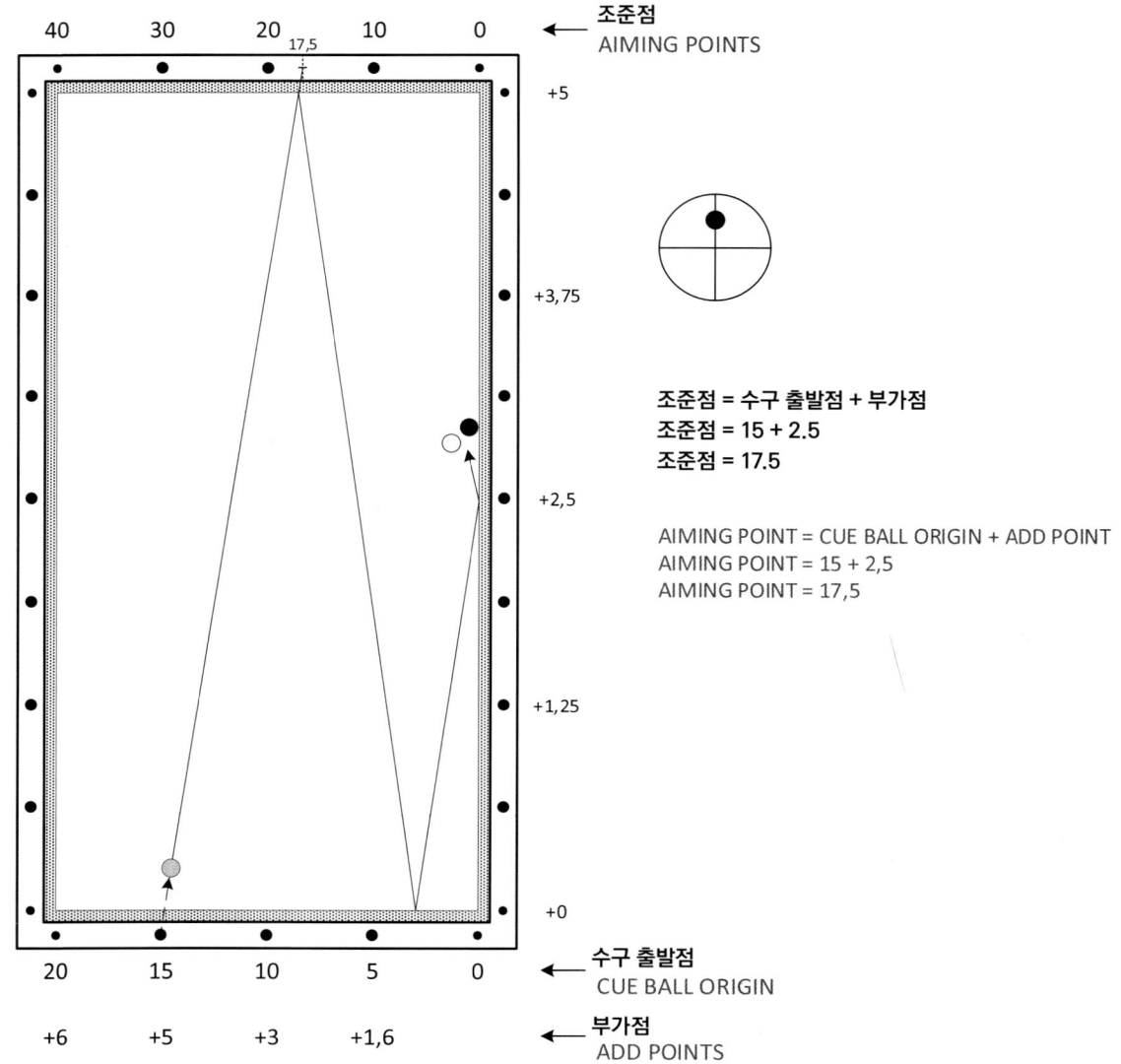

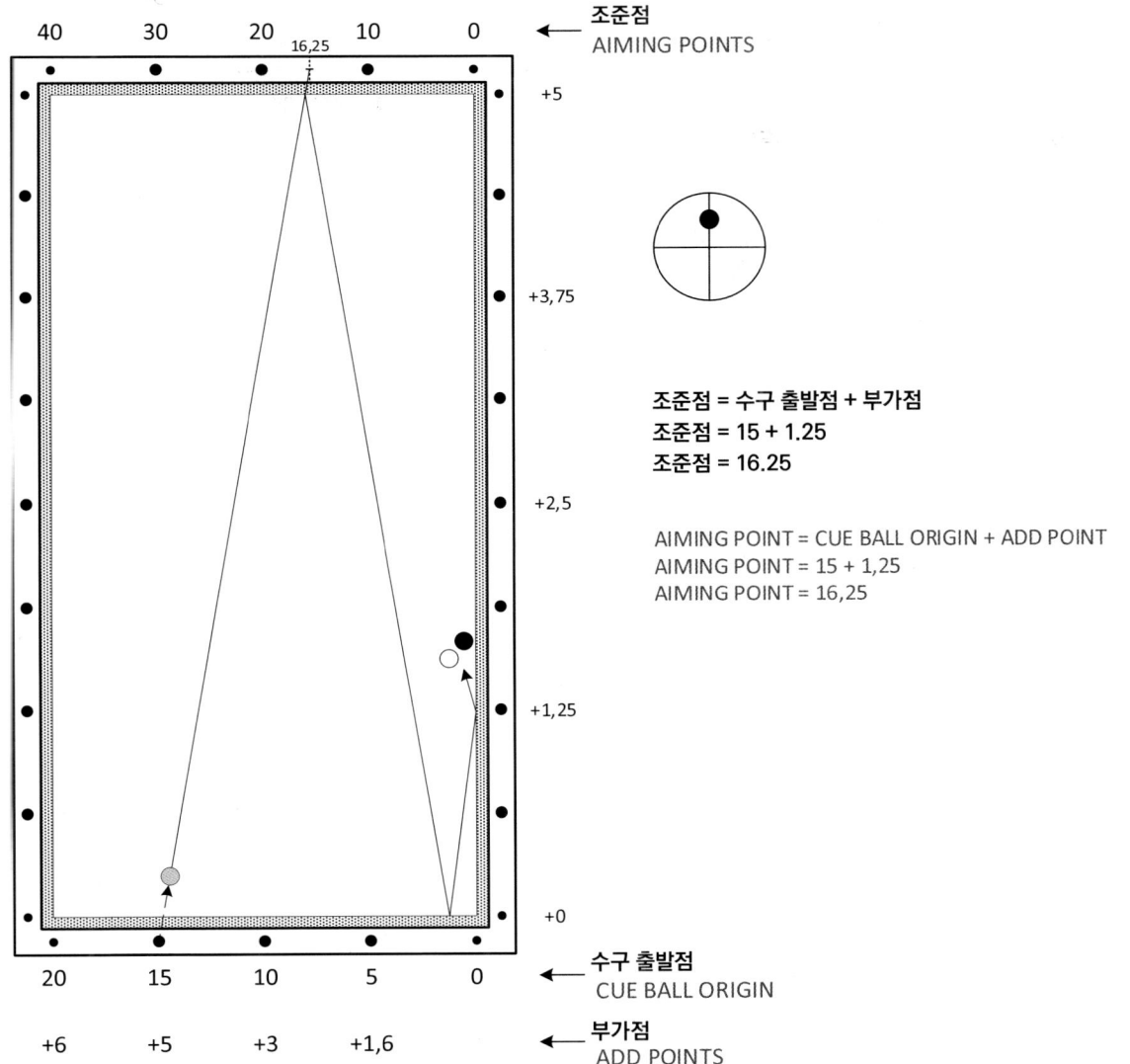

조준점 = 수구 출발점 + 부가점
조준점 = 15 + 1.25
조준점 = 16.25

AIMING POINT = CUE BALL ORIGIN + ADD POINT
AIMING POINT = 15 + 1,25
AIMING POINT = 16,25

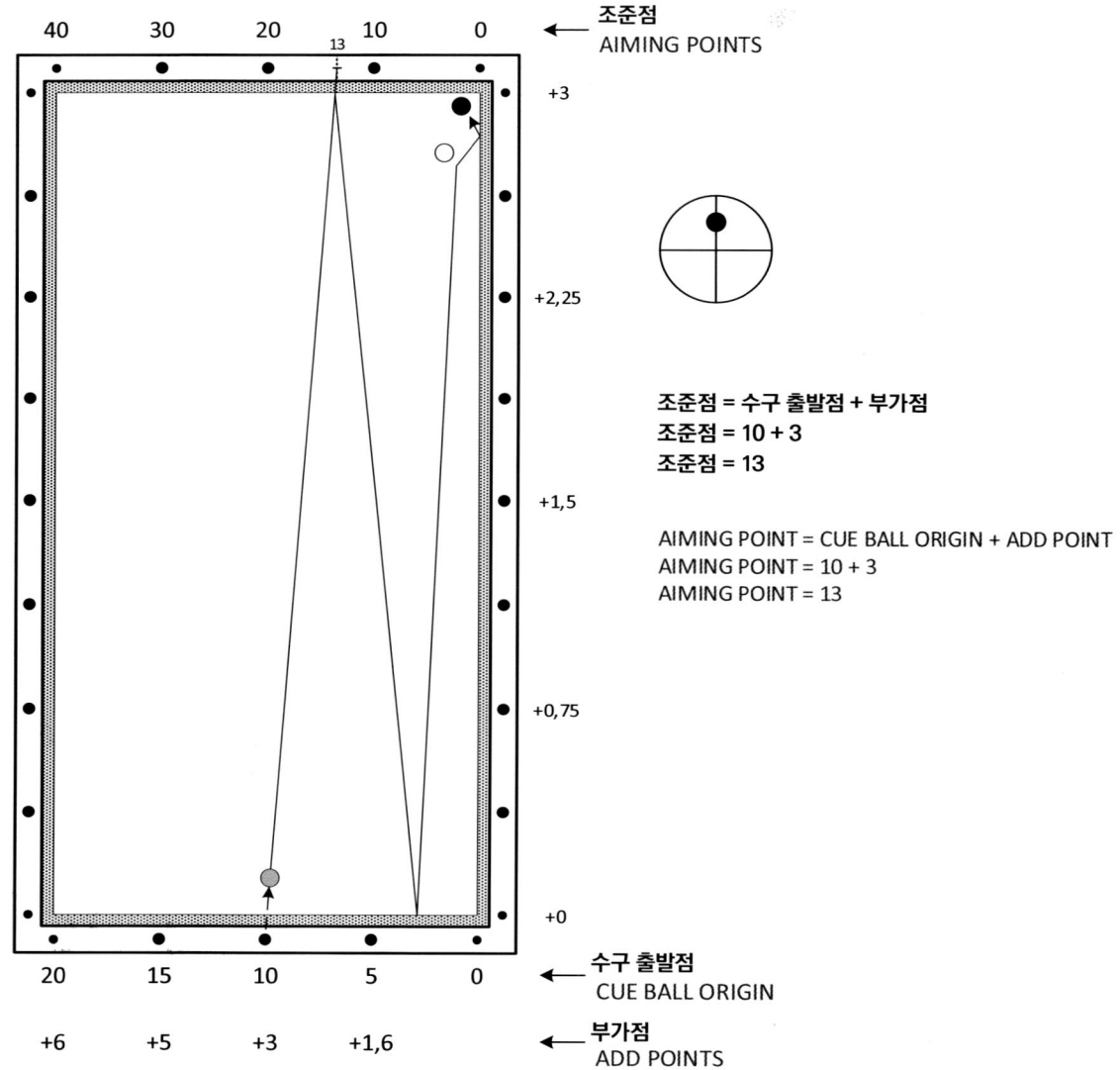

조준점 = 수구 출발점 + 부가점
조준점 = 10 + 3
조준점 = 13

AIMING POINT = CUE BALL ORIGIN + ADD POINT
AIMING POINT = 10 + 3
AIMING POINT = 13

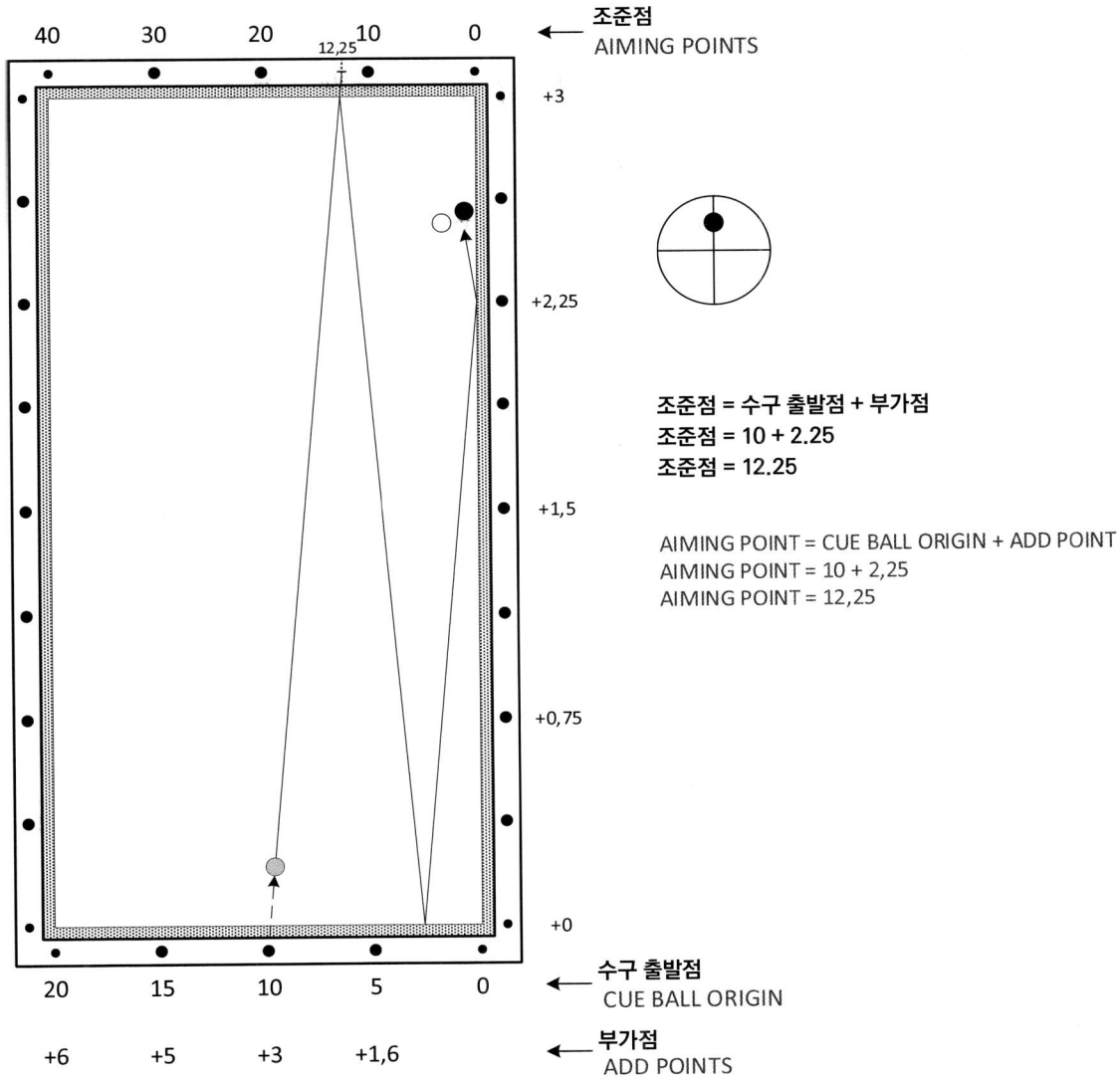

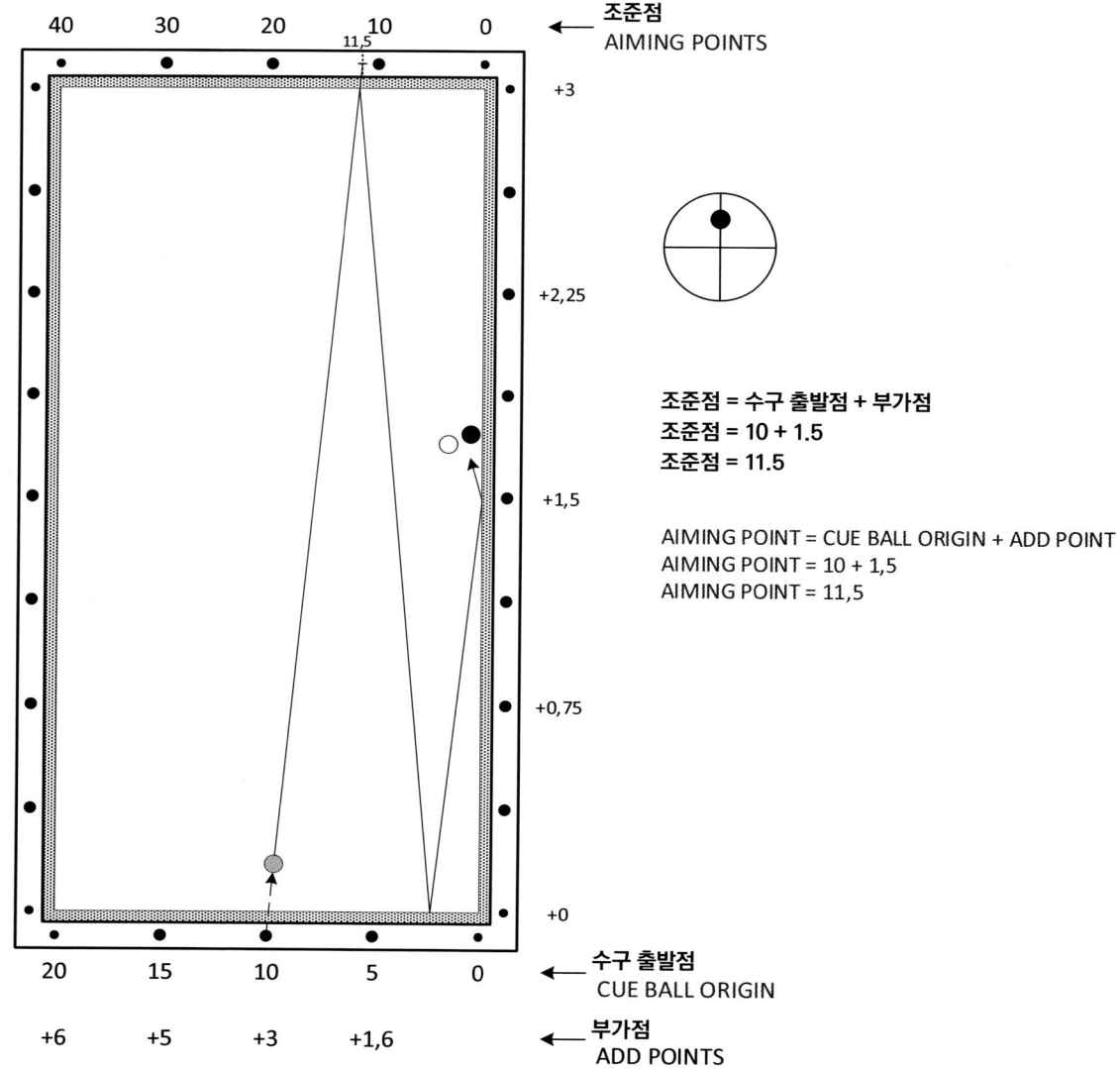

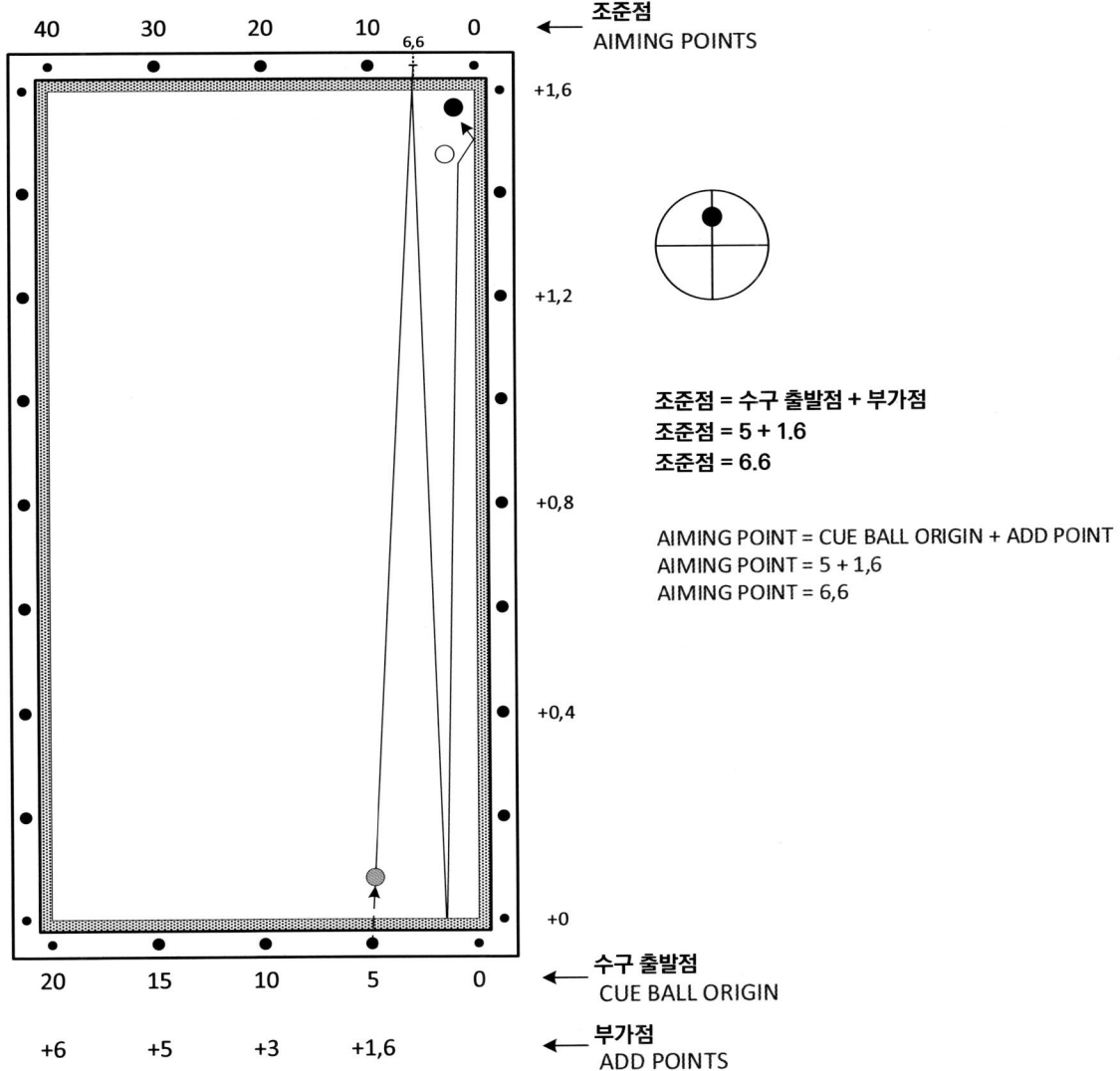

조준점 = 수구 출발점 + 부가점
조준점 = 5 + 1.6
조준점 = 6.6

AIMING POINT = CUE BALL ORIGIN + ADD POINT
AIMING POINT = 5 + 1,6
AIMING POINT = 6,6

용어

English	한국어
Add point	부가점
Aiming point	조준점
Arrival point	도착점
Cloth	라사지
Cue	큐
Cue ball	수구
Cue ball origin	수구 출발점
Cue-tip	큐팁
Cue tip contact point	큐팁 접점
Curve	커브
Cushion, Rail	쿠션, 레일
Dead ball shot	무회전 샷
Degree of spin	회전량
Diamond	(레일 위의) 포인트
Double rail	더블레일
English, Spin	회전
Follow-through shot	팔로우스루 샷
Long cushion	장쿠션
Shooting speed	타구 속도
Short cushion	단쿠션
Short-stroke technique	끊어치기 기법
Starting angle	출발각
Stating from the short cushion	단쿠션 출발
Stroke technique	스트로크 기법
Stroke, Shot	스트로크, 샷
Systems	시스템
Table	테이블
Table Value	테이블값(회전량)
Three-Cushion Billiards Discipline	3쿠션 당구 훈련

부록

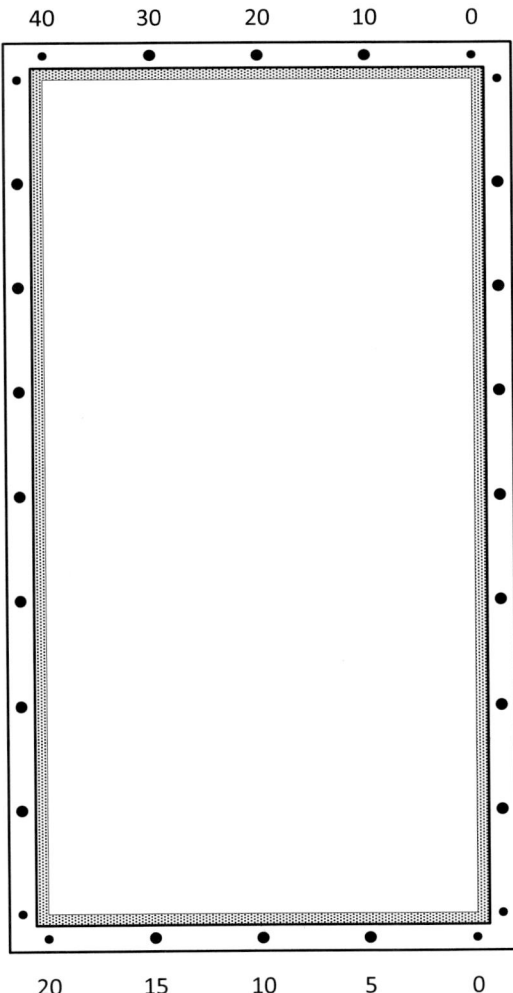
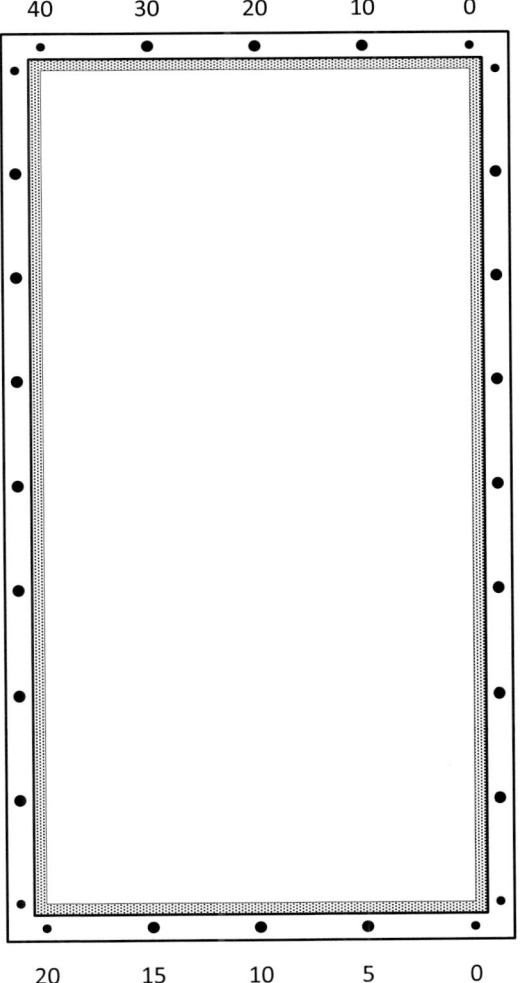

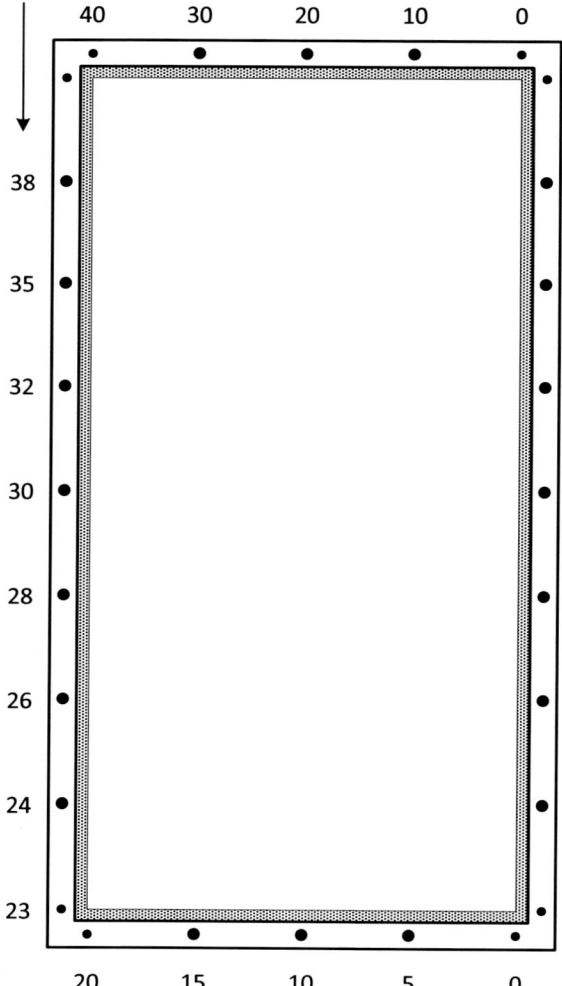
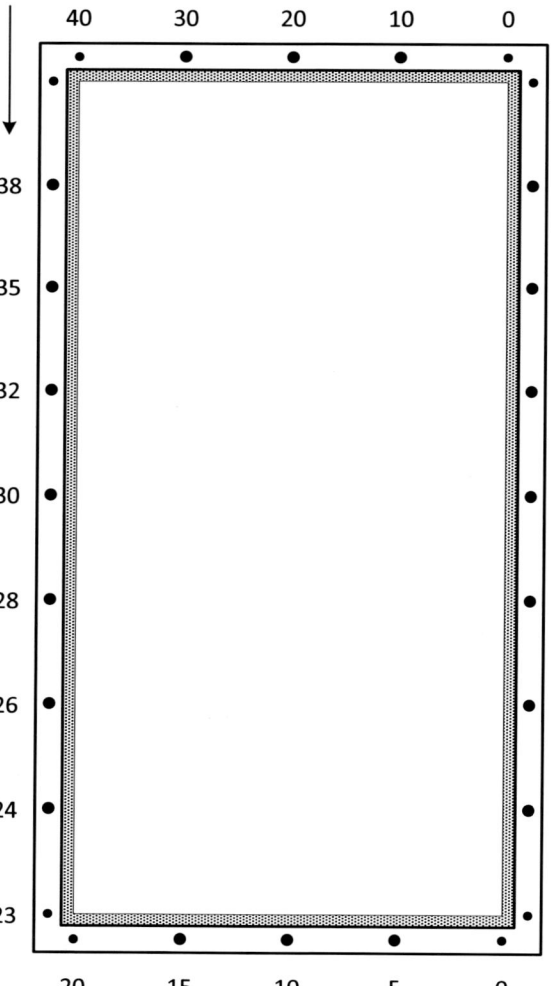

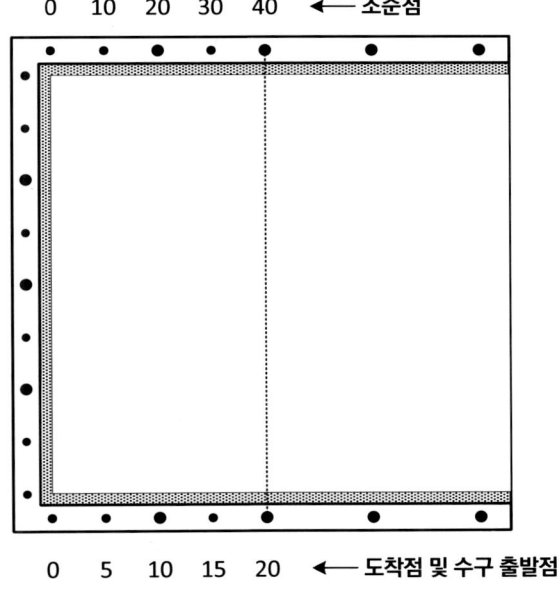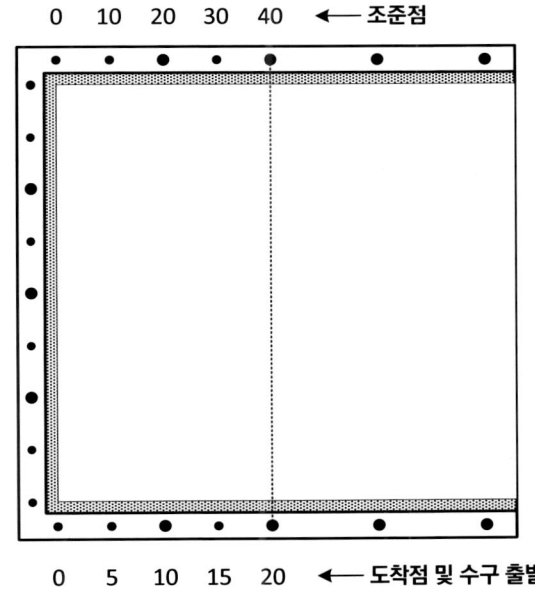

튜즐 당구 시스템

© 글로벌콘텐츠, 2020

1판 1쇄 발행 __ 2020년 04월 25일
1판 2쇄 발행 __ 2023년 08월 25일

지은이 __ 무랏 튜즐
옮긴이 __ 박천수·박지수
펴낸이 __ 홍정표

펴낸곳 __ 글로벌콘텐츠
        등록 __ 제25100-2008-000024호

공급처 __ (주)글로벌콘텐츠출판그룹
        대표 __ 홍정표   이사 __ 김미미   편집 __ 임세원 강민욱 백승민 권군오   기획·마케팅 __ 이종훈 홍민지
        주소 __ 서울특별시 강동구 풍성로 87-6 전화 __ 02-488-3280 팩스 __ 02-488-3281
        홈페이지 __ www.gcbook.co.kr 메일 __ edit@gcbook.co.kr

값 15,000원
ISBN 979-11-5852-277-3 13690

·이 책은 본사와 저자의 허락 없이는 내용의 일부 또는 전체를 무단 전재나 복제, 광전자 매체 수록 등을 금합니다.
·잘못된 책은 구입처에서 바꾸어 드립니다.